Boot Camp for the Broken-Hearted™

How to Survive (and Be Happy) in the Jungle of Love©

By Audrey Valeriani

Boot Camp for the Broken-Hearted

How to Survive (and Be Happy) in the Jungle of Love

By
Audrey Valeriani

New Horizon Press
Far Hills, NJ

Author's Note

This book is based on extensive personal interviews and insights from experts in the fields of personal and emotional health and relationship therapy. All names have been changed and recognizable characteristics disguised except for contributing experts.

Audrey Valeriani
Boot Camp for the Broken-Hearted:
How to Survive (and Be Happy) in the Jungle of Love

Cover Design: Wendy Bass
Interior Design: Eileen Turano

Library of Congress Control Number: 2007933789

ISBN 13: 078-0-88282-292-1
ISBN 10: 0-88282-292-6
New Horizon Press

Manufactured in the U.S.A.

2012 2011 2010 2009 2008 / 5 4 3 2 1

Dedication:

To all the women in my life who have influenced me —
for providing me with wonderful examples of the
kind of person to be,
scaring me into *not* doing what you've done,
protecting me from the harshness of life,
having the courage to tell me the truth about the world,
showing me how not to be afraid of hard work,
how to persevere, how to pick myself up and brush myself off,
and how to have fun.
I thank you from the bottom of my bruised,
reused, renewed heart.

Testimonials

"I asked your advice and it was so clear and simple. [I thought] why couldn't I think of that? You made me feel so much better and now I have a clearer head!" ~ JAC

"You made such a difference in the way I now think and handle my relationships. I am with a new guy now who's nice and attentive and sexy and I owe it all to your advice! Thank you so much!" ~ a reader from Massachusetts

"I think you are so nice to take your time out to talk with other women and your site is GREAT! I cried when I read your story... You are the first person who has really helped me, when I found this site it was God send. I didn't want to bash my man, I just wanted to know that other women can help me... I can't thank you enough!!" ~ a reader from Tennessee

"The Accidental Expert has been very supportive and has helped me get through some tough times with her advice... when I am feeling down and missing [him], she suggested I write down the bad things and when I look at it, it should help me realize I am doing the right thing... words can't say how much I appreciate it!" ~ DAM

"The Accidental Expert has helped me think about who I am and about taking care of myself and about the little girl in "my" pocket. Her advice helped me through a very difficult relationship and to move on to better things." ~ JTM

"The concise, wisdom filled, words of The Accidental Expert helped me move a relationship in the right direction. Life is better now." ~ BM

"The Accidental Expert has helped me learn that when I'm in a relationship I am always the giver and that I have a hard time receiving. I am now dating and have learned to step back and not give too much of myself and am learning that it is okay to say 'No.'" ~ a reader from Massachusetts

"... I found your insights so helpful and interesting! You inspired me to remain positive and make the most of every day... Anyway, I just wanted to let you know that you are a true inspiration, and I wish you the best of luck with everything." ~ a reader from Connecticut

Foreword

I have been dealing with relationships with people and relationships throughout my career as a psychotherapist. Armed with a Masters degree in Social Work, I began as a counselor in a Family Counseling agency. After several years, I started my private practice, where I have been seeing patients for over 30 years, working with adults both as individuals and couples. Singles come asking for help with relationships as much as couples do. Whether someone is coming with their partner or not, relationships are the main presenting problem. People are searching for help to get over a break-up, find a partner or make a relationship work. Everybody wants a good relationship.

Boot Camp for the Broken Hearted is a book for women to read and for men to appreciate women reading it. Audrey Valeriani helps women understand how important having a positive self-image is and to see what has influenced them so they won't blame themselves for not always having one. In fact, Valeriani takes the word blame out of the dictionary and replaces with appreciating yourself and your partner. She teaches women in a down-to-earth, straightforward approach, how to have greater self-esteem and its importance in a relationship. Reading this book is like having your best friend understand what you are going through and then having someone with real life experience teach you how to have a better sense of self and therefore a better relationship. Without that self assurance, any relationship you enter will be a battleground of the heart.

This book is a practical guide for women. The author writes in a witty, no-nonsense way with lots of how-to lists and revealing exercises. By reading this book, you gain deeper knowledge coupled with effective techniques to improve your communication skills, which are crucial for making any relationship work. Moreover, unlike many other books, it gives concrete advice on how to have a great sex life. And the reason it is so helpful is that the advice comes from men.

Boot Camp for the Broken Hearted is unique in that, as a woman, you feel understood and with that understanding, it helps you to understand men. The author makes it crystal clear that no one is the enemy. *Boot Camp for the Broken Hearted* is also exceptional in that it points out the daily problems that couples face and shows you how to handle them. With keener insights about how to create and sustain mutually fulfilling intimacy, Valeriani shows how women can communicate to men what she is all about in a way that they will listen – and what men want her to know about them.

If you are just out of a relationship, this book is for you. If you are looking for a relationship, this book is for you. And if you are in a relationship and want to make it better, *Boot Camp for the Broken Hearted* is for you.

Leslie Joseph, LICSW

Table of Contents

Preface

Are You Ready for Boot Camp?

You've been together for several years. In the beginning, you felt the butterflies in your belly every time the phone rang. When you saw him, your heart raced. He was so sweet and cute. Flowers, teddy bears, the wooing — oh, it was beautiful! After a few months, you settled into a routine. Friday was guys' night out; Tuesday was poker night. You went out together on Saturday night, but Sunday, of course, was for football. Then he became distant and a little more forgetful. There were still times when he was thoughtful — usually after many hints from you. You began to go in different directions, to want different things. You wondered, "How did that happen?" You began to feel taken-for-granted. Then the arguing began. You can't really remember how things escalated, but they did. You think, *What's wrong with me?*

As you remember it, you hardly fought in the beginning. Then after six months, it seemed like you argued all the time — over his obnoxious friends, the forgotten phone call, him working late and staring at that waitress. He was always defending himself, and you were always in tears. He accused you of complaining constantly for no reason, and you accused him of not caring about anyone but himself. Then *she* appeared out of nowhere. He says they are just friends, but you notice the glances between them when they think no one is looking. You become suspicious all the time, and question him constantly about her. He finally blows up and storms out in a rage. You call him all night but he is not answering his cell phone. You're worried and frantic, but deep down you know where he is. You think, *How could he do this to me?*

i

You've been burned many times but finally believe you met *The One*. He's charming and handsome and fun. The only thing that worries you is that he gets quiet and withdrawn — but he said it's because he's been hurt too. He told you right from the start that he's still reeling from his old relationship that ended three years ago. He asks that you take things slowly. You agree and expect things to change over time. But it's been two years now and you are still seeing each other about once a week. He seems to come and go as he pleases while you wait for him to call and make plans or you beg him to attend your friend's wedding with you. You finally ask him how he feels about you and tell him that you want more. He tells you he's not sure what he wants. You feel as though your life is over and think, *How can I get him to love me?*

Well, you did it again. Your loser magnet attracted another one. This one was so screwed up he even lied to you about what he had for lunch! Actually, this one was not quite as bad as the last one who actually introduced you to his entire family on the second date. Or what about the one you dated for a month last year who asked you to tattoo his name on your butt? And then the other *prince* who stole money out of your wallet and then tried to tell you that you forgot you gave it to him! You go out every weekend to bars with your friends. You smile and laugh and wear the trendiest clothes, but still attract the bottom of the barrel. You wonder, *Will I ever meet a normal guy?*

Introduction

<u>The Accidental Expert</u>

I walked into the therapist's office, broken and ready to let it all out —
after all, what did I have left to lose? I grew up in a depressing and hostile
environment, the youngest of three daughters; my two sisters were significantly older and moved out when I was just a toddler. Just after my nine-
teenth birthday, my mother died from cancer, my engagement broke up, I
was forced to put my dog to sleep, my father unexpectedly sold the house
which had been in my family since my grandmother came over from Italy
and I had no place to go. If that wasn't enough, soon after that I suffered
through some abusive relationships, additional family tragedies and then
my best friend died. It became too much. All of these things had driven me
to the point of hopelessness, desperation and rage. I sat down believing that
this therapy session was my last chance of surviving under all this rubble.
My heart was broken; my strength was gone; I felt unloved, betrayed and
inertly suicidal. Here I sat feeling scared and nervous, hoping and praying
that this would not be another disappointment. Still I struggled to listen and
understand everything my therapist said and tried to follow her every
instruction. After all, my life was on the line. After several sessions, we
began to make some progress. During one session, the therapist suggested
we try a visualization-meditation technique that I will never forget. First,
she instructed me to sit comfortably and close my eyes…

The Visualization

Picture in your mind a little girl who lives in your shirt pocket. Take her out and look at her standing in the palm of your hand. Notice how sad she looks. She's been mistreated most of her life. She's been belittled, hurt and abused. She's gotten dirty and wet, felt cold, hungry and lonely. Not only have other people made her feel this way but so have you — by ignoring her needs and prolonging her pain. Can you picture her little face looking up at you? Why were you as mean to her as everyone else had been? She looked to you for love and kindness and you provided none, instead blaming her for causing what was not her fault. Did you perhaps feel that there must have been a reason all these bad things happened and that she must have deserved such misfortune? Have you become so hardened and cynical by the let-downs of life that there's no compassion left inside your heart for someone else? For yourself? That's right. *That little girl is you.* Now try and remember all of the things that have happened in your life that hurt you. It's not fair, is it? All you've ever wanted was for the pain to stop, for that hole in your belly to heal. You've been looking for something or someone to make you feel better, to change your life. Well, that someone has been with you the whole time, *just look in the mirror.*

It's not too late. Now take that little girl and clean her up. Give her some healthy food and nice clothes. Make her look pretty. Tell her that she's wonderful and that you love her. Tell her that she can do anything and that you will help her to have a wonderful life *from this point on.* Then put her back in your pocket, next to your heart, and never forget she is there.

After doing this exercise, I felt my heart melt, my fists relax and all the fear and anger drain from my body. I felt so badly for that poor, scared little girl. After crying for a long time and then vowing never to treat myself so insensitively and unfairly again, the realization came that I wasn't alone. I did have someone. I had me!

After this incredible epiphany in the therapist's office, I became *hungry* to live, not just survive and to feel genuinely and deliriously *happy.* I read everything I could find about love, family, God, the meaning of life — you name it. But the beginning of my healing truly started when I became acquainted with the little girl inside me. That beautiful meditation saved my life. I wondered how many other women out there needed saving.

Who am I? Let me begin by telling you that I am a woman perhaps very much like you. I am forty-something-years-old. Growing up, almost every marriage around me either ended in divorce or was extremely dysfunctional. I had no example of a healthy, happy relationship between a man and a woman to guide me. As a result, I began to believe that true love was only found in the movies and that Cinderella had gotten married just so she could get back her shoe (after all, they were glass *and* custom made!).

In my twenties and thirties I had my share of experiences — good and bad. For years, my loser magnet was in perfect working order and able to reach far and wide. Like you, I've agonized over the stupid mistakes I made in relationships (being too clingy or too judgmental). I've been overly critical of myself and tried so hard to be the *perfect* woman for everyone in my life. I've fallen hard for the bad boys, ignored the nice ones and have mourned the loss of many a dickhead boyfriend! I finally asked myself, what was I doing wrong? Would true love *never* find me? Was it really possible to have a relationship with a man who would be as good to me as I was to him? Or to find someone who *really* understood me (and loved me anyway)? Was I even worthy of love? Nowhere did I find the answers I needed. I felt as though I was roaming around in the dark. Finally, after years of listening to everyone around me complain about their painful, unfulfilling relationships, I decided to stop this unproductive cycle of despair and disappointment and find the answers to the questions myself.

My adventure began by talking with friends, friends of friends, co-workers and even welcoming strangers in line at the bank. I asked waitresses in restaurants what their gripes were about men and eaves-dropped on the conversations of other women in ladies' rooms every-where! I solicited information from anyone who looked like he or she would talk to me.

Once I began interviewing women, I could immediately see a problem. I found that most of us still fell into the role of "martyr" (like our mothers) as we habitually put everyone else's needs before our own, which made me wonder how that affected us emotionally and what kind of fall-out would result from those feelings. My first step was to examine how we as women treat *ourselves*. I discovered that most of us don't take the time or *know how* to give our spirits, minds and bodies what they require so that we may *feel* and *live* life to its fullest. When we don't properly care for ourselves, how can we possibly do it properly for those we are supposed to love? It became clear then that there is a connection between loving one's *self* and loving *others*. The ideal *characteristics of love* (kindness, generosity, nurturing and respect) were the same for both kinds of love, so why then did we not convey them equally? What I found was, unfortunately, most of us don't consider ourselves as important or treat ourselves with the respect with which we treat everyone else in our lives. I became determined to find out why.

Continuing my research I asked women and men about the complexities of their relationships. Most men to whom I talked expressed concerns about sex (lack of or decrease in) and felt that they were misunderstood a lot in both their words and actions. One man told me, "We're not complicated. Men are simple" (a statement which when I repeated it later made a lot of women laugh). I talked to women about their most recurrent problems, listened to many stories in which they described being emotionally hurt by men and took notice of the similarities as they questioned (as well as became exasperated by) some of the things men do, like "not listening when I talk" and "leaving everything for me to do." What I realized was that most relationships were full of assumptions, misunderstandings and confusion. (I had my work cut out for me.)

Most surprising were some of the comments I heard from women who appeared very strong and independent. When asked how she would react to certain misbehaviors by her man (like leering at other women in front of her), one woman admitted, "I'd ignore it. I just don't want to cause any trouble." While discussing some serious trouble another woman was having with her man, she confessed that she stays with him because "it's nice having someone there to tell you they love you." She said she "couldn't take" being alone. (With the help of her friends and my advice, this woman *finally* extricated herself from this very unhealthy relationship and is now doing exceptionally well!) Finally, when asked what she thought men wanted from women, another woman responded, "Men want women to let them do whatever they want and not complain," and she said that was pretty much what she'd been doing (and she was miserable). Again, each of these comments appeared to me to reflect how each woman felt about herself and her *self-worth*. It became clear that the state of a woman's self-esteem served as a blue print for the kinds of relationships she would have over a lifetime.

Then I sought to identify the ways women and men routinely communicate, share their lives and love one another. To begin this examination, I read a lot about the psychological and social aspects of interpersonal relationships, which piqued my curiosity as to what *real* people like me were going through. I spoke with women in the beauty salon and in elevators, men waiting in line at a lunch place and people on the train going into and out of the city. An invitation to "tell me a story" went out to my contacts via e-mail, including a request that they forward it to their associates and acquaintances. I sent my friends to their social engagements armed with questions and *notebooks* so they could gather information for my research. I distributed surveys (via e-mail and by hand) to any man or woman who would take one (along with some extras to distribute to their friends, as well). The surveys asked what qualities they looked for in their partners, what feelings they experienced most in their relationships (happy, jealous, confused, etc.) and what they would *most* want the opposite sex to know. Interestingly, many *men* surveyed admitted to feeling insecure in relationships, and a lot of women wanted men to make them a bigger priority in their lives.

I looked for hard data to support my findings by scanning medical journals, university studies, news articles, books and magazines on the subject of love and relationships. It became clear that *biology* as well as *environment* had a lot to do with how men and women feel and behave (i.e., some things are instinctual; some are learned). I attended seminars and listened to experts give their best advice on how to improve relationships; some chose to examine behavior and advise couples how to compromise, while others advocated looking *inward* to their spiritual side for answers.

Once my research materials overtook my spare room, it was time to organize and categorize my data. After many months of reading and analyzing all of the valuable information I had collected (as well as testing out pieces of advice and ways of behaving on my friends and my poor, bewildered fiancé!), I was able to determine the enormous impact of self-esteem on relationships and determine the most common problems in daily life, to identify the ineffective approaches used by men and women in the past and then uncover *new* ways of dealing with those problems that would produce the best possible outcome. Here, at last, are the fruits of my labor!

Please note that the ideas in this book are not intended to work magic in a relationship that is abusive, destructive or ignored. Relationships are hard work! Potentially serious problems are highlighted later in the book and for those I recommend help from a licensed professional. Realistically, all relationships have their ups and downs and are hard work. My book teaches readers how to get along better with their partners on a daily basis, showing ways to maneuver through the little aggravations and how to keep things fresh and meaningful *from a standpoint of someone with a healthy self-image* (but don't worry, we'll work on that first). You and your partner need to have established a basic compatibility and affection for one another, as well as a genuine desire to be in a committed relationship involving mutual respect, trust and love. The observations within this book have resulted from gathering information *directly* from people like you and me. I will share with you what I learned firsthand about what men and women truly believe does and does not work in various situations. They told me what turns them on, what turns them off and what kinds of mistakes they made by misdiagnosing or ignoring the problems. Their invaluable input has enabled me to pinpoint the most common problems in relationships from both the *male* and *female* perspectives and to isolate easy, effective, field-tested techniques. You will be able to exchange your frustration, anger and resentment for positive, life-changing ways in which to love and be loved in your relationship.

Portrait of the Author as Young Girl:
Audrey in her Wonder Years

Part I — Basic Training:
Get Out of That Slump!

Relationships are complicated and can end for many reasons... cheating, lying, abuse, neglect, irreconcilable differences! Whatever the cause, when a romance is over it can be devastating. Your range of emotions can take you from upset and crying to angry and bitchy to even giggly at times (which usually leads back to tears). What's actually happening is that you are grieving the "death" of the relationship and whether you like it or not, this process is usually inevitable. Although it is especially common for women to go through this kind of mourning period, a lot of women have trouble coming to grips with this kind of sudden loss. Many will obsess about their former lover, hang on to their somewhat *altered* memories of the way things were and make excuses for their actions, never really getting to the root of the problems. Unfortunately, once they make it through this period, many will be eager to get into other relationships without taking the time or making the effort to examine their own behaviors. This will compel them to repeat the same mistakes with yet other men — only to be disappointed once again.

Well, I'm here to tell you that whether you are recovering from a failed relationship, feeling lonely or just unhappy with the status or quality of your sex life, this *can* be a golden opportunity for you. You've got a chance to make a fresh start and you should take advantage of it. Right now you can make changes that will finally stop that seemingly endless

1

cycle of confusion and despair. As you proceed, you will learn how to:

♥ Pump up with emotional support the person who deserves it most — you!

♥ Respond properly to the cryptic words and actions of the opposite sex!

♥ Build a meaningful and rewarding life — with or without a man!

You will also learn how to avoid landmines (resist toxic behavior that is sure to cause problems), when to go on search and destroy missions (what *not* to tolerate), when to stand down (how and when to let things go) and how to make him yell "Whoo-rah!" (in the bedroom). Your G.I.Q. will be top notch after reading this highly *classy-fied* information!

So ladies, are you up to the challenge? Are you ready to conquer your enemy, which is *not* men but a lack of understanding about yourself and others? Are you ready to embark on your search for the freedom that is love and happiness? Okay then, let's move out!

Chapter 1:
Anatomy of a
Broken Heart

A. <u>Understanding What's Happening.</u> *Falling in and out of love is a chemical reaction.* When we fall in love, our brains generate certain chemicals (e.g. dopamine and norepinephrine), which give us euphoric-like feelings, temporarily *blinding* us from most anything that may be construed as negative about our *paramour* (that's why they say, "Love is blind"). After a while, however, our bodies generate smaller amounts of those chemicals, which lead to a decline in that tingly feeling and sense of excitement. Usually, it can take anywhere from one to three years before these chemicals *naturally* lessen, but if your romance abruptly comes to an end, these levels can plummet and leave you feeling as though your rose-colored glasses have been ripped off!

Your heart is sick — much like your body can be. Just like getting the flu, your heart can get *sick* and your spirit can become *ill*; so you must take care of them as you would your physical body. So take it easy. Don't put too much responsibility on yourself for a while. You're on an emotional roller coaster and, unfortunately, with all of that comes a process. Like mourning the death of a loved one, while grieving the loss of the relationship, you may experience any or all of these seven stages of grief.

GRIEF STAGES	
1 *Denial*	You feel numb; may expect everything to go back to "normal"; the pain has not yet set in.
2 *Anger*	You're mad at him for leaving; at God or the universe for "making" this happen; at yourself for saying or doing something "stupid"; at everyone for no reason.
3 *Guilt*	You regret things that were said or not said, done or not done, which you are *sure* would have changed the outcome.
4 *Depression*	You're sad; there is weight loss or gain; anxiety; unable to cope with routine tasks; crying bouts; tiredness.
5 *Forgiveness*	You begin to come to terms with what happened and slowly let things go; you begin to forgive the other person *and* yourself.
6 *Acceptance*	You get used to your new situation; you are not upset all the time anymore; you begin to move on.
7 *Recovery*	You don't think of him so much anymore, and when you do there is little discomfort; you are ready to move on!

You may also experience physical symptoms as well. Your body can feel tired, almost stiff and may be resistant to any activity. Also, studies show that depression can lower your immune system which can make you susceptible to colds and disease. Mentally, you may feel confused, forgetful and scattered. You may be unable to concentrate, and following simple directions can feel overwhelming.

Change is not easy. Use this time for self-reflection and goal-setting. When we experience something that is potentially devastating, our minds tend to protect us from memories which can be too overwhelming or upsetting. For this reason, we may not always be able to accurately remember the facts about certain events. We may forget how irritating or cruel or controlling the person was, or imagine them to be more loving, desirable or kinder than they were in reality.

B. <u>Mental Conditioning.</u> *Let the Healing Begin.*

Now that you are beginning to have a better understanding of what's going on within you, let's examine ways to help you to begin feeling better. Instead of spending all your time thinking about your ex, going over and over everything that happened in your mind and just plain wallowing in your misery, it's time to take control over your thoughts and start focusing on you! Below, you will find a chart describing things to rely on in order to get yourself moving in the right direction. Practice these suggestions as often as you can and if you slip up, it's okay. Chock it up to a bad day, let it all out and start fresh the next morning.

HEART MENDING

♥ What to **focus on** to help you get over a broken heart:

Yourself	Don't think about what your ex is doing; keep your mind on YOU.
The Present	Concentrate on what you're doing *in the moment.*
Friends and Family	Let people who love you listen to you and help you.
Structure	Keep to your normal schedule as much as possible.
Your Spirit	Say prayers, affirmations; think positive.
Goals	Decide what you want, make a plan and go for it.

♥ What to **do** to help you get over a broken heart:

Have Faith	Believe in yourself and that you will be okay. Relinquish control over everything. Leave yourself in the hands of your higher power.
Keep a Journal	Write down everything — both good and bad thoughts. If you write your thoughts on paper, it will help you get rid of all the anger, confusion and heartache you have inside.

Practice Self-Control	Keep yourself focused on your responsibilities as much as you can by allowing yourself to get upset or dwell on your ex *only at certain and limited amounts of time.*
Exercise/Move Around	When you're feeling overwhelmed, get up and move your body. It has been scientifically proven that changing the location and position of your body can break your train of thought. You may feel stiff and weak, but physical activity will help clear your mind.
Eat Right	This is *not* the time for a strict diet, nor is it a time to indulge in all the ice cream sundaes you can eat. Some foods containing sugar, caffeine or alcohol can make you anxious, so be aware of what you're eating and drinking.
Keep to a Schedule	When you're feeling bad, there is a tremendous temptation to just stay in bed and lay around the house — but don't do it. Cruise on automatic pilot for a while. Right now, your only tasks are to get yourself up and go to work.
Read Everything That's a Positive Reinforcement	Review old books that inspired you. Seek out stories or articles that are uplifting, funny and insightful.
Smile/Laugh	It may sound peculiar, but studies have shown that when we smile our faces send messages telling our brains that we are alright, and soon we feel better. Laughing also relieves stress and improves our immune system (at first you may break into tears, but keep on smiling)!

Volunteer or Do Something for Someone Else	You'd be surprised how much helping someone else actually helps you! It takes your mind off of your problems for a while. You shouldn't commit to anything long term just yet, but try doing something nice for a relative, friend or neighbor. Whether you believe in karma or not, positive energy is a powerful thing, and I believe that *what you give out, you get back.*

If you are having trouble falling asleep at night during this time, try this visualization.

Lie in bed and close your eyes. Think of all the people and issues that are worrying you. One by one, picture each of them and then shrink them until they are really tiny and can fit in the palm of your hand. Then pick one up at a time and place them on your night table — pick up your ex, your boss, your mother, the bills — whatever — and place them on the nightstand next to you. Picture this little group standing together now, waiting patiently for you to address them again in the morning.

Worrying about things and rehashing events over and over does you no good — it just keeps you from getting a much needed good night's sleep. By (literally) taking them off your mind, you allow yourself to get some much needed relaxation without the fear that your problems will go unaddressed.

Besides getting enough sleep, it's also important to make yourself feel comfortable during this time. Wear your favorite clothes, snuggle with your softest blanket, eat your favorite foods, then take a bath and put on your pajamas! Think of yourself during this time as being *under the weather* and treat yourself kindly.

C. <u>Planning Future Missions</u>. *Think about what you want, and set some goals*:

In a later chapter, we will explore how fear, procrastination and/or laziness are the only things stopping you from having what you want. Basically, there are three steps to achieving a new goal: (1) Figure out what you want, (2) Take steps towards your goal every day, (3) Focus on it and don't give up.

Now ask yourself these questions: What do you want for your future? What have you denied yourself? What have you put off? What's important to you? What do you dream of being and/or doing? List your replies and write down the actual steps you can take to make them happen. For example:

GOAL	TODAY	THIS WEEK	THIS MONTH	IN SIX MONTHS	BY YEAR END
Become a Paralegal	Find a school or training	Get brochures; choose.	Get financing; work out details.	Go to class and study.	Graduate!
Go to Paris	Get brochures.	Save money.	Book with travel agent.	Pack and go!	Enjoy pictures!
Buy a Condo	Save money.	Talk to an agent.	Get qualified by the bank.	Look at properties.	Move!

<u>Tips</u>

- Understand what's happening to you both emotionally and physically.
- Allow (and help) yourself go through the whole "process" of ups and downs.
- Be gentle with and forgiving of yourself.
- Keep up with your normal routine as much as possible.
- Take time to examine your choices and do what's best for you.
- Review what you've learned from your experience.
- Set some goals and make your first move!

Hopefully, you're now feeling a little more optimistic and believe that life will go on. At this point, it is wise to figure out how you got in this predicament in the first place.

Part II: Identifying the Enemy — Low Self-Esteem!

Chapter 2: What is Self-Esteem?

You would think that loving someone would come naturally, right? You would expect that we would all be born with the right "tools" to get the job done, especially since we were, theoretically, conceived from the act of love. However, it is your level of self-esteem that determines how you view and treat yourself and affects your choices throughout your lifetime. Wanting or intending to love yourself and others is one thing, but knowing how to do it properly is quite another.

Self-esteem is not only feeling good about yourself, it's knowing how to:

- Fulfill your own needs by knowing how to make yourself feel better when you're down; supporting yourself and your lifestyle; making decisions in your own best interest; respecting and listening to your body.
- Get respect from others by establishing boundaries; setting examples of how you expect to be treated by others by treating yourself well; having a sense of pride and integrity.
- Handle yourself in any situation by cultivating and utilizing your skills and talents; knowing that what you don't know you can learn; facing your fears; never giving up.
- Love yourself and others by practicing kindness, compassion, gratitude, humility, forgiveness, generosity, faith and love.

9

Who needs to improve self-esteem?
- The girl from the low income family who feels that because she doesn't have much, she isn't worth much.
- The little rich girl whose parents pay the nanny to raise her while they tend to their own business, oblivious to their child's need for parental attention, interaction and love.
- The twenty-something who looks capable and in control, but never learned how to make her own way in the world.
- The thirty-year-old woman who still lives at home with her parents, waiting for a man to come along and take care of her.
- The middle-aged woman who, while raising a family and working long hours, dismisses her dreams and ignores her own needs.
- The mature woman who, after seeing the kids off to college and living through the death of her husband, feels that without others around her, she is lost.
- Many, many others.

What factors determine self-esteem levels?

Our upbringing. We are born seeking love and acceptance and unconditionally trusting those who show us love. When we're children, we naturally believe what is told to us by the adults around us and even our peers. If someone tells us something negative about ourselves, because we trust them, we believe what they say. Our minds logically believe the people who say they love us, so why would they tell us something that wasn't true? Perhaps because they don't know any better — maybe that's what was told to them when they were young. It could also be that they offered a personal opinion or made an offhand remark that was not meant to be taken seriously. Unfortunately, however, the reasons don't matter — some things we hear from loved ones just remain with us because they surprised, hurt or made us think. Those are the statements we take into our hearts and file in our minds as truths, which then become "toxic imprints." Unfortunately, what passes on is what our mothers learned from their mothers and what their mothers learned from their mothers and so on. Hopefully, as we evolve and learn to review our imprinted beliefs and decide what is true for ourselves, we will improve upon our methods of child-rearing and teach our children only that which is healthy and positive.

The world around us. As we grow older, even though our blind trust changes, unfortunately our toxic imprints do not. They remain a constant part of us. During our formative years, as we continue to trust the words of those whom we believe love us, our own opinions and ideas surface and often conflict with the old "toxic imprints." However, until we improve our levels of self-esteem and trust our own opinions, we will continue to assume that the negative comments of others are correct and second guess our own instincts and feelings.

Despite any generational "hand-me-down" ways of thinking, however, not only does our upbringing shape our self-esteem, what's going on around us in our neighborhoods, on television and in the world also influences us. All of these mixed messages are contributing factors to how we view ourselves which, in turn, has a profound affect on our lives.

Family		Media/Society		Environment
You're good. You're bad.	↓ ↓ ↓ ↓	*You're too fat. You need a man.*	↓ ↓ ↓ ↓	*You can't do it. You don't fit in.*

(processes, categorizes, memorizes) **SELF** (reviews, deletes, re-learns)		
positive thoughts	*everyday*	*conscious effort*
PRIDE (*a sense of one's own proper dignity or value*)	**DIGNITY** (*the quality or condition of being esteemed or honored*)	**RESPECT** (*to feel or show deferential regard*)

leads to ↓
↓

LOVE (*of self; for and by others*)

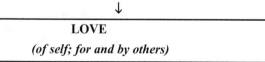

As you can see from the chart, ultimately we are each responsible for processing the information we receive correctly thereby securing our own happiness and well-being.

- Your level determines how you see yourself, which in turn determines what you expect for yourself and brings to you exactly that from other people and the world around you.
- Until you know how to love and take care of yourself, you probably won't be able to do that properly for others.
- Your visualizations about yourself, whether positive or negative, will manifest into the person you become and will help to determine how others see you.
- By having low standards, you will not be able to experience all the wonderfully positive things and people that life has to offer.
- Your beliefs and feelings will disseminate into the world and spread to others who also need positive reinforcement.

What will you gain by improving your self-esteem?
You will be able to:
- Handle work and family stress.
- Make better choices.
- Recognize and avoid negative behaviors.
- Communicate more effectively.
- Manage your emotions.
- Set priorities.
- Focus on health and exercise.
- Speak up for yourself.
- Develop and maintain positive relationships with loved ones.
- Improve personal skills and talents.
- Take on challenges and set goals.

How can you improve self-image?
Review and revise your way of thinking. Once we recognize the origin of our negative thought patterns (toxic imprints), we must decide that not all of what was told to us as children is true. We should then proceed to do some much needed mental closet cleaning, reassess what we've come to believe about ourselves and flag as *"wrong"* those so-

called truths that have done us harm or have negatively influenced our lives. I say "flag" because, unfortunately, since these ideas are imprinted in our minds, they will never be totally removed regardless of how much work we do to improve ourselves. From time to time, during our weaker moments or in times of depression or crisis, these negative messages will inevitably pop up. When they do, we have to remember that they have been labeled as "*wrong*" and replace them with new, more positive personal truths to which we can refer consciously and deliberately for inspiration and strength.

What happens once you've improved your self-image?

Constant maintenance and growth. After all of your hard work you will have a better overall sense of well-being, confidence and peace. However, as I stated earlier, inevitably one day when your guard is down your old, negative ways of thinking will take advantage of your vulnerable state and, again, try and convince you of their credibility. When this occurs, you should:

(i) *Recognize what's happening*: Say, "Okay here come those old feelings again. I know that these are part of my old, destructive patterns and are of no use to me anymore." Then say, "Stop."

(ii) *Remind yourself how far you've come*: Say, "I have worked really hard at improving myself and my self-image so I choose not to indulge these negative thoughts and refuse to allow myself to pay them any attention."

(iii) *Put yourself in the present*: Say, "Today, I am a new and improved person who feels confident and secure within myself. I know that I can take care of myself and that I am a good person who has a lot to offer the world. I know I am loved and respected and have the power to make a wonderful life for myself. This is me now."

How can you begin improving self-image right now?

1. Dismiss any preconceived notions about who or what a woman "should" be.
2. . Understand that *YOU* are many things; you are an individual like no other, made up of many things: ideas, opinions, feelings, preferences, beliefs, talents and a sense of humor.
3. Know that on a scale of one-to-ten, you were born a perfect ten.

4. You are only accountable to yourself — ultimately, only what *you* think matters.
5. Believe that you are in control of yourself and your life — you can choose whatever you want.
6. Realize that the past does not equal the present or the future — your life starts brand new every single day.
7. Eliminate:
    - Negative, unproductive, ineffective thoughts.
    - Self-destructive behavior.
    - Certain words from your vocabulary, like *should* and *can't*.
    - Thinking in terms of black and white — much of the answers are found in the gray.
    - Automatically trying to measure up to the popular social guidelines for living your life.
8. Begin to:
    - Smile (all the time).
    - Read any and all positive, constructive, feel-good material.
    - Hold others accountable for disrespecting or mistreating you.
    - Have faith; express gratitude; pray or meditate.
    - Stay quiet for a time everyday; open your mind and allow for inspiration.
    - Listen to your inner voice/gut instinct.
    - Visualize!

Earlier I shared with you a visualization that had a tremendously positive effect on my life and still does today. Swami Nikhilananda's article entitled, "Power of Thought: Slow Down Ageing by Thinking Young" discusses how the "projections of the mind" can influence what happens to the body. For example, if you want to get thinner, stop picturing yourself obese and start visualizing *your head on a slimmer body* going to the office, playing with the kids, talking with your husband, etc. Of course, visualizing alone will not make you lose weight, you must accompany it with eating properly and exercising; however, seeing a goal as a reality in your mind can help make it attainable for you.

Visualization can help you to build self-esteem as well. You can picture yourself completing a task, communicating positively with others, walking confidently into a meeting or even attracting a man. For example, you are all dressed up and sitting at the bar with friends. How are you sitting? A man comes over to order a drink. What do you say? How does he respond to you — positively — picture it! Then imagine you are having a conversation and he is interested in you. How do you feel? What do you say?

And you can use visualization to help with other situations as well. Suppose you are trying to work through a problem with a friend. Picture yourself talking with the person, expressing your ideas, listening to her side and finally bringing the disagreement to a conclusion. By doing this, you can consider the various situations that may occur during your talk, which will ultimately conclude in a satisfying resolution.

Another example of when to use visualization technique is when you are preparing to go on a job interview. Picture yourself sitting in the office with the boss. How are you seated? What are you wearing? How are you speaking? What are you disclosing about yourself? Is your behavior appropriate? Visualize the situation so that when you are actually there the interviewer will be interested in hiring you.

And as I touched on earlier, visualization can also help to resolve the issues of your past. Sometimes when we think back on a particularly hurtful event, our memories may omit some important details that would otherwise make us feel better or, alternatively, bring a painful truth to light. There were many times when I made myself visualize a painful situation — one that kept haunting me — in order to go back and remember exactly what went on back then, what my options were at the time and to see if I could bring about closure (which I did). For example, years ago I used to feel badly about the day my mother passed away. I felt like on that day I didn't say or do enough to make her know that I loved her and would miss her. When I went back in my mind twenty years ago to that day and place, although it was heart-wrenching, I was able to visualize all that was going on and that, given the circumstances (meaning the hustle and bustle of the staff, the devastation to the family and my young age and naiveté), I became satisfied that I indeed said my good-byes as best I could on that awful day.

What does your self-image project on to others? How does it make you appear to men?

As you can see from the examples to follow, you do have some control over the kind of man you attract and how the relationship progresses.

Example 1: You haven't met the right man for you and feel like you never will. You get down on yourself and often feel lonely, almost desperate to meet a man. You go out to bars dressed provocatively and talk to the men who approach you freely, dropping sexual hints and acting as if you don't care about anything but a good time (so they'll think you're fun to be around and not a "nag").

Outcome: More often than not, you *will* get attention, but only for a short time. You probably send out the "desperation vibe" which men can sense from 500 paces. They see that your self-image is low because you put yourself on display and have an attitude of a party girl, which to them means that's all you're good for.

Example 2: You've just started dating a man with whom you'd really like to have a serious relationship. One night you invite him in after he takes you to dinner and he sees that your apartment is messy and unorganized. You shove a pile of clothes on the floor to make room on the couch and put some dirty dishes in the sink. As you feverishly look for the television remote, he sees your checkbook on the table, along with a pile of papers and unopened mail. Your phone rings and you stop and chat with a friend. You then turn to him and begin to "make out."

Outcome: He sees you as someone who's scatterbrained and doesn't have much control of her life. He thinks that you aren't capable of taking good care of yourself, never mind someone else and a household. He also sees you as primarily interested in keeping up with the social scene and having a good time, so he's not taking you seriously.

Example 3: You're sitting with your new boyfriend and a group of his male friends, listening to them talk and tell jokes. The language gets very racy and even a bit insulting, but you say nothing, instead laughing along with the others as if you were "one of the guys" just having fun.

Outcome: He probably thinks you're easygoing and fun, and feels like he can say anything in your presence because you don't have any limits, which to some extent can be a good thing. However, he feels comfortable enough to use any type of language around you; this may include derogatory remarks when he's upset with you, which is a sign of disrespect.

Example 4: You go out for an evening with friends, dressed stylishly showing off a little leg in a tasteful knee-length skirt. You are groomed nicely and your posture is perfect. You are relaxed and meet several men with whom you talk about news, world events, careers and family, avoiding bad language and negativity, but still showing a warm sense of humor.

Outcome: You appear as though you are a woman who takes good care of herself. Because you take pride in your appearance and how you communicate with others, he believes you have high standards. He listens intently to everything you say, hoping to get to know you better. He talks courteously to you, giving you compliments and making an effort to say all the right things. He's polite, a little nervous and hopes to live up to your expectations.

Now, you decide what kind of woman you want the world to see.

Walking the Walk

While going through your self-esteem evolution, you may pinpoint certain qualities you admire in others and would like to possess yourself. So how can you acquire such a characteristic?

Well, as they say, "Imitation is the sincerest form of flattery," which just happens to be one of the best ways to learn a positive, new trait! Professional life coaches have long advised people to not only "talk the talk" but to "walk the walk." That means it's important to actually act out what you believe, rather than simply talk about it. I know — easier said than done. Although you may not know exactly how to do this, one way to take on a positive new attribute (i.e., confidence) or change a behavior that is not working for you (acting as if you don't care when you do) is to choose a role model with the quality you admire and observe how that person puts it out there.

For example, sometimes when I am talking to women, they will say, "You are so vivacious" or "You are so confident," and I reply, "Well, I wasn't always like this." And it's true. Years ago I felt like a scattered mess. Deep down I yearned for confidence and the ability to share my opinions with others in a helpful way, however, I never understood how to truly cultivate those qualities in myself. It was not until I decided to find role models who possessed those characteristics that I was able to observe, practice and finally, make them my own. I studied how a few women whom I admired responded to others in certain situations. I watched how they communicated verbally and non-verbally, how they entered a room, their posture and noticed their sense of style. Then, as situations presented themselves to me, I remembered how my role models responded and then consciously replicated their words and actions. Ultimately, what happened was that by practicing and believing in what I was doing, I captured those same positive qualities for myself. As a result, today I feel at ease, satisfied and more confident than ever before. Be the person you want to be! Teach yourself to be secure, assertive, joyful and reap the benefits of a healthy, happy and well-rounded life.

Try this technique: Choose a role model whom you admire and begin to *try on* their admirable qualities for yourself. This new behavior will probably feel a bit strange at first, so just *fake* it for a while. Think of it this way. When you're learning how to bowl, you feel very awkward when you first pick up the ball and take those four, choreographed steps down the lane. But after you do this a few times, the steps become easier because you've practiced them. Then once you become more comfortable doing the activity, *you'll make it your own*. It's the same when learning a new positive characteristic. You will get used to it and eventually it will become a natural part of you. This is, in fact, the best way to build confidence. At first, you must force yourself to face situations with a confident facade, even if on the inside you feel shaky and nervous. (Think of it as an acting experience.) After a while, you will begin to actually feel what it's like to be confident.

Here is a chart that shows the correlation between your level of self-esteem and what it brings to you. As you will see, it's important to work towards feeling good about yourself so that as you come to believe you deserve only good, you will draw it to you.

SELF-ESTEEM & YOU

Self-Esteem Level	What You're Really Saying	The Results
VERY LOW	**I hate myself; I'm not worth much; I don't deserve much.**	**You get the bare minimum from yourself and others and feel as though this is the best your life will get.**

LOW	I don't like myself; I expect some good things but never get them.	You get the minimum from yourself and others, but you wonder if there is a way to change things.
ROLLER COASTER	I guess I'm okay; I expect some good things and may get some from time to time.	Your mood ranges from slightly depressed to sometimes content. When something good comes along, it's usually a surprise to you and makes you feel uncomfortable.
ELEVATED	I'm a good person; I like me; I want and have good things come my way.	You are generally content and satisfied. Often you get treated well and find what you need comes your way.
HIGH	I am a great person. I love me. I expect only the best from myself and others and know that fate will see that I am taken care of.	You are happy and satisfied. You usually get what you need, and when you don't get what you want you know it's because there is something better on its way to you.

Chapter 3:
Finding Your Forte

How Do You Define Yourself?

As you grow into the person you want to be, you will naturally acquire certain personality traits or characteristics that will become a part of you. As these develop and you mature, you will have experiences that will also continue to mold the person you are. Although it may be true that you are the product of your positive and negative life experiences, it is *not* true that how you define yourself is determined by what you do, where you work and to whom you are related. There is a major difference between the two as you will see from the example that follows.

Consider these two lists made by our imaginary friend Mary. Which one do you think best *defines* her? Which *describes* her?

I am...	I am...
The child of alcoholic parents	Loving
The youngest of three sisters	Honest
Born in poverty and despair	A hard worker
A wife	Intelligent
Single	Joyful

When defining yourself it's important not to get caught up in labeling. In the last example, the items on the left are simply facts that describe Mary and her life. The items on the list on the right show things about her defining character - things which she works at and believes in being and exhibiting.

Later, when you read about the importance of "movement" you will understand that some of the defining things about you will change, depending on what phase of your life you're in. For example, when you're a young adult in your twenties you may not be as secure or as confident as you will be when you're in your forties. And when you're older you may not have to work as hard as you did earlier.

Defining yourself involves getting to the core of you as a person and does not include any terms that describe details pertaining to your past or present. Just because life has led you in certain directions, made you a part of some things and allowed you to take on certain roles, those things do not *define* you, they *describe* you. Please take a moment to fill out the chart which follows.

DEFINING YOU

What Describes You?	What Defines You?

The Effects of Stress on You and Your Relationships

Trying to improve yourself while dealing with relationships and day to day responsibilities can cause anxiety and stress. Almost everyone you meet at one time or another will admit to feeling "stressed out" or exhausted for one reason or another. When you greet people and ask "How are you?" listen to their answers. How many times do you hear: "Fantastic!"; "Well-rested!"; "Dying to take on more responsibility!"? Not very often. A lot of the times, what you hear is "I'm stressed."

Stress, as defined by Judy Foreman on www.MyHealthSense.com, is "a mentally or emotionally disruptive condition... usually character-ized by a fast heart rate, a rise in blood pressure, muscle tension, irritability and depression." Studies show that stress can lead to obesity and insomnia, as well as heart disease and, perhaps, even Alzheimer's disease and cancer. Nowadays, stress can be caused by problems at work, relationship conflicts, juggling too many responsibilities, finances or as a result of caring for your family. What's interesting is studies showed stress in relation-ships takes a bigger toll on women than men.

In August, 2002 a research study was done on couples who after arguing with their mates, were evaluated by trained professionals. Evidence showed that, "Marital strife was much tougher on women than men. Women simply experience a bigger stress response to men than men do to women..." The women in the study showed a faster and longer lasting response to hostility. What's more disturbing was that those women also showed a lowering of certain functions of their immune systems!

When stress is felt, your "fight or flee" senses kick in and adrenaline is released into the bloodstream, which causes a rapid release of glucose and fatty acids into the bloodstream. Additionally, to help you while in this state, your senses become keener as does your resistance to pain. However, while these important protectors are busy coming to your aid, other functions like growth reproduction and your immune system *temporarily* shut down until the stress is gone. For this reason, *chronic* stress can lead to an increase in your chances of getting sick and sexual dysfunction, because since the stress is unrelieved, those systems remain shut down for longer periods of time.

Constant overreaction to stress can also overload the brain with powerful hormones that can damage and kill brain cells. According to the Franklin Institute's report on the Human Brain, what happens is the sympathetic nervous system (SNS) helps you deal with stress and emergencies (again, the "flight or flee" response) while the parasympathetic nervous system (PNS) centers on relaxing you. When stress is felt, a "tug of war" begins between these two systems. After a while your relaxation hormones stop, but the hormones that react to the stress do not and in the process can "injure and even kill cells in the... area of your brain needed for memory and learning."

So what are the effects of this persistent feeling of ill-health on your self-esteem? How can you possibly feel good about yourself when you don't feel good physically and mentally? Aside from the serious internal repercussions, it's no fun feeling tired and irritable and, unfortunately, these feelings will be conveyed through your words and actions towards friends and loved ones. Here are some signs of stress that you may recognize.

STRESS SIGNS
- You spend too much time working, and lose touch with friends and family.
- You can't remember the last time you had fun.
- Your skin is irritated or has broken out.
- You feel anxious and impatient.
- You get recurring stomach pains and headaches.
- You have trouble sleeping.
- You have trouble concentrating.
- You have panic attacks.

If you find you are frazzled, some excellent de-stressing techniques are: stretching, exercise, long baths, listening to relaxation tapes, controlled breathing and visualization. One of my favorite ways to relax is to curl up on my bed with my cat, snuggle, rub noses and purrrr! Animal therapy has been proven very effective for humans. Pets' unconditional love and affection (not to mention those cute wagging tails) can do wonders after a hard day or even an extended period of illness! Of course, if nothing in your familiar surroundings can make you feel less stressed, maybe it's time for a vacation!

Panic Attacks

Along with feeling stressed, you may also experience an occasional panic attack. A panic attack is a sudden feeling of fear or anxiety during which a person can experience dizziness, rapid heart beats, shallow breathing, trembling and even fainting. According to studies, one-third of adults experience an occasional panic attack even though they are usually happy and healthy. Such an attack can be brought on by highly stressful or unfamiliar situations, major life changes, excessive worrying, a bad memory, having a baby or for no reason at all! Researchers just don't know for sure yet. However, studies show that there are also a number of *physical* problems that can exist along with panic attacks such as irritable bowel syndrome, cardiac problems and chronic fatigue syndrome.

In women, panic attacks can begin in the twenties and thirties but can increase greatly between forty-five and fifty-five (midlife). For those who suffer frequent attacks, the disorder can be extremely crippling and limiting to life choices. The good news is that panic disorders can be treated through therapy with a trained professional or medication. According to R. Bruce Lydiard, M.D., Ph.D., professor of psychiatry at the Institute of Psychiatry at the Medical University of South Carolina, "With cognitive behavioral therapy, psychologists teach patients behavioral techniques that help them overcome the panic."

Whether your anxiety is related to stress from your relationship or something that just *happens* to you, when you're "under attack" your loved ones may not be aware of your condition. Partners may also be put off by some of the self-imposed limitations set by victims of panic disorders because they, in fact, become limited as well in terms of doing certain things with their loved ones who simply can't participate in some activities. This lack of understanding can cause problems between lovers, so it's best to bring the problem out in the open and alert your partner when you're feeling upset. It may also be wise to have a *plan* in place, so that your partner knows what you need (or don't need) to help you through a panic attack when it occurs. You might want to ask for a glass of water, some space, excuse yourself to take a walk, a hug, hear a funny story or reach out for some silent hand-holding. Whatever works best for you to bring you out of the attack. You and your partner should talk beforehand, so this way when anxiety occurs your partner will be aware of what's happening and understand that soon, with a little help, you will be back to your old self again.

If feelings of panic occur frequently or you have a full blown disorder, *do not be ashamed*. Find the right doctor and consider support groups to help you deal with your high sensitivity to stress and anxiety. A professional trained in such areas should be able to draw out the cause(s) for your panic attacks and prescribe the treatment that's best for you.

Chapter 4:
Testing the Waters

Movement

Have you ever felt the stress and frustration from wanting to change something about yourself or your life but not knowing how to find the right approach or where to start? Have you been depressed and listless, because you feel stuck in a situation with no way out, knowing you are not satisfied with your life and yearning for something to just *happen* to change things for you? I felt this way for years, and after much crying, complaining and fussing I finally found the way to resolve these horrible periods. When you feel this way, what's actually happening is that the *inner you* is trying to tell you to change your current situation, because you are not happy. What you have to do is what I call "Movement."

The concept of movement is simple. It's just doing *something*. I believe that fate is perfectly willing to guide us, but cannot do so if we are sitting still. It's just like someone wanting to show you the way to their home, but you won't even get in the car. You have to be on a moving path — even if it's in the wrong direction — for you to be steered in the right one. And that comes through trial and error and being open to inspiration.

For example: you are working at a job you dislike, not meeting any "good" men and feel as though you are accomplishing nothing in your life. What do you do? Well, you can sit around, complain to your friends, wishing and waiting for Mr. Right to come along and whisk you off to begin your happy life, or you can make it happen yourself.

First, think about what you want to do, where and how you want to live and the person you want to be. Then just take the first step towards one of those things and the rest will follow naturally, albeit slowly and subtly. Here are some situations to which you may relate. You will notice that in each one, no matter which path you choose, the initial movement is the reason you ultimately reach your destination.

After thinking about your life you decide:

Scenario 1: You hate working in an office and decide *I love to cook, I'll take a cooking course and become a chef.* Looking into various available schools, you find one you like and can afford. You sign up, begin to learn to cook and enjoy it. For a while, you continue to work in the office during the days and take cooking lessons in the evenings. Then you complete the course and begin applying to restaurants for a job. You find a job as a sous chef, you leave the office for good. You begin to meet new people and have achieved a goal.

Scenario 2: You hate working in an office and decide: *I love to cook, I'll take a cooking course and become a chef.* You look into various available schools and find one you like and can afford. You sign up and begin to learn to cook, and hate it. You meet an attractive and fun man in the class and begin a relationship. Now, your office job doesn't seem so bad and you begin to feel better about your life and its possibilities.

Scenario 3: You hate working in an office and decide: *I love to cook, I'll take a cooking course and become a chef.* You look into various available schools and find one you like and can afford. You sign up and begin to learn to cook, and hate it. You don't like cooking or the teacher or even your classmates. You leave the class, a little disappointed, but can at least check off "cooking school" from your wish list. You begin to get a deeper understanding of yourself and what you want and don't want and decide that you are more interested in decorating than cooking, so you begin to research design schools.

In each of these scenarios, your "movement" produced a different result. However, no matter which one you chose, you learned something about yourself, made a change of some sort and got closer to your destiny. Along the way you became inspired, enlightened and were steered towards a path of some kind, but the initial *movement* was the key. Nothing would have happened had you not taken the chance and signed up for the cooking class in the first place.

See? Here's another example. Your relationship of seven years broke up for good. You get up and go to work everyday but feel a little lost. After a while you begin dating but can't seem to click with anyone. You eat a lot of fast food now (no one to cook for) and feel as though you're getting fat and drinking too much. After eight months, you discover that you are lonely, bored with the "bar scene" and sick of just about everything.

Here are some possible realizations and actions:

Scenario 1: Each day you go to work, stop and do an errand or two, then come home. You take the time to cook yourself a meal each night, watch television or read and go to bed at a decent hour. You become comfortable with yourself and with being in control of your life. You're at home one Saturday evening and your best friend calls and begs you to accompany her to a social event, which you really do not want to attend, but you do it for her. You go, have fun and meet a nice man whom you begin to date.

Scenario 2: Each day you go to work, stop and do an errand or two, then come home. You take the time to cook yourself a meal each night, watch television and go to bed at a decent hour. You become comfortable with yourself and with being in control of your life. You're at home one Saturday evening and discover that you are hungry for more information about changing your life and making things better. You get dressed and go out and buy every book you see in the "Self-Improvement" section of the bookstore. You begin to read. You discover that there are parts of your life that you want to share to inspire others. You design a website, featuring everything you've learned in your life experiences, and begin to connect with people from all around the world.

Scenario 3: Each day you go to work, stop and do an errand or two, then come home. You take the time to cook yourself a meal each night, watch television and go to bed at a decent hour. You become comfortable with yourself and with being in control of your life. You're at home one Saturday evening and decide that you are ready to "get out there" but are not sure how. You decide to write down your thoughts and try to make some sort of a life plan. You discover that your thoughts are actually a story and you begin to write. You discover a new passion — writing.

Now, you would think that choosing to stay at home more would be considered "sitting still" and not movement, but it is not. The change from running around to becoming more domestic and taking better care of yourself, in fact, *was* the movement. In each case, your first decision to slow down and reflect on your life led to the enlightenment and other life-changing events. And in this example, each one of these scenarios is exactly what happened to me and what brought my words into your hands right now!

Earlier we discussed "defining" yourself and what that means. I mentioned that movement would change your personal beliefs and characteristics as you journey through your life. In my case, who I was changed when I began writing and helping others — that realization was a moment in my life and with that change of lifestyle came a change in my beliefs about myself and others, which brought about a new definition of who I was.

The idea of movement may sound simple but can make you feel a bit uncomfortable. However, if and when you decide you are ready to begin to move your life into a new direction, remember this key point: Whatever it is you are considering, if you become apprehensive, stop and ask yourself, "What's the worst that can happen?" then make note of all of your options and go for it!

> *"Life is a series of roads. Just when you feel that you have traveled a road far enough, a new and more interesting road appears on the horizon." ~ Pamela J. Leavey*

What's the Worst That Can Happen?

A question most of us hesitate to ask (although when we do it's often surprisingly calming) is, "What's the worst that can happen?" Of course, with all the factors that we must consider in a query such as this, the answers can range from slightly off-plan and a little inconvenient to the equivalent of the end of the world as we know it. Nevertheless, when planning a major change in your life why not ask the question and try to consider what you might have to do in each of the possible scenarios? By doing so, if your *ideal* outcome is not met, you will have considered the other options from which you can choose and will have alternate plans in place.

I have a friend in her mid-forties who's been dreaming about relocating out west for some time, to a place where she has friends and possible employment opportunities. Her present situation is this: she's making a living as a secretary in New England and hates her job. She is attractive, fun and single, but she can't seem to meet any men she likes. She owns a condo but it is expensive. She hates her commute into the city and the cold weather. Basically, she is depressed, lonely and looks bleakly on her future. So if she dreams about moving to California, why doesn't she make the move? Fear of the unknown? Fear of losing what she has here? Fear of failing? I told her to (1) decide that happiness is important and decide what you truly want, (2) make a plan, (3) ask yourself "What's the worst that can happen?" and (4) begin to put the plan into action.

In my friend's case, I suggested that her plan would need to include (1) contacting friends at or near her new location (she told me that several people have already told her she could stay with them until she was ready to live on her own), (2) selling or renting her condo (she said she knows of an agent who would help her), (3) saving some money for moving and living expenses (she would just refrain from vacationing and shopping for a while) and (4) packing and deciding on a method of transportation (she said she would sell some stuff and drive out there hauling the rest of her belongings behind her). Once at her new location, she would look for a job and a place of her own.

From her responses, I realized then that she has explored the idea. To try and figure out why she hasn't yet acted on her plans and to relieve her fears, I asked her to consider the "worst case scenario," another step towards realizing her dream. She told me they were (1) missing her mother, (2) staying with annoying friends, (3) meeting no men there either, (4) getting stuck with a crappy job and (5) living in a tiny apartment. Once we discussed her fears, we could then come up with alternatives available to her if her fears were to become realized. I told her to *weigh the risks against maintaining the status quo.* We discovered that she had a lot of back-up options, namely that she could try moving to California and returning to visit her mother whenever she could. If California didn't work out, she could go to her sister's place in the Midwest and try situating there, or to Dallas to see other friends, maybe even come back east and stay with friends or at her mother's house and start all over again. Or she could even set her sights on a new destination and try things there. In each of her options, she had support from friends and relatives, which made her risks minimal — at least when it came to a place to live. Emotionally and financially were other things to consider and she made her list of options for those areas too.

As I explained to her, a person can't move forward in her life if she doesn't even move! Sitting in one place too afraid to make the wrong choice is far worse than trying something and failing. At least when you're in motion, you're heading in some direction which can change, whether by your own choice or circumstances. You start out with good intentions going in one direction, and may end up in a place you never even considered — happier than you've ever been! All because you were brave enough to take that first step! I believe you eventually end up where you're supposed to be… which can only happen if you are not sitting still, frozen in fear. As long as you have something to fall back on — alternative plans B, C and D — taking the risk of movement will feel a little less scary.

Think about this. What about the people who have risked it all? Consider:

- A man, who managed to grab a few small parts in Broadway plays, slept on the stage at night and had a little to eat before making it big (Al Pacino)!
- A woman who lived in her car and sang at bars at night, barely making enough money to eat, before becoming a professional singer (Jewell)! .
- A girl whose parents were drug abusers, whose mother eventually died of AIDS, was homeless and eating out of dumpsters, but by the age of nineteen became a student at Harvard University and the subject of a movie on Lifetime Television (Liz Murray)!
- A divorced woman, who suffered through a period of poverty and depression, wrote her dream novel while earning a living and taking care of her daughter (J.K. Rowling)!
- A woman who was born in a charity ward in Los Angeles, raised by foster parents by whom it was alleged she was sexually abused and then became one of the 20th century's most famous celebrities (Marilyn Monroe)!

What separates these people from those excuse-making *victims of circumstance* is the fire in their bellies — their perseverance, faith, hard work and their utter refusal to give in to fear and give up on their dreams under even the most dreadful circumstances.

You don't have to want to move across country or devote your entire life to acting to begin movement or ask yourself, "*What's the worst that can happen?*" You may want to change jobs, buy a dog or paint the house. Despite what you want to change in your life, it all begins with a single step and some insight into what other options you may have should the goal you envisioned not work out.

From time to time when I see my friend she says "Yes, yes, I know...I know..." and then smiles. But she continues to listen to her married friends who enjoy their loving families as they warn her of losing the security of her lonely apartment and unfulfilling job. She goes to her office each morning in the big, cold city and sits alone at dinner each night. She will get by but will she ever experience true happiness? Maybe. Maybe not. She'll pay her bills, continue to see friends, go on vacation and meet various men, but what of her dreams and what could have been?

Getting Back Up

Oftentimes, when you've been "knocked down" a few times in life it gets harder and harder to pick yourself up and gather the motivation and enthusiasm to get back out there again. But I believe that things happen in our lives to teach us what we need to know and guide us. And although we can choose to do what we want in life, ultimately I believe that our individual, natural talents help lead us down the path to our final destinations.

Next, I pose some interesting questions to consider when you're feeling too weak from disappointment to take another crack at love. Give some thought to your answers, to help you find your way through this unhappy phase in which you now are and find a renewed sense of interest in the opposite sex.

DISAPPOINTMENT ASSESSMENT
- What have I learned from this recent experience?
- Why was this supposed to happen?

- What didn't I see?
- What were my instincts telling me that I ignored?
- What are my new goals?
- What ways can I achieve these goals?
- What do I know now that I didn't know before this happened?
- How am I a better person for having gone through this?
- What can I teach others from my experiences?

> *"When one door closes another door opens; but we so often look so long and so regretfully upon the closed door, that we do not see the ones which open for us." ~ Alexander Graham Bell*

Back in the Dating Saddle Again... Yes, You Can Do It!

Today when it comes to finding a date, you have more choices than ever. There is the usual way, of course, where you "meet a guy and go on a date." There is "blind dating" (through friends). There is internet dating (you meet in a chat room). There is phone dating (party line/hook up). There is computer matchmaker site dating and even what they call "speed dating."

But how appealing are any of these once you've been out of the dating scene for a while? In order to get back in the proverbial saddle, you should consider all of your choices and figure out where you will be most comfortable. Although there are pro and cons to all of your choices, it may be a matter of trying them all out in order to find what's right for you.

Meeting a guy by chance may not happen very quickly. A random meeting of a handsome stranger in a bar doesn't really give you much information about the person other than how he looks and talks. However, *kismet* is the traditional way... I once met a guy while sitting in traffic on the highway. We talked through our open windows and ended up exchanging telephone numbers — turned out not to be my best decision, however! And another time I met a guy at a nightclub who on our first date exposed himself to me in the elevator of my apartment building! Back then I could really pick 'em! For those who believe that their true love *will* somehow find them, make it easier by getting yourself out there and taking a class or going to the gym or visiting your local church, synagogue etc.. People who share the same passion for something often find themselves passionate about one another as well.

Being set up through friends can be fun and also scary. Your friends often think they know you and your preferences, but when it comes to setting you up, it could have disaster written all over it. It's a big chance to take and one that, if fails, must be handled with care so as not to hurt the feelings of your friends or the person with whom you were matched and now must reject. I once set a friend up with a guy *I* met. I thought they would hit it off and they did — for about a week. Then she couldn't run away from his needy, clingy paws fast enough. (She still yells at me every time he calls her!) But this can happen to any of us... I was once set up on a blind date with a guy who, in his attempt to kiss me, put his huge, wet mouth all over the lower half of my face — yuck! In any event, the positive aspects are that you can make new friends, visit new places, and may even meet someone with whom you *click*. Again, it's chance, but it can be fun and worth the effort.

There are also chat rooms and party lines now where people get acquainted by talking. In this arena I can't help but wonder how much of the truth is actually being spoken. Nevertheless, ways of "hooking up" seem to be new opportunities to meet people. However, practice caution and common sense when communicating your personal information with anyone you don't know.

Speed dating is another new way of meeting people. Here, you sit in a restaurant, club or function room and one at a time meet about a dozen people in a timed fashion. Everyone rotates among a group of people and are given about five minutes to talk and learn some basic information about the other person. At the end of the time allotted, you decide from a list of names you keep the people you are interested in and see if you are on their list as well. If you both agree, then you set up a date. For a woman who doesn't want to waste time, this seems like a good way to meet *a few good men* in a single afternoon!

And then there are the matchmakers. Examples are: Yahoo singles, eHarmony and Match.com. Years ago, this kind of internet dating was considered only an option for those who were "desperate" or "unattractive." Today, with the busy schedules of business people and other professionals, it seems to make sense to have your dates screened for you to look for things you have in common with another person. Once you sign up on a site, you fill out a questionnaire and usually submit a photo. Then the "experts" work their magic and come up with a bunch of potential suitors from which you can pick and choose whom you would like to meet. They do this by matching up keywords which clients' type in their profiles. They also search for common interests and base matches on as much as twenty-nine criteria items, including age, region and level of intimacy being sought (casual, monogamous, marriage-potential). I think this should be considered part of your dating options. I do, however, believe you should still go out, take a walk, smile at the guy at the bookstore, encourage friends to help you meet new people and explore any option where you feel comfortable and think may be a fun learning experience.

So now that you're considering venturing out there again, how will you know when you meet the right one?

Are Your Expectations Too High?

As children, many of our parents read us books about a helpless princess who waited for her handsome prince to ride up on his white horse and rescue her from her tower. As we grow up, we are introduced to love and romance through movies, television and love songs. Unfortunately, as we mature and meet *real* people, many of us become disillusioned and find that no one can live up to those imaginative and impractical representations. And, as if that wasn't enough, we also become conditioned through the media and advertisers to seek out society's "archetypes" — people with characteristics that we believe to be most coveted. We become brainwashed, if you will, to seek out what we think men and women are *supposed* to be. This kind of conditioning sets the standards of our "wish list" for the ideal men and women. Then, when we fail to attract those ideal beings or can't meet those standards ourselves, we feel as though we are not good enough. This is commonly referred to as "fairytale syndrome."

In the article, "Sex, Love and Romance in the Mass Media" by Mary-Lou Galician, the author describes other types of relationship "fantasies" including:

The soul mate fantasy: Believing that there is only one soul mate out there for you... and that when you meet him, you'll know instantly that he's The One. So as you go along meeting men, you decide after only a few minutes that, "No, that wasn't him" and walk away. In this scenario, you run a high risk of rejecting a good man who is shy and awkward, but kind, loving and respectful, and with whom you could make a wonderful life.

The master-servant fantasy: Dreaming about the prince who marries the peasant girl and rescues her from a life of drudgery. You may think, *One of these days, I'm gonna meet the man of my dreams and then I'll (fill in goal here)*... Why can't you do it yourself? Can you see that while you're *waiting*, you're putting your life on hold and basing your future on something which, in all probability, may never happen?

The love is forever fantasy: Getting stuck in unhealthy relationships because you don't want to "give up on love." You may believe that "anything worth having is worth fighting for..." But when does the fighting end? Think about it. Love shouldn't make you suffer or feel miserable or hurt. Been there, done that! To me, ideologies such as "love hurts" and "suffering for the sake of love" are bull!

My fiancé is the cousin of my best friend. She introduced us and upon first meeting, I thought he was nice enough, but not my type... oh, I had a hundred reasons to run back to my ivory tower, believe me! Then he called to ask me to dinner, to which I agreed only because I felt obligated — after all, he was my best friend's cousin! I didn't want to hurt his feelings or feel awkward around her. After our first date, I liked him enough and we got along well, but I still thought it best to consider him a friend. Again though, out of a feeling of obligation, I agreed to another date and by our third date, I fell in love with him and, well, here we are today — goofy and deliriously happy! What happened was that after we had the chance to talk and learn about one another, I opened my mind to the possibility of "us" and realized he was a sweet, kind, trustworthy, responsible and sexy man!

Another thing to remember as we search for someone special is that *we are just as good as anyone else* — even celebrities and the rich and famous. So often we imagine our "selves" to be so different from them in terms of how they feel and what they can accomplish. So many of us think that celebrities walk around feeling wonderful all the time because they are regarded as beautiful and talented and are known and loved throughout the world. But don't be deluded into thinking that they lead "charmed" lives!

Do you ever picture someone like actress Angelina Jolie and murmur, "God she probably wakes up every day and thinks 'I'm amazing!'?" After all, she's gorgeous, is loved and envied by millions! Well, that may be true, but did you know that when she was a child she was teased by other kids whom she's said made fun of her "distinctive features, for being extremely thin and for wearing glasses and braces?" What's more, her initial attempts at modeling failed which added to her low self-esteem. She has said that as a child she was troubled and depressed, openly speaking about "her teenage self-loathing" which included thoughts of suicide. In an interview on CNN, she admitted to "cutting" herself. (Cutting is inflicting physical harm serious enough to cause tissue damage to one's body.) Angelina said, "I collected knives and always had certain things around. For some reason, the ritual of having cut myself and feeling the pain, maybe feeling alive, feeling some kind of release, it was somehow therapeutic to me." As she grew more successful, she began visiting underprivileged countries and was profoundly touched by the children and conditions she saw there. She quickly stopped hurting herself and complaining about "minor things" and became more content with herself and more confident in her ability to help others.

What we believe to be true about others (especially celebrities) are our own contrived beliefs that reflect our own insecurities, assumptions and imaginations.

Chapter 5:
Why We Do the Things We Do

We've already established that the way we grew up and what we were exposed to as children are key factors in determining our self-esteem and creating who we become as individuals. Those essential elements, in turn, directly affect our life choices and how we interact in relationships. If our self-esteem levels are low, then it is likely that we will settle for the choices that are obvious or handed to us, not expecting too much from others and believing that we deserve no more than the bare minimum. If self-esteem is high, however, we will naturally look after our own best interests and will only allow people into our lives with higher values and self-worth. Knowing this, it then makes sense to believe that once we improve our self-image, our standards and outlook on life will be uplifted, and when making decisions our natural inclinations will be to seek out the best possible options available. So do young women today have an advantage over those of us, say, from a generation ago?

My friends and I grew up watching television sitcoms in which Mary Tyler Moore proudly held her own in the boorish business world, Edith innocently defied Archie's intolerance and Maude argued for social reform. We read about the "women's movement" in Cosmopolitan magazine, while Cher broke new ground with her unabashed sexuality and singer Aretha Franklin taught us about "Respect." Over the years, the struggles of our older sisters made it possible for us to open doors, to attain more than they had, to soar. As we grew up, yes, we dreamed of meeting our Prince Charming, but many of us also envisioned working in an office in the city, or becoming a doctor or a lawyer. We felt adventurous and brave, and going out into the world seemed exciting and rewarding. Women had new energy, and began to believe that they could *do* anything and *be* anything. Indeed, over the years we made important strides in our quest for equality with men in business and in society, but what about in relationships?

Recent research tells us that, as women, most of our domestic, nurturing and organizational qualities are instinctive; however, we also *learned* ways of thinking and interacting with others from our mothers, who had, of course, learned from their mothers. But what *had* we learned? Thirty years ago, most of us saw our mothers cater to our fathers, while not paying attention to developing their own minds and neglecting themselves. They did what was expected of them. But were they happy? Some of us took note of their silent suffering. As one woman said, "I'll never forget that look on my mother's face... she couldn't have been happy." We told ourselves that things would be different in our relationships and they are, to some extent. But had the freedom and independence that had *finally* bubbled to society's surface made us wiser and more connected to our *inner* selves or did it just give us more *outside* choices? Had those achievements influenced our roles as loving and lovable companions? These were some of the hot-button questions I posed to women as I began conducting personal interviews for my research.

As I spoke with women as young as thirteen and as old as *never mind*, I began to see evidence that our gender evolution was a bit lagging when it came to love relationships. In my interviews with women forty and older, I saw that they had been influenced by our pioneer sisters (at least in some way) and knew how important *image* and *respect* were to women. Yet, some of them admitted to continually putting themselves, their needs and desires second to those of men. I wondered, *Why are these women — who are functioning intelligently and successfully in the world — keeping the little girls in their pockets from expressing themselves and from experiencing everything life has to offer?* Could the examples set by our mothers be the reason why a lot of women find it hard to *maintain* their own identities once they enter into marriage or commit to long-term relationships?

The advice given by many of our grandmothers when getting married was to "take care of your husband and be a good wife." Years later, a woman's duty was still to give of herself, sacrifice for the happiness of others and try to be a good mother. And today, I fear, it's not much different. "For better or worse, for richer or poorer..." Well, what happens when the "worse" occurs because he's cheating or the "poorer" is due to his gambling all the money away? Do we stay silent and just make the best of it? Of course, there is a certain amount of compromising, but when it comes to stifling our opinions, concerns or needs just to keep the peace in a relationship, I think that's a big mistake. During the course of an ordinary day, how often does a woman murmur, "I should just pick up the mess he made" or "I should not talk about this because it will upset him" or "I should forget going to the gym today because I have too much to do?" In my opinion, we ought to forget the "shoulds," not the gym! I say, do what you need to do to keep yourself satisfied and happy. Don't lose who you are by slowly slipping into the shadow of your partner. Living solely to serve the needs of others may appear to solve immediate problems and avoid uncomfortable confrontations, but in reality, it slowly chips away at the essence of a woman's identity. After consistently ignoring her own needs and preferences over a period of time, a woman may forget them altogether and begin to define herself in terms of who she is to others. Then her partner wonders, "Where is the woman I married?" and she asks, "Why doesn't he appreciate all that I do?"

As I continued my research, I found that some of the younger women with whom I spoke appeared to be no more evolved than the older ones. They seemed to be a new breed of female: unprepared, naïve, and oblivious to all of the hard work women before us had endured in order to get us out of the shadows and into a more accomplished and respectable light.

Look how far women have come:

WOMEN'S PROGRESS

1960s	Betty Friedan's book *The Feminine Mystique* is published. The *Civil Rights Act* is passed, banning discrimination on the basis of color, race, national origin, religion or sex. *National Organization for Women* (NOW) is founded to ensure equal rights for women.
1970s	Gloria Steinem launches *Ms. Magazine.* The *National Women's Political Caucus* is founded in Washington, D.C.
1980s	New guidelines from the *Equal Employment Opportunity Commission* prohibit sexual harassment. *Dying to be Thin* is published; *anorexia nervosa* recognized.
1990s	*Violence Against Women Act* is established. The *Women's National Basketball Association* (WNBA) debuts.
2000s	Dove launches *Campaign For Real Beauty.* Empowering movie and television roles for women. Plus-size models go mainstream.

So, if what we feel and think is partly a result of what we were exposed to as children, and if we agree that women have truly evolved in the last half century, what does that tell us about the attitudes of girls growing up today?

Chapter 6:
Illusionary Icons

Have you noticed how obsessed some young women appear to be with having the perfect body, perfect face and perfect hair? Why are these major priorities? Age, of course, is one reason, but could it also be the dozens of makeover and plastic surgery shows on television that promote beauty and perfection? The constant marketing of all kinds of products for women (and men) on radio, television and in magazines completely consumes the airwaves and billboards, luring young women with false promises of happiness and everlasting love and almost *hypnotizing* them into buying their magical potions and gadgets. Their messages are delivered to us in exchange for riches: "Look like your favorite movie star in a few weeks and be set for the rest of your life!" What kind of impact does that have on their self-images? It's definitely not teaching them to love themselves in their *natural* states! Our young women need to *believe* that they don't have to think or look or behave a certain way or do what the so-called "trendsetters" dictate just so advertisers and retailers can make money (who are *they* to set the standards anyway?). As one sixteen-year-old told me, "You *gotta* look good… there are beautiful girls everywhere." Those kinds of deceitful messages are shameful and potentially harmful to young people who try futilely to reach the media's ideal archetype.

Hollywood star and British actress Kate Winslet recently voiced her outrage at the "glamorization of ultra-thin and size zero models and actresses." She said, "It's so disturbing because young girls are impressionable from eleven up to… twenty even. They're trying to figure out who they are and they want to be loved, and what I resent is that there is an image of perfection that is getting thinner and thinner, and it's truly upsetting to me." The actress said that she doesn't allow any magazines featuring "rake-thin" models into her house for fear her daughter will see them. Winslet said, "It's only a matter of time before she becomes aware of it, and it frightens the life out of me." The actress said she hoped she will be an inspiration to others because, as she said, "I'm a normal person, I'm doing all right. I've got a lovely husband and children and I didn't lose weight to find those things, and those things are what should be important."

I am also concerned that a lot of girls feel they need to have a *man* (actually, a *boy* at that age) in their lives in order to feel complete. Again, part of the reason is age — the dawn of hormones — but could it also be a result of reality shows where a *dozen* women compete for *one* man by using any means necessary? These shows have turned meeting and winning the heart of a man (a.k.a. "falling in love") into a spectator-driven, cut-throat event featuring ruthless women who act as if men were almost extinct! Now, I admit that as young girls we wanted to have boyfriends and we used makeup (remember that black eyeliner and blue eye shadow?), but I also remember that all of that seemed to be just a *part* of our lives as budding young women. We were also curious about the *world*, about finding out who we were *inside*. We actually contemplated what we would *be* when we grew up.

One reason for the somewhat distorted thinking of young women today could be that they are not being taught by society how to be proud of who they *are right now* and how to respect and take care of themselves. Because of the wide variety of options available to young women today, I think they become overwhelmed by the enormous amount of opportunities out there and paralyzed by a fear of making the *wrong* choices. These impressionable people need encouragement and to be taught to think on a more individual basis. They need to consider what's best for *them* and be shown how to establish a *balance* in their lives. They need to know that physical attributes *aren't* everything and that there's a meaningful place in their lives for education and family and fun, as well.

Parents today work very hard and can only hope that their kids will listen to their words of wisdom and experience about what's really important in life. However, it's a losing battle when these young women then go out into the world and are bombarded with opposing messages.

At least we had some examples of good and bad behavior. We were taught not to let boys get fresh and watched women in the movies slap men's faces when they were rude. Girls today are told by their mothers to behave respectably, and are then exposed to music videos full of men objectifying women (who, by their words and actions, apparently acquiesce). As young adults, my generation listened to rock-n-roll music about teenage angst (like "Satisfaction" by the Rolling Stones) and dancing (like the Beatles' "Twist and Shout"). Songs with positive messages like Helen Reddy's "I Am Woman" and Gloria Gaynor's "I Will Survive" gave us inspiration and strength. Now, I am appalled as I drive the car listening to my thirteen-year-old niece sing along to popular songs, with their degrading language and obscenity and whose words express sex acts and violent behavior. As I swerve to avoid crashing, reaching quickly to change the station, she says, "What are you doing? I love this song!" Please know that when I state my case, I am *not* advocating censorship here. Nor am I in favor of producing a class of male-bashing women — far from it. I am talking about *taking responsibility* for teaching our young people the difference between what is true and appropriate for them and for *real life* and what is put out there for "shock value" and entertainment purposes.

I believe that we need to spread the word to our young women that they have a choice *not* to be that woman in the video dancing half naked and that they will still get a boyfriend (and one of better quality). We have to teach them how to be comfortable in their *own* skins. We have to tell them that it's okay to refrain from using (and listening to) offensive, disgusting and violent language, and that some women singers are dressed like strippers because they are *on stage* and that yes, blow jobs *are* sex!

Are Girls Being Pressured into Sex?

When I was a teenager and confused by my blossoming body and hormonal chaos, it was natural for me to wonder about sex and to have anxiety about when to have intercourse for the first time and what it would be like. In my generation, a teenager's biggest fears were getting caught by parents, being thought of as a "slut" and getting pregnant. Although as young women we felt pressure to have sex with our boyfriends whom, of course, we cared for and wanted to please, but because of our fears, some of us were able to put off intercourse until we were ready and better educated about contraception. Unfortunately, there were other girls who blindly indulged, had babies out of wedlock and endured the judgmental stares of the neighborhood gossips.

Those days seem a lifetime ago, even more so as I read studies relating to women today and talked with young women about their attitudes towards men and sex. It seems to me that the twelve and thirteen-year-old girls of today are more like the seventeen and eighteen-year-old girls of my generation. There is an uninhibited "in your face" attitude among young women about a subject that was approached with trepidation and spoken about in whispers not so long ago! Many of these girls don't seem to be afraid to get caught. They don't fear being judged (except as a bad sexual partner) and they don't fear pregnancy. Some even think that they are technically still virgins as long as they only engage in *oral* sex. A study published in 1999 in the *Journal of the American Medical Association* found that sixty percent of college students said "oral-genital contact" did not constitute having sex. I disagree. Is intimacy present? Are you touching another person's sexual organ? Is there an exchange of bodily fluids? Then smarten up — of course it's sex!

In an attempt to learn how sexually transmitted diseases (STDs) travel through teen populations and in conjunction with the National Longitudinal Study of Adolescent Health, the National Center for Health Statistics reported that many young people don't consider indulging in oral sex to be as important as having intercourse. In a study which included both male and female subjects, *more than half* of young people admitted to engaging in oral sex. The chairman of the Medical Institute For Sexual Health confirmed this growing trend and expressed concern over "how much girls [really] enjoy [giving] oral sex," then added, "I'd like to know a whole lot more about the pressure boys put on girls."

According to MSNBC, a survey taken in Indiana of teenage girls between the ages of fourteen and seventeen, found that more than forty percent admitted to giving in to sex due to pressure from others and to avoid angering their boyfriends, ten percent said their partner forced them to have sex, and five percent said they'd had sex after being offered money or gifts.

What this means is that although girls may realize that having sex is an important step for which they may not quite be ready, they are nagged by feelings of obligation to comply with the wishes of others who use manipulation and/or the threat of violence to get these girls to go outside their comfort zones and perform sex acts. And the impact of this kind of exploitation can be devastating to the self-esteem of these young women.

As is the case with any area of social evolution when it is explored and discussed, there comes more frequent viewing, acknowledgement and eventual acceptability of the activity. Once you hear about something over and over again, don't you treat it as mundane and unremarkable? Most young women today "know it all" and feel unaffected by sex and treat it as though it's not a big deal. So, following that logic, if it's no big deal, then what will draw interest to it again, what will make it fun and interesting, what will make it exciting? It may be performing sex acts at parties, in front of friends, with same sex partners and with people who are not in a relationship. And I have to wonder how those girls feel about themselves when they look in the mirror the next morning. This state of "reckless abandon," I fear, can only last so long. There are severe personal consequences that result from putting on that kind of "show" for your friends and hastily exposing the most intimate pieces of yourself to others.

A July 1999 *Washington Post* article reported that "suburban middle-school students were regularly engaging in oral sex at one another's homes, in parks and even on school grounds." An April 2000 *New York Times* article quoted a Manhattan psychologist as saying "it's like a goodnight kiss to them" when describing oral sex among seventh- and eighth-graders. The students told the doctor that they were saving themselves for marriage but were having oral sex in the meantime, because they thought it was safe. Who tells children these things?

Health officials are extremely concerned about any exchange of fluids among unprotected teens which can cause increased spreading of STDs and other diseases. According to the Department of Health and Human Services, Centers for Disease Control and Prevention, although transmission of the HIV virus through oral sex is still being studied, there *have* been a few cases of HIV transmission from performing oral sex on a person infected with HIV. According to the National Institute of Allergy and Infectious Diseases, other diseases such as the human papilloma virus, herpes simplex virus, and hepatitis B can be transmitted in this way. Also gonorrhea, syphilis and chlamydia, which are bacterial infections, can also be passed through oral sex.

Aside from a better sex education, we need to show our little sisters how to properly nurture, respect and love themselves *as well as* the partners they will choose in life. How do we do that? We need to encourage them to reach their full potential and teach them how to be strong enough to handle whatever life may bring them, including standing up to the pressure from others to make them do things they don't want to. Life will be tough, disappointing and heartbreaking at times. We need to show our young women how to get back up after being knocked down and how to live their lives with purpose and dignity.

Part III: On the Front Lines — Teaching Our Sisters the Right Stuff

Chapter 7: The Essentials

Exercise and Self-Esteem

When you're sad or depressed, do you run around frantically doing errands and keep busy? Or are you, like me — someone who doesn't feel like doing a thing... not going to the store, not cleaning up the kitchen and especially, not exercising! A woman with a "positive personality trait" is more likely to engage in exercise, which in turn maintains and improves her self-esteem, than someone with a more negative self-image.

In their study, "The Reciprocal Influence of Self-Esteem and Exercise" by Monica A. Frank and Susan Gustafson, the authors explain that research done on certain groups of adolescent and adult women proved that "maximal exercise show[ed] acute increases in fatigue and self-esteem, and decreased tension and vigor." For those women in the research study who were part of the walking group, they found an increase in self-esteem, but for those women who were not, there was evidence of a "significant" decrease in self-esteem. So those that exercised were tired but felt better and less stressed, while those who were not physically active still felt badly about themselves!

The authors concluded that those with positive self-images were likely to exercise and vice versa: "Engaging in the behavior of exercise, in turn, leads to a greater positive self-[image]..." Armed with this knowledge, the dilemma posed to them after the study was to figure out how to get women with low self-esteem to exercise.

The Lowdown on the Slimdown

The only real "standard" when it comes to your weight is the way it affects your health and well-being. No other rules need apply. If you are someone who is overweight and would like to lose a few pounds, there is no real secret to doing so, although the *snake oil salespeople* out there want you to believe that there is. Some people who are extremely over-weight may have the option of a procedure called gastric bypass surgery, however, reputable physicians will tell you that the procedure is a drastic solution and should only be used in extreme conditions where a person's health is dangerously at risk.

For the rest of us, eating healthy foods and exercising is key. Sorry, there is no magical cure. The answer is *balance*. It's what our mothers have been telling us for years: eat fruits, vegetables — a bit of everything from each of the major food groups (if your physician allows) — in moderation. If you are used to eating big meals, in order to eat healthier and lose a few pounds, cut down on your meal size. A good rule is to make sure your portions of food are about the size of your own fist. You may still feel some hunger at first, but your stomach will eventually shrink a little and you will start feeling fuller even though you will be eating less food.

Another suggestion, which I practice, is instead of eating three major meals a day, I eat a little of the good stuff all day long. That helps fuel my body and I feel full! For example, I might have low fat peanut butter on a slice of whole wheat toast and a cup of tea in the morning. Then a banana around half past ten. Then lunch which is usually either a salad topped with tuna or a yogurt and some fruit, or if I'm really hungry, chicken or steak kabobs and a salad (and no treats). Late in the afternoon I have another snack which can be a piece of fruit or a bag of yogurt-covered peanuts, and later on for dinner I have a small amount of pasta and broccoli or meat and vegetables or a salad.

One trick that always works for me when I want to lose a few pounds is to change my "routine foods" and eat different things for a week or two. For example, if the foods I listed above were my "routine foods" — the kinds of foods I usually eat — then I would just change it up a bit. Instead, I'd have an egg or oatmeal in the morning, then a sandwich or soup or cottage cheese for lunch, and fish or a healthy stir fry for dinner (and maybe cut way down on breads and sugar for a while). What happens is that my body, which is used to processing the same foods in the usual way at a certain speed, is surprised by having different foods to break down and process. By shaking things up in this way, my metabolism is slightly altered, and I can see and feel a difference in my body after only a few days.

When it comes to desserts, I say it's perfectly fine to indulge *on occasion*, which means that once in a while I take a bite or two of something decadent and that's it — no more. By doing this, I don't feel as though I am missing out on what others are able to enjoy. Also, try to eat your treat slowly, enjoying the taste and the *moment*. That's what I do, and it works!

Along with eating right, you have to do some kind of exercise to burn calories and stay healthy. Scott L. Diamond, Ph.D., director of Penn's Biotechnology Program and a professor of chemical and biomolecular engineering at Penn's School of Engineering and Applied Science says that "… exercise helps protect the vessels, by stimulating an anti-inflammatory program when the vessels are exposed to elevated blood flow. We're not talking about running a marathon here, we're just talking about getting the blood moving at high arterial levels." So walk, run, take a dance class, play a sport — do something. Anything. And as we said before, you will see more positive results than just your *physical* body.

Does Food Affect Mood?

Now that we have established that exercise and diet can affect your self-esteem, what about what you eat and drink? Can those things affect your self-image and, in turn, affect your relationships with others?

It's been proven that some foods can make you feel energetic, some can calm, while others can make you sleepy. For example, when you eat turkey, serotonin is increased in the brain, which gives you feelings of listlessness and drowsiness — you know how you feel after eating Thanksgiving dinner, right? Well, turkey has tryptophan in it, and the presence of tryptophan leads to the natural production of serotonin in the brain, which is a natural chemical that makes us feel good. Also carbohydrates, such as cereal and pasta, can produce an increase in serotonin, and again bring that satisfied, tired feeling. That's why they're called "comfort" foods. Also, large meals high in fat and calories can slow the body's absorption and increase the blood flow to the stomach, thereby producing a sluggish feeling. So maybe that fast food for lunch is why at half past two in the afternoon you feel like you need a nap.

Conversely, protein-rich foods, such as tunafish, can result in an increased feeling of alertness and make you better able to concentrate. Also high in protein are lean meats, beans, tofu, nuts, cheese and eggs.

It has been reported that women are more sensitive to these kinds of changes in the body than men. Nearly eighty percent of women at some time in their lives have experienced PMS (pre-menstrual syndrome, in case you don't have a uterus). Mood swings during PMS are due to hormone changes which, they say, can reduce the brain's production of serotonin (that natural chemical that makes us feel good). So when our levels are down, we become irritable, anxiety-ridden, clumsy, forgetful, crazy people! That's when some of us reach for things like coffee, sugar and even cigarettes, all of which can induce a release of serotonin for a temporary high and a break from the turmoil. I know when I have PMS, I feel restless, I get easily aggravated and cry during the coffee commercial where the guy comes home from serving in the army and sneaks into his parents' house early in the morning to surprise them and his old dog comes running to him…. sorry I digress — that one always gets me!

And then there is… *aaaahhhhh* chocolate! Chocolate has always been a delicious treat for most of us, but now it appears there is evidence that chocolate can temporarily improve our moods due to its high levels of sugar, fat, phenyl ethylamine and caffeine. Score! Fat and phenyl ethylamine are associated with an "endorphin" release. Endorphins are often referred to as "natural pain killers" and are produced by the body. You know that rush you get just about halfway through a long run or when your energy "peaks" during a workout? You get a feeling of tingles throughout your body — those are your endorphins kicking in! Science now says that eating chocolate can stimulate the release of serotonin and endorphins in the body, which combine to produce a euphoric feeling. This may explain why some people crave chocolate (like me) all the time! Finally some good news — I love science!

Your body clock can also affect your mood if you have not fed yourself properly. For example, "morning people" are most alert in the morning. Their energy levels drop during the afternoon and evening at which time their best bet is to reach for protein-rich foods. "Night people" are usually sluggish in the morning and should make protein-rich foods part of their breakfast, such as eggs, cheese and yogurt. Unfortunately, I am not a morning or night person! (My fiancé complains that on Sundays I can easily sleep late, take a nap and then go to bed early — I tell him, it's a gift!) My energy level rises mid-day (which is when I like to exercise), which means that my eating a little bit here and there all day long helps me to carry on until bedtime.

Water

Besides eating the right foods, scientists and doctors are always telling us to drink more water! Nutritionists believe that eighty percent of us are technically dehydrated. Most of us drink coffee, tea and sodas which make the body lose water. Did you know that water makes up:

- Almost two-thirds of our bodies?
- Eighty-three percent of our blood?
- Seventy-five percent of our muscles?
- Seventy-four percent of the brain?
- And twenty-two percent of our bones?

Water is also necessary for digestion. It helps detoxify the body by carrying waste out of the body. It improves your skin, reduces headaches and is healthy for your heart. Findings in the *American Journal of Epidemiology* stated that women who drank more than five glasses of water a day were forty-one percent less likely to die from heart attacks.

Water is also a *natural appetite suppressant*, so when you're feeling hungry, drink a glass of water! Water is especially important for pregnant women, nursing mothers and athletes. Water is also valuable in preventing *urinary tract infections* (ouch!) by flushing impurities out of the body. I have to admit that most of what ails me on a regular basis is due to my failure to drink fluids. If you are like me, you have a hard time drinking a plain glass of water, so add a slice of lemon or orange or mix in a splash of cranberry juice (also good for you) and enjoy. When I want something to take away the chill, instead of hot tea or coffee, I make this same concoction using warm water. It's just as delicious!

Color Me Happy

It has been said that colors can affect our mood and energy levels. One tip some experts say can help us feel better on our "down" days is to choose an outfit in a great color. Offices are often painted in soothing colors with a hint of a bright accent here and there to spark creativity, while prisons are usually painted beige or gray to keep prisoners subdued and low-key.

The chart which follows shows the generally accepted relationships between color and mood. It may also be true, however, that your own interpretation will determine which colors produce a certain mood in you. It's all in the eye of the beholder. Use this model as a guideline to determine which color will help you to attain your desired mood or figure out why you may be feeling upset or low.

COLOR & MOOD RELATIONSHIP

Red	Passion, Energy	Increases blood pressure and heart rate; can produce feelings of intimacy, stimulates the appetite.
Blue	Peacefulness, Tranquility	Soothing; slows pulse rate; can lull us to sleep; can also suppress the appetite.
Green	Calming and Refreshing	Natural; the dominant color in nature; promotes healing.
Yellow	Cheerful	Fun; grabs attention; represents joy and imagination.
Orange	Warm	Friendly; less dramatic and passionate.
Purple/Violet	Romantic, Feminine	Considered an exotic color; represents royalty, spirituality and wisdom.
Brown/Beige	Natural, Manly	Can bring on sad and wistful feelings.

Gray	Gloomy	Represents solid strength and longevity; can bring back bad memories.
Black	Intense, Stressed	(Absence of color); represents power and authority; thought of as stylish and timeless.
White	Pure	(Absence of color); represents cleanliness and innocence.

Chapter 8:
Building a Wonderful You

Now that you've learned to accept and respect yourself, in order for you to comfortably interact with people and leave your mark on the world (in whatever way that may be), you need to learn how to *be* yourself. But what does that mean? It means being at ease enough to feel and act in a way that comes *naturally* to you.

Be Yourself

Who you are is made up of many things: your feelings, tastes, style, viewpoint, how you think and what you like to do. Ask yourself these questions:

Are you religious or spiritual, or do you believe in science and logic?

How do you view politics, the economy? Are you concerned about the environment, poverty, war?

Are you outwardly affectionate towards those you love? Are you involved in the lives of your family and friends? Or are you shy, somewhat of a loner?

Do you feel strongly about certain issues and simply have to tell people how you feel? Or do you keep your thoughts and ideas to yourself?

Are you thirsty for knowledge? Do you like to read and write? Are you inquisitive? Suspicious?

What makes you get up in the morning? What inspires you? What brings you joy?

What are your passions? How do you like to spend your spare time? Do you enjoy watching movies or going to concerts? Do you like sports? The Red Sox? The Yankees?! *(This one is very important!)*

All of these things (and more!) make up who you are inside. When you meet someone, it's easy to put yourself and your needs aside to show someone that you care. But never give up your essence — what makes you YOU — to try to please someone else. Some women think they should, for example, stay quiet around a group of men talking or refrain from laughing too loudly or even stop hugging people because the person with whom they become involved might not like it. Think about this. What if:

- Isadora Duncan stopped dancing?
- Eleanor Roosevelt kept silent?
- Rosa Parks moved to the back of the bus?
- Lucille Ball suppressed her zany sense of humor?
- Oprah gave up her dream of broadcasting?
- Elvis stopped gyrating?!

The world would have lost out on greatness! These people were all true to themselves and, as a result, touched the lives of millions of people and many generations. So nurture your talents and embrace who you are! Who knows where your passion and imagination might lead?

Embrace and Accept Your Self

Don't obsess about your looks or hair or berate yourself because you're not model-thin or don't always say the right thing. So many of us put ourselves down on a daily basis, and it's just so unhealthy. Have a realistic view of yourself. Never stop trying to be your best, but don't pick yourself apart all the time. Stop telling yourself you're not good enough and don't keep comparing yourself to others. In September 2004, Jamie-Lynn Sigler, star of the HBO series *The Sopranos*, gave a heartfelt talk at Colgate University about her struggle with anorexia and bulimia a few years earlier in an effort to help other women who may be dealing with similar problems. And it was recently revealed that while battling the diseases, she was so unhappy that she considered suicide. She said that she kept saying "Why can't I be normal? Why can't I be happy? I have everything. I just don't understand. I don't want to live anymore." The chair of the Colgate Activities Board commented that what Jamie-Lynn spoke about was "something everyone had or has issues with: self-image."

Frankly, most men don't even notice those *few* extra pounds or that imperfect hair day, and as far as your intelligence goes, you can always improve that by reading and learning new things. So from now on, every morning when you wake up, look in the mirror, smile and say, "Hello gorgeous!" (and be sure to greet your friends in the same way!) Cut yourself some slack. Be gentler with yourself and *embrace* your feminine characteristics — your curls, your curves, your verve! As women, we are our harshest critics and hold ourselves to ridiculously impossible standards.

Cultivate Your Own Style

Another way of treating yourself with love and respect is to take care of your health and your appearance and take pride in your own *uniqueness*. Sculpt your choices so they reflect who you are and what's special about you. You are one of a kind and can decide who and what you want the world to see. Make selections in your wardrobe and makeup that will make you look and feel your best *without* going overboard or trying to live up to the expectations of others. Wear clothes that accent *your* positive features and that are comfortable — not everyone is tall and fits into a size four. Find dresses that compliment your fuller figure. Wear jackets that elongate your shorter torso. In other words, dress for your body type.

For example, pear-shaped women usually have narrow shoulders, a defined waist and generous hips and thighs. The best look for this body type is fitted on top, a defined waistline and a loose fit around the hips. Round shaped women are usually bustier, with a generous middle and slender legs. For this body type, you should wear longer tops and avoid those that bunch in the middle and wear clothing that draws the eye to the leg area. Straight shapes usually have upper and lower torsos of equal length and flat bottoms. Here it's best to avoid thick belts and to wear v-neck sweaters and low-waisted skirts. For larger women, the best pants are boot-cut or flared. Heavy women should avoid anything too baggy or too tight and look for dresses that flare out at the waist.

It's important for *everyone* to remember to:
- Wear the right color for your skin tone.
- Avoid high-waisted and pleated pants.
- Make sure your clothing fits you.

When it comes to your face, try to bring out your skin's natural glow by using the proper facial cleaners and moisturizers or dabbing on some of those new skin brighteners. Enhance your beautiful eyes with a little shadow and your lips with some subtle color. Experiment with cosmetics or stay *au natural* — whatever works for you! And experts say it's best to try and go with your hair's natural state, whether it be wavy, curly or straight. Of course, with proper care and maintenance, nothing is impossible! For best results, consult a professional and keep your grooming up-to-date.

When you take good care of yourself, you send a message to your brain that you love and respect yourself, thereby enhancing your self-esteem. What that means is, *if you feel like you're all that, it will show* — you will *exude* confidence! You may *never* attain that "centerfold" look, but that's okay. Men will *always* have their fantasies — no matter *what* you look like — but most admit they would much rather have a great woman with naturally *unique* features than Ms. Perfect. When asked if they prefer large, fake breasts or natural ones, most men admitted that, although they will admire (*stare at!*) the big ones, they said that *natural* was better — and not just in the case of women's breasts. They said faces that looked altered by surgery or appeared "pulled" or "stiff" weren't as attractive or interesting as were the quirky, unique ones. Believe it or not, perfection can get boring after a while!

So embrace your individuality. When your man and those around you see your confident sparkle, they will feel your power and treat you accordingly.

Find Your Scent

Scent is a very powerful force in the *science* of attraction in animals and in humans. According to a *Time* magazine article entitled "The Chemistry of Desire" by Michael Lemonsick, scientists are studying the function of chemicals produced by the body called "pheromones," which are effective in causing a sense of attraction. Beginning at puberty, both men's and women's bodies give off pheromones naturally and, although we don't "smell" them as we do, say, food and flowers, they do have a strong effect on us. Studies have shown that these scents not only have a lot to do with sexual attraction, but also how people *react* to one another even in the most subtlest of ways. With this science to back them up, perfume companies have begun adding synthetically manufactured pheromones to their products, advertising that *their* scents are *guaranteed* to attract the opposite sex!

According to a report on WHDH-TV in Boston, it's been proven that certain smells can trigger emotional and physical effects. For example, chamomile is said to relieve stress, peppermint to keep us alert and eucalyptus is commonly used to clear nasal congestion. In the science of attraction, there have been a number of reports claiming that lavender, as well as the smell of cinnamon buns, pumpkin pie and licorice can all boost a man's erection!

The Smell Report issued by the Social Issues Research Centre claims that women are highly sensitive to male pheromones, particularly around ovulation, and that the male pheromone "androstenol" has been shown to attract women. However, when not *freshly* emitted the smell can be received by women as "highly unpleasant." Women are also said to be sensitive to the scent of musk, which exists in products for *both* men and women. So if you are wearing a perfume containing musk, you may be much more likely to arouse more women than any males in the area! And one last thing to consider, while some scents may attract the opposite sex, it is important to make sure that your intended knows that *you* are the one smelling so good! When in a crowd, the arousing scent may not be able to be traced back to the person wearing it.

When we use perfume or cologne, each concoction mixes with our own natural chemistries. That's why one scent can smell differently on two separate individuals. Sample a variety of products until you find a fragrance that is subtle and mixes well with your body. And believe me, he will let you know when you find the right one. It can become your *signature* scent.

"Where should one use perfume?" a young woman asked.
"Wherever one wants to be kissed," I said. ~ Coco Chanel

FULL "ESTEEM" AHEAD!

It was a beautiful Spring day, and I was having lunch with friends in the park for the first time this year. We talked about the usual things: men, American Idol, shoes and, of course, weight. Instead of the same old dramatic confessions about how one of us hadn't gone to the gym in a week or ate a whole pound cake for dinner, sitting there surrounded by warmth and sunshine, we began sharing stories about the times we actually defended our imperfect bodies against the unsolicited comments of loved ones — each of our stories ending in, "Can you believe she said that to me?"

My friend Tina told us about how she and her boyfriend invited her mother out for Chinese food at a local restaurant one evening. Her mother declined the trip but asked Tina if she would bring her some dinner on her way home — crab rangoon to be exact. After dining with her boyfriend and taking the time to drop off dinner to her mother, Tina and her boyfriend returned home to a ringing phone. She answered it to hear her mother on the other end say, "Do you know how fat your butt is? And you should think about stomach stapling…" Tina then added, "and when I was a kid it was my nose!" Our mouths fell open. We were mortified for her, but we laughed.

Another friend Janey told us that when she was in her twenties, she went to Weight Watchers with her mother, who would habitually compete with her for pounds lost and body shape. And if Janey wore anything other than a turtleneck and corduroy pants, her mother would tell her she looked like a tramp!

Then Darlene said that her mother recently embarrassed her in front of a whole room full of relatives by criticizing her about being in her mid-thirties and not being married or having any children. We all shook our heads in support. She added, "Doesn't she think I want that, too? I mean, what good is berating me — that won't make it happen any sooner."

Then we recalled an interview where even Jennifer Anniston said that she was self-conscious because her mother told her that her eyes were too close together and that "if it wasn't for that she could be pretty." Makes you think.

As we laughed over our stories (while secretly feeling one

another's pain), we wondered why people who supposedly loved us would say such things. Why would our own mothers and sisters make such obviously hurtful comments?

Are they just stupid?

Do they intentionally try to knock us down so they can feel better about themselves?

Should these people simply not have had children?

We then speculated on the repercussions of such unconstructive criticism. Tina said, "I think comments like that give us complexes. I know it did for me. Ever since I was a kid, I've always been self-conscious of my huge nose, and the only thing that's keeping me from plastic surgery is the pain factor. I may have my nose straightened yet."

Janey said, "Hello? Low expectations? No wonder I married that jerk" (her ex-husband). "He seemed like Prince Charming then!"

If it happened to Jennifer Aniston, I guess it happens to everyone, right? But why? Well, we may never know the reason why people say the things they do, whether malicious or well-meaning, however, one thing is for sure. The impact of what a young woman hears about her body and its effects on her self-esteem lasts a lifetime.

Imagine if you will, a generation of women raised with healthy self-esteem, have a realistic and true appreciation of their bodies, enjoy their uniqueness and don't feel self-conscious or afraid or anxious around people. Women who are able to enjoy their own company, are more spontaneous and less inhibited and are capable of handling their relationships in positive, constructive ways. Women who encourage and help one another and know that giving a compliment to someone else doesn't take away from themselves. Role model women who recognize and accept the beginnings and endings in life, have no regrets, feel no shame and have a joyous attitude, and as a result feel peaceful and calm, live life to its fullest, revel in the silence and love themselves.

Have Confident Body Language

Besides the fact that most men are attracted to women who come across as relaxed and confident, it feels *good* to express your feelings and thoughts in an uninhibited fashion. In other words, learn to act and react freely and naturally. Say what you think, gesture with your hands and make facial expressions if you want to. Do what feels comfortable; don't suppress your natural urges. The ease with which you communicate will rub off on those around you. According to experts, our non-verbal language communicates about fifty percent of what we really mean, voice tonality thirty-eight percent and words themselves contribute only seven percent.

Consider this:

- Walking briskly and standing up straight makes you look confident.
- Folding your arms across your chest can make you look angry or defensive.
- Tapping your feet or biting your nails can make you seem impatient or nervous.
- Avoiding eye contact may make others see you as deceitful.

Smile. Make eye contact. Listen intently to others and respond when it's your turn with conviction. Watch other women around you. Compare those who sit still and speak in a monotone fashion (boring!) with those who smile and incorporate enthusiasm in their voices and actions. Notice which women are *animated* and draw your attention. Who seems more enchanting to you, Goldie Hawn and Julia Roberts or the Queen of England? Now *that's* what I'm talking about.

> *"Creativity represents a miraculous coming together of the uninhibited energy of the child with its apparent opposite and enemy, the sense of order imposed on the disciplined adult intelligence." ~ Norman Podhoretz*

Indulge the Ego and Exercise Your Independence

When a man says, "She's got it goin' on," he usually means more than just her appearance. Let him see you as a *whole* person who knows how to make herself happy and can *do her own thing*. My fiance once told me that when he came to pick me up on our first date he was very impressed (*thank ya... thank ya very much*). He told me that when he entered my home, he looked around and saw that I had a lot of interests — he saw my writing materials, design magazines and exercise equipment. The truth is that most men don't want a clingy woman who just sits around waiting for a guy to "take her to the party." He's more inclined to go after one who throws the party herself!

I know a woman who took a trip alone to Arizona for a week of exquisite spa treatments and loved it! When she came back, she looked refreshed and radiant. Another woman, Trish, told me that once a week she treats herself to lunch and a facial or a manicure-pedicure combo with her best friend. Time for *you* could be a walk on a lovely Spring day. Take a twenty-minute break during the workday to replenish your spirit. Shop, exercise, read, collect things. Don't sit around and wait for someone or something to make you happy. Get out there and have some fun. Good things are sure to happen for you along the way. Don't just say, "Wouldn't it be nice to..." Do it!

Also, sometimes when a guy comes into the picture, a woman may start to ignore her friends and change plans at the drop of a hat for *him*. Has that ever happened to you? A lot of women I spoke to said, "Oh, yeah, as soon as she got him... I didn't hear from her anymore," and "She only calls me now when they're fighting." Don't be that woman. That is a sure sign that you're losing your independence and making the wrong choices for the wrong reasons. Of course, circumstances will arise when plans have to change and your friends (or your man) should understand as long as you don't make a habit of backing out of things just because you get a better offer. Explain your dilemma with sensitivity and apologies ("I'm so sorry. His mother just came into town unannounced" or "I've got a once-in-a-lifetime chance to sit in the front row to see [insert your favorite performer here]!") and be sure to reschedule as soon as you can. You most likely will need your friends to be there for you someday, so be respectful and loyal to them now.

> *"True friendship is like sound health; the value of it is seldom known until it be lost." ~ Charles Caleb Colton*

Need People

The disadvantage to being independent is coming across as not needing anything from anyone. This is *not* a message you want to convey to those you love. As much as you *know* you can take care of yourself, when you love someone you must make them feel that you need them for support, affection and companionship, among other things. If you are someone like me who is used to supervising everything, you may get a little carried away with the concept. It may be difficult to let your guard down or ask for assistance when you need it, but as I stated earlier, there is nothing wrong with allowing someone to see your vulnerability.

Some people do everything in their power not to appear vulnerable because of a lack of self-confidence, fear of the unknown (what might happen if they did), a discomfort with change (in personality or status) or an inability to let go of the past. Whether your reluctance has to do with a deep-seated fear, insecurity or your title as CEO, it is important to give up control once in a while. If not, you may miss out on an exchange of ideas with others, support and compassion from loved ones, participating in social occasions, tuning into your own feelings and experiencing new adventures.

My fiance once commented on my independent nature, saying with great frustration, "I know you may not *really* need me, but could you at least create the *illusion* that you do?" A lesson learned!

Set and Stay Your Course

Despite what the so-called experts might say, when meeting a new man, it does no good to play games. Are you looking to go out and have fun as friends, or are you looking for a relationship with the hope of marriage and children? Why hide your true feelings and waste time with someone who doesn't ultimately want to work towards a common goal? Now, I'm not saying to announce on the first date that you are looking for a husband. What I am saying is to hold true to what you want and be honest.

Eddie, the married, thirty-year-old co-host of *Double Take* on WSOC-TV in the Carolinas says, "Once you know what you want, if the person you're with can't or won't give that to you, then there's nothing wrong with saying, 'It's decision time... sometimes you reach a crossroads and have to choose a path." What's more, if you are afraid to allow your intentions to be known and settle for someone who has a different future for themselves in mind, then you are only keeping yourself from being available when your *real* soul mate comes along and ultimately being happy.

By being upfront about what you want and going for it, you are allowing yourself to feel and experience emotion to the nth degree. The spirit of living is *feeling* what life brings — all the highs and the lows and everything in between. If you are already in a relationship where you think you may have quenched your dreams and desires and how you really feel, it's never too late to shake things up. Declare your intentions, and begin the ride of your life!

"People who know me know I'm strong, but I'm vulnerable." ~ *Catherine Deneuve*

Say What You Mean; Speak from Your Heart

How do *you* interpret the words and actions of others? Are you the kind of woman who lets everything go and ends up getting walked on? Or are you the kind of woman who takes no crap? Well, it may surprise you to learn that it's not healthy to be *either one* of these types. Do you bring up past mistakes every time you argue with your man? Or hold everything in until you eventually explode? Well, you shouldn't — that's unfair to him and unhealthy for you. Are you someone who says "no" when you really mean "yes" (like when he asks, "Do you mind if I go out with the guys?"). Mixed messages are very unproductive. An honest exchange of feelings and ideas is essential to both parties feeling fulfilled.

As you cultivate your independent spirit, remember that there is a better chance you will get what you want or need if you ask for it. No hints, no games, just cut to the chase. Forget coy (unless you're in the *bedroom*). If you mean no, say no without expecting him to fight to change your mind, just as you should listen to the words that are said to you without speculating as to hidden meanings and ulterior motives. The point is, we all want each other to be happy, but assumption and pacification aren't the proper ways. Unfortunately, however, what is commonly said by women and men is not understood in its proper context. Consider these common statements made by women and men and how they are actually received by one another.

PERCEPTIONS & IMPERCEPTIONS

Statements Made	What is heard
"I'm going out with my friends."	Men hear, "I'm going to do girl things like shopping or gossiping with my friends."
	Women hear, "I prefer being with my friends now instead of you."
"How do I look?"	Men hear, "Please tell me I don't look fat or I'm going to have to change my clothes and then we'll be late."
	Women hear, "Is my zipper up? Will I embarrass myself?"
"What's the matter?"	Men hear, "You look like something is wrong so just tell me now because I won't stop asking and we'll only end up screaming at one another…"
	Women hear, "Now what are you complaining about?"
"I'm not in the mood."	Men hear, "I reject you; don't come near me."
	Women never hear this.

	Men hear, "We're not having sex."
"I'm tired."	Women hear, "Don't ask me to do anything because I'm gonna plant myself on the couch and ignore you."
"I don't feel well."	Men hear, "We're not having sex."
	Women hear, "I need your help."

Often times when we are communicating with the opposite sex, we:
- *Anticipate* what we think will be said to us.
- *Incorrectly interpret* the meaning behind the words.
- *Base our responses* on those incorrect interpretations.

Our incorrect assumptions, which are based on insecurity and fear, promote confusion and conflict. By becoming secure within ourselves (i.e., having a high self-esteem), we are able to hear the words and their intended meaning without assuming negative implications and without imagining hidden messages that simply are not there. We are also better able to recognize a statement that is meant to be misleading or argumentative and will know how to address the comment in the proper time and without fear or defensiveness. For example, years ago I might have heard the words from my fiance, "I can't wait to see Jimmy and Bill" to mean that he's dying to get away from me. Now I know he's just anxious to go out and have some fun with old friends. I also may have interpreted a statement like, "I guess I'll just have to do this myself" as a remark meant to make me feel as though I was not doing my part, whereas now I ask him, "Are you trying to ask for my help?" and the matter is resolved quickly and amicably.

There are definite choices to be made when deciding how to handle a particular situation that, if dealt with appropriately, can increase communication, joy and intimacy in a relationship. When the wrong choices are made, the space between a man and a woman can grow wider and cordial conversation between the two can seem impossible.

Authors Dr. George R. Bach and Ronald M. Deutsch tell us that stating your true intentions is vital to two people getting along. They recommend that couples respect each other's *right* to honesty. Truthful communication is admirable as well as *healthy* because holding things in can lead to anger and resentment (which may cause physical ailments). Be straightforward. If you really don't want to spend every Sunday with his mother, tell him, but make sure to speak with tact and sensitivity. The reaction you'll get from your man will be based on *your approach*. For example, if you begin in an agitated voice saying:

> "I'm tired of wasting every Sunday sitting around with your mother when there are plenty of other things I can be doing,"

then you will get a defensive reaction from your man such as:

> "Well, excuse me if all of a sudden my mother isn't good enough for you! I'm sorry we're wasting your precious time!"

Alternatively, you will achieve better results if you calmly set aside time to discuss with your partner how you feel (though not on the eve of your visit to his mother) and say something similar to the following.

> "Honey, I'm feeling tired this week and I'm finding that by spending every Sunday at your mother's house things around here are becoming overwhelming for me. I was thinking of taking this Sunday to catch up on some chores and maybe adjusting *my* visiting schedule to every *other* weekend with you. I was also thinking that, since you work hard all week too, maybe you should take some time for yourself... on the occasional Sunday when you want to go to a football game with the guys, I can be with your mother and give you an afternoon off..."

Basically, when discussing a sensitive issue, remember to:
- ♥ Speak calmly and sensitively.
- ♥ Don't defensively announce a change in plans at the last minute.
- ♥ Clearly state the reasons for your opinion, and offer alternative suggestions.
- ♥ Don't use insulting or degrading language.

Believe me, in the long run, both of you will appreciate the sincere, straightforward exchange. It will save a lot of precious time and should result in the both of you getting pretty much what you want. And this kind of candid communication enhances your self-esteem by reflecting your commitment to speaking up for yourself as well.

Do Your Part to Stimulate
the Cycle of Love and Comfort

In conducting interviews and surveys as part of my research, I discovered the ways in which men and women differ in how they process information and express themselves. In order to make all of these differences work, a man and a woman have to be able to fulfill each other's needs in a natural, give-and-take manner, so it's important to determine where to begin.

I think we can agree that what's most important to women is: love, respect, support, attention and loyalty — which translates into *they need to feel special*. And as we are learning here, what matters most to men is: love, gratitude, trust and sex — which means they need to feel appreciated and desired. So how is it possible that these two human beings with primarily different needs ever come together or get along?

Let's say that you've just met a man. He is sweet and treats you with respect and you treat him the same way in return. As your relationship progresses, he does nice things for you, which you appreciate and reciprocate. Then you fall in love. He is loyal to you and makes you feel special — reassuring you that you are the only woman in his life. You feel loved and secure and show your appreciation through trust, support and sexual intimacy. And they lived happily ever after, right? Not so fast.

As you know, there are times in every relationship when you have misunderstandings and arguments and all of a sudden he's not so nice and you're not in the mood. In order to get through these rough times, it's important for you to understand that he may get careless or stressed, and he must understand that you may get irritable or overly sensitive. *It's how you react to one another through your words and actions during these times that will either get you through these difficult phases or put you on the road to a deteriorating and unhealthy relationship*. Although it is perfectly understandable to take a stand and make your case, you still need to address the comfort and needs of your partner, despite your difference of opinions and the imperfections that go along with your gender differences. Then when times are good, you'll realize that had he not been respectful of you and made you feel special, you would not have been able to appreciate him or make yourself vulnerable to him. And had you not appreciated the things he had done for you, he would have stopped caring and ignored your needs.

How Your Communication Technique Can Enhance *the Cycle*

Are you really someone who spends her time communicating in a positive way with your partner? Simple, everyday courtesies and respect can make a world of difference in your relationship. Consider these questions honestly and you be the judge as to what areas may need improvement.

- Are you open to showing your feelings?
- Do you feel comfortable when discussing serious or intimate issues?
- Do you know how to control yourself and/or resolve a situation if you become angry or upset?
- Do you look into his eyes when you talk?
- Are you okay when there are silent pauses between you?
- Can you tell when your partner is upset or hurting without him telling you?
- Do you speak to him in a different way and tone than you do to friends or co-workers?
- Can you express yourself non-verbally as well?

Think about how you greet your boss, a teacher, the Mayor, a stranger. You don't even know these people and yet you are respectful and well-mannered to them, right? Well, your daily communication with family and friends should be even *more* polite and respectful than that. After all, you love these people! Include in your daily vocabulary "please" and "thank you" and compliment, encourage and support your partner with words (and actions) whenever possible.

There are always positive things to say to your partner, no matter what the situation. I recommend incorporating simple phrases like these in your relationship.

- "I admire you because you really know how to get a job done."

- "You look very handsome in that suit."
- "Your touch makes me melt."
- "Thank you for cleaning out the basement. Now I have room to organize things."
- "You are the best guy in the world."

    Also, special greetings and pet names can really make a difference in positively reinforcing your love and appreciation for the other person, as well as de-stressing tense phases through which all relationships go at one time or another.

Be Passionate about Your Life and Your Work

Passion in your communication with friends and loved ones and in other areas is not only an attractive quality, it can make your life richer and more interesting. You know when you get excited over a new man? All that energy and interest and desire you feel is passion. If you're part of a small percentage of people who have a job you love — one you have chosen rather than a job you just work at to pay your bills — then you know what I mean.

An article by Katherine Hansen called "10 Powerful Career Strategies for Women" highlights these important points which I believe can enrich *any* occupation. They are:

- Get as much education and training as you can.
- Use the internet and take advantage of all the information available.
- Sharpen your communication and interpersonal skills.
- Network with people in organizations and at social occasions.
- Learn self-promotion.
- Develop your talents by using them in some way (practicing).
- Consider becoming a business owner.

I also recommend:

1. *Learning the art of negotiation*: It's important to know how to negotiate and compromise in personal relationships and in business in order to get what you want. You must know your target (whom you are negotiating with), plan the most advantageous approach (tough, vulnerable, sweet, etc.), understand the issues involved (know your facts)

and pick the right environment (feel comfortable in your surroundings).

2. *Thinking outside-the-box*: What this means is to open your mind to any and all possibilities. Don't just do what is customarily done in a certain situation. If you think of another way to accomplish your goal, then go for it. For example, the "norm" may be to sell your cookies in bakeries or door-to-door; however, you may wish to sell them at the checkout of a posh department store or even near the local post office!

3. *Standing up for what you deserve (whether it be a courtesy, promotion or pay)*: Vital to a high level of self-esteem is your ability to request or demand the appropriate compensation for your actions. Whether you are owed back wages for work, an apology or some recognition or credit for your efforts, it is important to learn how to speak up for yourself and proudly and accurately state the reasons why you are due such remuneration.

4. *Asking for help when you need it*: This is sometimes seen as a weakness; however, it really shows strength of character and initiative When you are in the midst of a project or situation and have come to a point where you have exhausted all of your own resources, it is wise to go to a source who can give you what you need (whether it be information or otherwise) so that you can continue working towards your goal and ultimately realizing it. Knowing how to achieve your goal is a matter of determination, creativity and intelligence.

5. *Taking risks*: You know how they say, "You have to spend money to make money"? Well, taking a risk not only involves money, it can also mean giving up something you are comfortable with, changing your way of thinking and making yourself vulnerable. For example, in order to go from being a secretary to the owner of a coffee shop, I would need to invest my own money as well as accept a loan from the bank, give up some luxuries such as changing my hours from a comfortable nine-to-five to a longer 7 A.M. until whenever, and allowing myself to be open to success or failure. While these seem like big risks, however, these steps simply *have to be taken* when I weigh how much I want to start this business against settling for not chasing my dream.

6. *Inspiring others along your way!* I like to look at the world as a place to share experiences and help one another whenever we can. Something I may learn from someone should then be passed on so that another person can benefit. And someone who may have helped me

along the way may be able to learn from my additional research or experiences somewhere down the line. I believe it's all a cycle of knowledge and love. There is no need to be selfish!

And when incorporating all of these things into your home or work life, remember that women can be just as dedicated and hard working and talented as men. What's more, there are many more opportunities for women than ever before, so your choices are virtually limitless. There is no longer a need for women to compete with men on *their* terms. I've said that if I had it to do over again, I would have opened a sexy auto mechanic shop and outfitted my fellow *female* mechanics in bikinis while they worked! Think about how many men would have come in to have their cars fixed — I'd have been rich! Now *that's* thinking outside the box!

Set Limits and Keep Your Word

While you mold your image and build your nurturing skills, you should also have an idea of how you wish to be treated in return. Don't ever let a man (or anyone else) walk on you. No matter what they say or do, *men don't like doormat*s. Trying to make yourself indispensable to him by doing or giving too much (especially if he hasn't even asked you to) will only leave you empty, seeming desperate and may ultimately make you feel as though you are being taken advantage of. If this happens, rectify the situation immediately by establishing some boundaries, but be warned. Don't just be a talker. You won't get the proper *respect* if you don't follow through.

As parents we are told by experts that children won't take anything you say seriously if you just threaten to punish them but don't follow through; eventually they could stop obeying you altogether. The same holds true in any relationship. One man named Rich admitted to me that he always got away with his inappropriate behaviors (e.g., lying) because his former girlfriend would cry and *threaten* to leave him but never did. He said he knew she would always forgive him so there was really no *incentive* for him to change his behavior. Notice I said former girlfriend. After all that, *he* ended up leaving *her!*

I have had this conversation with women many times. A woman will come to me and complain about something her man is doing and then bluster and make threats about what she'll do if it keeps up. So I ask her if she means it, and oftentimes she laughs and says something like, "Wouldn't I love to" to which I respond, "Then do it." More laughter usually follows. By the end of these conversations, I try to get these women away from the extremes ("I'm leaving him" versus "I'll just have to live with it") and focus on a real solution to the problem somewhere in the middle — a logical and reasonable response to an unacceptable action that can be communicated without threat and can be followed through with a little effort.

For example, you may need to set limits when it comes to everyday chores and responsibilities. If you need your partner to put his dirty clothes in the hamper instead of leaving them all over the floor (if, in fact, you do his laundry), let him know that only under those circumstances will you wash them. When the time comes, if his clothes never made it to the hamper, then don't worry about washing them. Maybe when he runs out of clean clothes he'll learn the lesson. Another example might be if you repeatedly ask him to call you if he's going to be late for dinner but he doesn't. When this happens, make your own dinner and enjoy. When he comes home later looking for a meal, explain to him in a sensitive voice that you waited for a bit, but he didn't call. And since you had *no idea* how long he would be, you went ahead and ate because *you* were hungry. Then, set a time to dine together the next evening, and try again. Communicate accurately and be sure to keep your word. Again, this follow-through reflects your obligation to take care of your own needs.

> *"Promises may fit the friends, but non-performance will turn them into enemies." ~ Benjamin Franklin*

Are Your Drama Queen Antics Driving Him Away?

When communicating with your partner, avoid being impulsive, critical and lacking self-control. Some say women who behave in such a way are creating drama to draw the attention of others (especially men). Others say it's a narcissistic thing. Yet one thing is for sure, not many people can take too much drama for too long a time. At first it may fuel passion and interest; however, after

---

a while it gets boring and tiring and downright unattractive. Consider the obsession a number of us have with celebrities and think about the drama that surrounds them. They are constantly in the spotlight — what they're wearing on the red carpet (not always flattering), their relationship mistakes and all of their bad hairdos! Most of them, however, don't feed into all of that and ignore the hype produced by gossip-mongers and the media.

I know when I was younger, I was more of a drama queen than I am today. I did not have a hold of my emotions and was very insecure, always looking for someone else to show me that they cared and give me the answers to my problems. As I matured, I realized that behavior was not working in my best interest and I got the help that I needed to change. Today, I admit that I am still a bit of a drama queen and even have a "Drama Queen" sign hanging in my bedroom (a gift from my fiancé). But now it's more due to hormonal changes than anything else!

Answer the next questions and see if you are a member of the *DQ Society*.

- Do you moan and groan loudly and conspicuously when you're sick?
- Do you argue in public with others?
- Do you talk loudly when speaking with one person so that everyone nearby can hear you?
- Do you leave people or places with ease or make an exit as the center of attention?
- Do you threaten people or take them to court?
- Do you disrespect wait staff or other service people?
- Do you always assume the worst?

Some words of advice: most men don't like drama queens. At first they may be intrigued, however, after a while they will naturally look elsewhere for a woman who knows herself, knows what she wants and comes across as a more peaceful and centered human being. And if you're one of those people to whom "drama" just happens, that's okay. It's how you handle the events in your life and what you allow to affect your life and your relationships that will give people the impression that you are in or out of control... hence, a drama queen.

Listen to Your Inner Voice

As emotional creatures, one gift that we as women should appreciate is our ability to get a "feel" for people through our sensitivity. Don't be someone who jumps to conclusions, but if you have that "feeling" deep down — and you know what I mean — don't ignore it. It's commonly known as "women's intuition."

A woman to whom I spoke, Jill, told me that it took seven years for her to find out the truth about the man she had been dating, although she had a feeling that something wasn't quite right for a long time before that. During their relationship, there had been phases when they would lose touch for short periods of time. He would eventually contact her though, and they would begin to date again. During their last round of dating, Jill experienced an uneasy feeling which though she ignored still persisted until, inevitably, a slip of the tongue one evening convinced her to investigate her suspicions. As they were talking on the phone, he casually mentioned that he had moved. She, of course, asked for his new address. He told her, "Just send any cards, letters or packages to my office." As that remark festered, Jill began to remember other things he said that didn't quite fit. Finally, convinced *something* was going on, she checked various addresses and other information on the Internet and found out that *he had actually gotten married several years before — and even had a baby on the way!* Jill, of course, was devastated and felt so badly about what had happened that one night when he was visiting, she confronted him with her discovery by telephoning his wife and handing him the phone!

In the February 2004 issue of *The Journal of Alternative and Complementary Medicine*, HeartMath published its research findings involving the roles the heart and brain play in intuitive behavior. Their studies found that the heart rates in their subjects increased significantly a few seconds *prior* to them viewing disturbing images and returned to calm, steady beats a few seconds *prior* to viewing more peaceful images. This, of course, was evidence that their bodies *correctly anticipated* what was about to appear before them. Further studies also proved that these physical changes were greater in *female* test subjects than in males. So your sudden sense of discomfort may be your inner voice trying to tell you something, and you should find out what it is. It may be minor, or in extreme cases it could be information that could change your life.

A report on the news program *48 Hours* in July 2004 featured a woman named Kathi Spiars who was married to Steve Marcum (real name Eric Wright) for twelve years. Throughout her marriage Kathi ignored her uneasy gut feelings and believed her husband's numerous over-the-top stories, one of which was that he was a former member of the CIA. Finally, one night after many years of feeling apprehensive, she decided to investigate. She found out, among other things, that his parents were alive (he said they were dead) and that he had two other wives (to whom he was still married) and also children (he told her he was a one-time divorcee with no kids)! Even more frightening, she found out that he had been accused of *murdering* a man in another state—and the investigation at the time was still in progress! Of course this *is* an extreme example, but the message here: *trust your instincts*.

> *"I feel there are two people inside me - me and my intuition. If I go against her, she'll screw me every time, and if I follow her, we get along quite nicely." ~ Kim Basinger*

Be Grateful

I believe it's important to be thankful for all of our natural gifts, the love of others, for who we *are* and all that we *have* — to whomever or whatever we believe in. Look around; things could be a lot worse! I know that we all have days when we just let petty, little things in our lives get us down — a missed bus, a stain on our favorite suit, a horrible day at work, but don't let it upset you too much. You may not believe this but *every time* I start to feel sorry for myself, a mentally or physically-challenged person, all alone and determined to get to his or her destination, passes right before my eyes. I'll be walking to my car, in a bad mood and irritable, and coming towards me is a man in a wheelchair trying to catch the bus for work. That image stops me in my tracks and humbles me.

Recently, scientists began researching the link between religion and good health and happiness. Dr. Michael McCollough from the Southern Methodist University in Texas and Dr. Robert Emmons from the University of California conducted the Research Project on Gratitude and Thanksgiving and said that their research indicated that "gratitude plays a significant role in a person's sense of well-being" and not just as it pertains to religion. They found that:

- Daily exercises in gratitude resulted in higher levels of alertness, enthusiasm, determination, optimism and energy.
- The test group experienced less depression, was more likely to help others, exercised more regularly, and made progress towards personal goals.
- People who felt grateful were also more likely to feel loved because they were open to allowing more positive influences in their lives.

Being grateful is very important. I believe that when we embrace gratitude and humility, we get the most out of everything we have been given, and our appreciation brings more goodness and love to us. One of my favorite quotes is:

> *"To speak gratitude is courteous and pleasant, to enact gratitude is generous and noble, but to live gratitude is to touch heaven."* ~ *Johannes A. Gaertner*

Everything's Relative

While it is important for us to appreciate our loved ones, it is also wise to measure from time to time the health of our personal relationships. But how does a woman determine if she truly has a good relationship? Obviously there are no clear-cut rules or set guidelines — if there were, we wouldn't all be so confused! And your idea of what constitutes a good relationship may differ from mine or someone else's. What one woman may complain about may seem wonderful to another. What works for one person, may not work at all for another.

For example, your friend calls you complaining that her husband is messy and stays home a lot. You might think, *That sounds great to me; my husband is a neat freak and is always out with his buddies.* Another woman may feel controlled by her man as he takes an interest in how she looks, where she goes and what she does, while her friend, whose husband seldom notices her, feels as though she is neglected. In the extreme, if in the past you've been in a physically abusive relationship, then what you have with your new man who just calls you derogatory names will seem like a good relationship.

So how do we judge what is really good and bad? Make it personal.

If your relationship and your man meet your needs and you are happy —
despite what other people say is the "norm" — then it's a good relationship. If you are consistently upset or confused or hurt, then you can
safely say that yours is probably not a healthy relationship.

The following chart shows that the *consistency* of how you are
treated affects your *mood* and outlook, which determines the *health* of
your relationship.

MOOD & RELATIONSHIP HEALTH

consistency	Always- Usually ↓	Usually -A lot of the Time ↓	Most of the Time- Always ↓
how you *are* *treated*	Abusive Disrespectful Neglectful	Helpful Affectionate Supportive	Respectful Unselfish Loyal Reliable Loving
mood	Miserable Unhappy	Okay Content Optimistic	Happy Joyful
health	Bad	Average-Good	Very Good

As you can see, the more often you are treated with the proper care,
the better you feel and the higher the quality of the relationship.
Accordingly, the way you treat your partner will also set the parameters
for your relationship. Ideally, both parties should be consistent in their
intimacy, love, respect and support for one another.

Feel Your Power

As we learn how to properly treat those we love, we also have to
remember to be true to ourselves as women. Being supportive and
confident and responsible does not mean relinquishing your female
attributes. "Acting like a lady" can be sexy and attractive to men and
spark confidence inside you as well. As you go through your daily life,
relax and feel the depths of your femininity. Take your time — walk
slowly and confidently and speak softly and deeply. Remember the

glamorous Hollywood movie stars like Ingrid Bergman, Audrey Hepburn and Grace Kelly? Now those are some powerful feminine images! Their appeal was not only because of their beauty — they simply oozed style, confidence and sophistication.

According to the "Top 99 Most Desirable Women" compiled annually by AskMen.com, votes are cast taking into account a number of criteria. It said "the women on the list possess a combination of looks, intelligence and personality that set them apart" which means that those women considered most desirable were most likely in touch with the power of their femininity. And when commenting on the fall/winter collection of a fashion designer, a CNN reviewer said, "Oscar De La Renta plays with the power of femininity in his fall/winter collection. His collection is geared towards the confident woman, sure of her role in society and secure in her self-image." The "power" portrayed by De La Renta's collection was not found by using a "mannish" construction of his suits, but in the feeling of ease and comfort with which women could wear his suits, thereby making the wearer feel and come across as powerful.

Speaking courteously and listening to others are also behaviors that convey power and are appealing to men as well. Basically, what I'm saying here is you don't have to be outrageously *over-the-top* or outwardly competitive with other women in order to capture a man's attention. Subtly works too. Demonstrate your respect for and sensitivity to others, practice your good manners and reveal your other gentle qualities — it will only add to your mystery! One man gushed that he was incredibly turned on by the way a certain woman *moved*. He said, "she was *so feminine...* she was just beautiful."

Believe It

As you learn to build your power and use your intelligence and common sense to make the best decisions for yourself, you must also *believe* that you can accomplish anything you put your mind to. The key is to (i) figure out what you want, (ii) take steps towards your goal every day, and (iii) focus on it and don't give up. A wonderful author named Louise Hay urges us to change the negative tape that's playing in our heads — the one that tells us that we are not good enough and that change is bad. She says to accept that there is nothing we can do about the past, but that we do, in fact, have the ability to improve our lives in the *present*. (For more on inspirational affirmations, I sincerely recommend Louise Hay's book, *You Can Heal Your Life*.) So believe that this moment right now is unlike any other moment in your life. You can make of it what you want: happy, sad, productive, relaxing — anything!

Thinking positively will surely improve your focus and determination and enable you to accomplish your goals. Muhammad Ali was once quoted as saying, "It's lack of faith that makes people afraid of meeting challenges, and I believe in myself." Experts tell us that fear of the unknown and fear of failure are major factors in preventing people from becoming successful. So the first thing to do when tackling a new challenge is to make up your mind that you *can* do it. Next, make a plan. You may begin feeling overwhelmed by the task or even the *idea* of the task, so identify what your initial step should be. The most difficult thing you'll have to do is to make that first move. It may be something as simple as making a phone call or retrieving a book from the library. But once you do it, you will see that you *can* and *did* accomplish something, and the next step will seem less intimidating. Just push yourself past that paralyzing feeling you get when confronted with "too much." As one woman put it, "I've never allowed my body to limit me as to what my mind wants to do."

Recently, I heard about a woman who, after her kids were grown, wanted to help out some young teenagers who needed a place to live and some positive guidance. She began by becoming a foster mother to a teenager. After that, she opened her home to more young people. A few years later, she got so much support and recognition for her honorable work that she was able to successfully start a shelter program where people could go for a variety of assistance!

You never know where your journey will take you or how much good fortune it could bring to you and to others. It all begins with just a few baby steps. After that you will be marching towards your dream and will end up running to embrace it with open arms. With confidence and a pure heart, you can do anything!

"A determined soul will do more with a rusty monkey wrench than a loafer will accomplish with all the tools in a machine shop." ~ Robert Hughes

ARE YOU AFRAID OF SUCCESS?

At this moment in my life, I find that I am fortunate enough to be realizing some of the goals I set for myself both personally and professionally. However, instead of feeling ecstatic about my accomplishments, I find myself having mixed feelings. Sometimes it seems as though I fear succeeding almost as much as I do failure. But why would a person who has been working so hard towards a dream suddenly be afraid of realizing it?

Well, with success comes change, which can include finances, family status, location and/or celebrity. This "moving forward" can bring on uncomfortable feelings with new, unfamiliar situations. Also, there is what I call the "phony factor." Some of us may ask, "Who am I to think I can do this?" We begin to doubt our abilities to handle the new role and our qualifications that got us there. We may also be faced with scrutiny from others; both criticism and compliments can be difficult for a lot of people to handle.

Besides the unfamiliar territory and our new functionality, often there is more work to be done in order to maintain the success we have achieved, as well as to set another goal and work towards that. Anticipating what's next can seem like another mountain to climb. Lastly, when we fail, we have a built-in excuse to maintain the status quo. Although we may complain about our failures, we may be secretly content to continue in our routines and live among what is familiar to us. We are aware that once we achieve our goals, that "safe zone" will be gone.

In order to help myself out of this *anxiety-ridden state of sheer terror*, I discovered several things to consider that helped me to relax a bit and feel more comfortable with my newfound success.

- Moving forward is evolving, and that is a chance for learning and growing. Embrace the challenge. Find proper role models to observe, follow their strategies and learn from your mistakes.
- You are not trapped; what you do is your choice. Ultimately, you are only accountable to yourself. You can change your direction at any time.
- Keep things in the moment. Take it slow. Break things down into baby steps. Make lists to ease your mind. Don't think about anything other than today's responsibilities.

> • Leave it all in the hands of fate. Give up control beyond your own hard work. Do your best and believe that whatever is meant to be, will be.
> • Enjoy the adventure. Life passes by quickly, so allow yourself to be proud. Celebrate and enjoy your achievements. Smile, cheer, giggle, dance, do a cartwheel!

Let 'Em See Your Joy

Have you ever seen a woman so happy that she almost glowed? That's joy. But how did she achieve it? Debrena Jackson Gandy, author of *All the Joy You Can Stand*, explains that pampering ourselves will only take care of our exterior selves; choosing to do and be in the company of what strengthens and nurtures us will bring us *inner* happiness. That means, surround yourself with positive role models and friends who have similar values and beliefs. Cherish your awake hours and make the most of the time you have with the people in your life! With each minute of your life, make a mental scrapbook to treasure and, if you have a bad day, find the lesson in the experience. Be receptive to others who share with you their gifts of wisdom and support and do the same for them. By trusting in others, you give up trying to control everything — allow life to flow! See each day as a new adventure, looking forward to the surprise of what's to come. That way, as with the big events in your life, you can get *excited* about the little things in your life, such as sipping hot cocoa under the blankets while viewing a great movie, watching the sun set after a hard day, and even beating all the red lights on your way home! *Take time to enjoy the moment with all of its silence, warmth, comfort and peace.* An actress once said that Goldie Hawn just bubbled with joy. She said that Goldie's passion for life was even evident first thing in the morning on the set as she would smile and say, "Isn't this the *best* cup of coffee ever?"

Joy comes through in our smiles and in our eyes and enables us to attract even more love and affection into our lives. Remember: *what you give out, you get back.*

Chapter 9:
Guiding Our Young Sisters

What to say to her when she's crying over a broken heart: "Love will come in and out of your life. Over the years you will understand why certain people touch your life. Some are meant to stay for a long time, others just to teach you something you need to learn or to help you in some way. When you feel your heart is breaking, understand that you will survive, that something better is on its way to you, and be thankful for the experience of having loved in the first place. As you go through this process a few times, you will become more and more confident in yourself and your ability to love and be loved. And trust me, years from now you'll be sitting around with your girlfriends reminiscing about old flames and probably won't even remember old what's-his-name!"

What to say to her when she's obsessing over how she looks or how much she weighs: "Like most women, you are being too hard on yourself. Right now looking like the other girls may seem important, when in the grand scheme of things, it's not. Most of the kids your age are feeling the same way as you do — everyone wants to fit in. Some things you may think are obvious, may not even be noticed by others. If you show that you are satisfied with yourself, then even if an imperfection is noted, it'll be no big deal. You are still growing and changing, so treat yourself kindly right now because you have a long way to go before you get anywhere near a finished product. You are a work in progress! You are an attractive person both inside and out, so calm down and trust yourself to make the right choices. And remember that almost all of us have to learn how to build self-esteem and have had to deal with crooked bangs and the small volcanoes erupting on their foreheads!"

What to say to her when she feels pressured to go along with what the boys want: "Right now most girls your age feel like attention from boys is really important. However, attention from boys at this age can be fleeting. Once a guy gets you to go along with him or do something he wants, he's done — there is no need for him to invest any more time or interest in you. Men like the "chase" and are titillated by the mystery of what a woman is or what she *may* do. Not being able to pin a woman down keeps them coming back! Never do anything that you don't want to do, and think long and hard about pushing yourself to do more than what you're actually ready to do. Think about what you want your image to be — how you would like others to see you — because it will represent, at least for now, who you are. Wouldn't you rather be the girl they *dream* about rather than the girl they *dish* about?"

What to say to her when she's upset because another girl made fun of her: "Usually, when girls make fun of one another, they are either envious or insecure; they need to put someone else down in order to feel powerful or make themselves feel good. It's not fair but it does happen. And what you have to remember is that what others think of you doesn't really matter because their attention towards you is brief and their opinions of you can change overnight. So why waste time being upset over the casual comments of someone else (who is not perfect herself) when what only matters is what *you* believe to be true about yourself? Try to ignore what they say. Smile, hold your head up high. If you believe that 'what you give out, you get back,' then those who speak ill of others will eventually get their due!"

What to say to her when she makes fun of other girls: "You should never go on the offense and attack someone with words (or actions). How would you like it if you were in her shoes? You should never judge others or throw in anyone's face that how you look or what you have is better because at any moment everything could be taken away from you. Women should stick together and help one another instead of breaking one another down... And why would you want to make someone feel embarrassed or ashamed? Are you insecure about yourself? Do you think putting others down makes you look superior? Well it doesn't. That's just inappropriate and mean, and acting that way makes you look like a bully. You should want to be the best person you can be and being hurtful to others is not being your best. And remember, anyone laughing *with* you today could turn and laugh *at* you tomorrow!"

What to say to her when she feels like she has to be aggressive or violent in order to stick up for or "represent" herself: "When someone says or does something to you that you think is disrespectful, there is no need to react with violence. What's important to remember is that you can walk away or tell someone how you feel without losing control. Think about how the other person is acting and how what she says makes her appear — ignorant, insecure, uneducated and unkind. What's coming out of her mouth is making her look like a fool, so be embarrassed for her, then walk away and release that person from your mind and your life. And if you ever have to physically defend yourself in such a situation, then do what you must in order to just get away and immediately tell someone in authority about the incident."

Bullying

When you were in school, were you part of the popular crowd or were you among those unfortunate, gawky drama club members who were picked on, ridiculed and tortured every weekday of their life between 8:30 A.M. and 2:30 P.M. and prayed for an overnight growth spurt and summer vacation?

When I was in grade school, I was tormented by some girls in my class to the point of a mini-breakdown. By my first year of high school, I learned to shut my mouth, avoid direct eye contact with the "tough" girls and keep a small group of friends close by. By my junior year, I gained a little more confidence and managed to become part of the group of kids who dominated school events, and by senior year, I must admit, I was more relaxed but secretly glad all of the anxiety was nearly over. Thinking back on some of the fear I felt in those days, I still get a little uncomfortable; however, compared to violence the kids today face, I had it easy! When parents send their children to school now, it is akin to sending troops into battle without the proper protective gear! Who would do such a thing?

According to a report on MSNBC, the number of girls arrested for aggravated assault has doubled over the last twenty years — and those are only the reported cases. Recently, the news has featured many reports of "girl fights" happening all over the country, which may be a surprise to parents but is really nothing new to the young women in schools today. They deal with intimidation and the threat of violence every day of their lives.

I asked a group of soon-to-be Boston high school juniors and seniors if the news reports were accurate, and they told me the problem was very real. "There are girl gangs, now," reported one girl. "They jump you after school, on your way home." When I asked how she would handle such a situation, one girl responded, "I would just tell my people and we'd handle it." By her "people" she meant her friends — the only protection she and others like her feel they have. "Wouldn't you want to tell the school or your parents?" I asked naively. "What are they gonna do?" replied another girl. "You can't rat; it's just not done." I asked, could this "code of silence" be changed if they had more school support and security around them, and one girl said, "Sometimes the school has young people — like college students — talk to us. They're the ones we can relate to, who know about our music and stuff like that... but no, I would not tell, not now. Maybe if I was younger, I would."

When I asked the group why they think "girl violence" has escalated to the point of gangs and sometimes even the use of weapons, they agreed with the reason given by some researchers: the change in sex roles. Men used to be the ones who were seen by society as the predators and the protectors. Today, women see female "heroes" on television and in the movies "kicking butt," expressing their anger and outrage in an aggressive and violent manner — just like men! Women's roles in society are no longer restrictive and passive, and anything ladylike might be viewed as old-fashioned and weak.

Then I turned to my twelve-year-old friend Ana for her perspective. When asked about her experience with a bully, she responded, "I tried to talk to [the girl] at first, but then I didn't trust her so I went to the guidance counselor. The guidance counselor talked to us separately and then brought us in together. The girl said she didn't want to be my friend, so I said OK. Now we just ignore each other." I asked her if other girls in her class also report bullies. She said, "No. They don't tell, but I don't care who knows if I do. I'm not afraid." And I think that's the answer. You can't let your fear keep you silent. That's what the bullies are counting on.

So as we encourage our children to speak out against intimidation and violence in school, what is being done to help them? Some public schools around the nation are being asked to develop "safe school plans" and to provide annual reports on the learning environment of the school to the Superintendent. Some are scheduling monthly classes designed to help students recognize and deal with bullying, as well as more access through guidance counselors and older students to help resolve problems.

Besides changes in the schools, what can we do? Well, parents should regularly talk with their children to find out if they are afraid at school or if *they* are the ones bullying others. If your child comes home laughing about some stunt he or she pulled on a kid at school, listen to what is being said, figure out if it's a matter of friends joking around with one another or if it's something more serious, and then talk about its appropriateness. Bullying can make the bullies laugh as though it was a nonsensical event, but leave the victims scarred for life.

Other ideas might be for schools to (i) provide an anonymous "information box" or other system so students can report any kind of violence or intimidation without retaliation; (ii) hold parents accountable/require family counseling for problematic students; (iii) expel and/or involve police regarding repeat and serious offenders; (iv) provide more obvious police presence at recess and after school around the neighborhoods of the most problematic schools; and (v) just like the domestic violence law in Massachusetts no longer requires an abused wife be the one to press charges against her husband, let school authorities become the complainants and prosecutors of a bully's violent actions. Now I know that any new measures will take additional commitment and money, but the schools have cookie drives and casino nights for other reasons — so why not for the safety of our kids? We need both the private sector and the cities and towns to pitch in both financially and through law. And, of course, we need students to help as well.

So tell the girls to listen up! They don't have to live in fear of a bully. Tell them, "Get the support of the adults around you and start taking care of yourself! Speak up. Tell your parents. Tell the school. Make a pact with your friends that you will report the bully and stick together, and do not engage in the violence yourselves. Stand together and raise your voices until you are heard and feel safe!"

"A woman is like a tea bag- you never know how strong she is until she gets in hot water." ~ Eleanor Roosevelt

Finding Your Purpose

As we mature, we grow less concerned with the opinions of others and more aware of the conflicts that can arise within ourselves, especially as we begin to realize our mortality. We begin to question the meaning of our lives, why we were born, what purpose our lives should serve. Eventually, most of us get to a point where we wonder why we are even doing what we are doing at all, and many of us wonder if we weren't meant to do something great. So how do we find those answers?

Finding your purpose doesn't mean that you need to perform some death-defying feat or discover a cure for cancer or attain celebrity status. In simpler terms, it means finding out what you were meant to do — what you want to do, what you feel passionate about — and having the resolve to express and enjoy it, no matter what. Although many people may not believe in having a set destiny, however, it can be argued that we all have special passions and natural talents that are different from one another and enable some of us to excel more than others in certain areas and that make us happy.

You'll know when you have found your purpose because of the feeling inside of you. The reward may not be monetary or even recognized by anyone else; it's all a matter of attaining a sense of completion, of accomplishment, of personal satisfaction — a sense that all is as it should be in your life.

For example, as a child I always wanted to become a teacher. I played "school" all the time correcting fictitious test papers and screeching at my naughty students (my parents used to come into my room and tell me "Take it easy on the kids, will you?"). In my junior year of high school, our guidance counselor informed me that the teaching profession was flooded and it made no sense for me to pursue that career. The following year my mother passed away and I needed to get a job right out of high school to support myself, so of course I thought that was the end of my dream. Years later, I found that I loved writing — it poured out of me naturally — and I became interested in helping women to overcome their problems (i.e., low self-esteem). As it turned out, through my books, articles, private coaching and website, I am, in fact, teaching! So although my initial choices seemed to lead me away from my "destiny," somehow the events of my life put me back on track to fulfill what I believe I was meant to do — teach!

You should also consider that your purpose may not be a career or vocation. It could be you contributing something to the world that somehow makes it better for someone else or simply feels right to you. So how can you find *your* purpose?

PURPOSE CHECKLIST

✓ *What do you enjoy doing?* It could be building things, taking care of children, painting, eluding danger, talking!

✓ *What are your skills and talents?* Perhaps you have a knack for arts and crafts or are good at playing a certain instrument or getting people to confide in you or thinking clearly in a crisis.

✓ *How can you best utilize your abilities?* Find a job that fits your skills, such as a customer service representative if you enjoy conversing with others. Be a stay-at-home mom or day care worker if you love caring for children, or a counselor if you are a good problem-solver. Share your gift of music with the world if you can sing or play the piano. Help build homes for the homeless or design inspirational signs if you love working with wood. Become a firefighter or a police officer if you enjoy a challenge or taking risks. See the connection?

✓ *What gives you a sense of accomplishment and pride?* Seeing the finished product? Bringing joy to others? Helping to solve problems? Knowing that you made a difference?

Faith

In order to find our purpose or our "calling" in life, we need to follow our paths with determination and faith. We know that determination is not giving up in our efforts to accomplish something, but what is faith? Aside from a belief, trust or confidence in a higher power, it is also having the same feeling about ourselves. When we have faith in something or someone, we are trusting that whatever we have come to believe to happen will happen, and whatever goal we are working towards will be achieved. When we have faith in a higher power, we believe that it will guide us and take care of us. And when we have faith in ourselves, we can therefore believe that we, *ourselves*, will be there to take care of us and will try our best to fulfill our needs.

I think most us of fall into the category of people with average faith. We will have days when we are sure things will all work out and also have days when we pull the covers over our heads and want the world to go away. But when those times of serious doubt and hopelessness arise (i.e., serious financial problems or grieving the death of a loved one), how do those of stronger faith cope and where do they get the strength to fight off those desperate feelings?

STRENGTH TO COPE

- *Maintain their resolve while believing things will get better* by focusing on the end result and never giving up.
- *Not listen to bad advice and make their own decisions.* They ignore the critics and naysayers and go forward with what they believe is right.
- *Do something that they may not want to do, but which is for the good of the situation or themselves.* Basically, they put the benefit of their actions before their own human, uncomfortable feelings.
- *Go to outside sources for help.* That means talk with others, vent in order to expel any temporary negative feelings or doubts, meditate and pray.
- *Express their opinions and fight for what they believe.* They fight off the pain and disappointment and speak the truth as they believe it.

In an article by Janice Shaw Crouse, Ph.D. entitled "Women of Faith, Women of Power," the author cites an example of faith from the movie *Chariots of Fire* when the champion runner was asked, "Where do you get the power to run races so fast?" and he replied, "It comes from within." Faith enables people to find the strength from inside themselves to move forward in the face of illness or threat of failure or death or even simply in the midst of a barrage of negativity. By improving your self-image, you build your inner power in the form of confidence, self-assuredness and faith.

Faith in yourself will see you through to achieving your goals and realizing your dreams, just as it did me. At my darkest hour, I was angry at everything and everyone for letting me down and "ruining my life," but I was especially angry at myself. When I finally released all of my anger and realized it was not too late to forgive my own negligence and lack of self-love and accept and protect myself, I felt a sense of faith begin to build in me and I finally felt as though someone was looking out for me — me!

What I am trying to get across to you is this: *you must trust and believe in yourself.* Whatever you want to do or be, believe it to be true. Don't waste time worrying over all of the reasons why you can fail or all of the obstacles that could get in your way. And as you walk towards your goal, give it your all. Don't entertain negative or cynical messages and don't settle. If something you want is actually something you need and was meant for you, it will happen. If not, don't get upset. Continue on your path because something even better is in store for you, so hold on!

I Thought They Only Made Soap!

The company Dove has recently recognized the need to educate young women on the importance of a healthy self-image and has dedicated itself to helping them accept themselves in their natural, healthy forms by setting up what they call the *Dove Campaign for Real Beauty.* Established in 2004, its mission is "to change the status quo and offer in its place a broader, healthier, more democratic view of beauty." *Brava!* To accomplish this, they first conducted and released global research on women in ten different countries and how they define beauty. Their first global study found that:

- Two percent of women surveyed described themselves as "beautiful."
- Three-fourths of them rated their beauty as "average."
- Half of them thought they were overweight.

So why such low self-esteem? Well, Dove decided to dig deeper. It seems no surprise that one study they conducted found that mothers have the "most powerful influence on a girl's feelings about beauty and body image." After all, our mothers are our first connection to the world; we often physically model after them and even subconsciously take on their views and feelings about ourselves and others. Among Dove's findings, sixty-one percent of women said that they wished their mothers had talked with them more about self-image when they were younger. Dove's Dr. Etcoff said, "Women around the world have sent us a clear message about their wishes. We now need to help them find a way to talk about it, both with other women and with their daughters."

Dove's Self-Esteem Fund was created to support confidence-building programming for girls and young women globally. Philippe Harousseau, the U.S. Marketing Director for Dove said, "Our research has shown that too many girls develop low self-esteem from hang-ups about their looks and consequently, fail to reach their full potential later in life." It's what I've been saying all along: *your level of self-esteem has a direct impact on your life choices!*

Dove's second global report entitled "Beyond Stereotypes: Rebuilding the Foundation of Beauty Beliefs" included 3,300 women between the ages of fifteen and sixty-four in ten different countries. It found that:

- More than ninety percent of girls wanted to change at least one physical attribute.
- Most had an issue with body weight.
- One-quarter would consider plastic surgery.
- And thirteen percent acknowledged having an eating disorder.

So does this mean that in order for women to have healthy self-esteem they need to feel that they are physically beautiful? It seems so. But by what means do they judge their beauty and where does this idea come from? Well, most experts say it comes from society's stereotypical images to which young women (and men) compare and judge themselves. And it's too bad, too, because if no one told you that something was ugly or unattractive, wouldn't you be left to decide for yourself? And don't you think that you would consider a wider variety of possibilities than what is provided by society (and the media) to people today (e.g., beautiful women are skinny, have perfect facial features, thick hair, white teeth, etc.)?

In order to be pro-active in their efforts, Dove designed a short film depicting "how [our] idea of beauty has become so distorted." In it viewers watch (through time-lapse photography) how an average-looking women is transformed into a glamorous model through hours of make-up, hairstyling, lighting and camera tricks. Dove has also changed its advertising to include more healthy-looking, natural women using their products, and on their website they feature interactive quizzes, have created forums to initiate discussions and have established workshops for young women to explore the various forms of beauty and build self-esteem.

We need to stop the cycle now. Let's help people change the negative thought patterns and actions of our young people into positive, assertive ones that will bring lasting benefits to their lives.

Real Women Who Make It Work

Rachel:

Rachel is a forty-four-year-old woman who owns a boutique with her boyfriend. They've been together for twenty years and despite the stereotypical view of "wives," Rachel is anything but ordinary. She is honest, outspoken, funny and worldly. Here is her take on how she makes it work:

"Well... I mean... it's so simple. Men aren't over-thinkers like women. We tend to analyze everything over and over again until we have exhausted a "nothing" issue. When I actually have an issue, he hears me because he knows I don't have a lot of them, so he doesn't shut me out. Pick and choose your battles and make sure they're real, not some made up drama. Don't waste his precious time with stupid nitpicking. Save that stuff for your friends. [And remember to] take care of his manly needs, [because] if you don't or you act like it's a bother, he's not going to like

doing it with you either, and then he'll start to feel unwanted, insecure and then... may look elsewhere. And I believe in send[ing] him off to work thinking about work. Just "hook him up," and he's good to go!

Flirt with each other, give a little wink across the room, a tap on the buttocks as you walk by, a little flirty gesture that just says "Hey.. .I'm aware of you and how cute you are right now." When we first started dating, we used to call each other daily to say "I'm crazy about you." Now we call each other a few times a day and say, "I just called to say I love you and I thought of something funny today," or "I was walking by a flower market and it reminded me of when we were last in Paris together," or "I just called to see how your day is going so far." Then listen to [his] response. It's not a competition. Communication means both partners talk and listen, but there [seems to be] no more listening. People are just too busy giving in to all the non-important people. They forgot to "people place." Place who is number one in your life, and pay attention to them. Give them your best, undivided, loving attention and embraces. That's what love is. Sweet selflessness! Be kind to one another, respect each other and be best friends. Confide in each other and trust one another and don't invite nosey #*&%^ people into your relationship. Yours is an intimate, private relationship that should be protected! Treat it like the treasure of gold that it is! [AND] P.S. Take care of your ass size. If you don't find yourself attractive, then how do you expect him to? Right?"

<u>Carolyn:</u>

Carolyn is forty-eight-years-old. She is bright, funny, and works nights as a secretary while her husband works days. They have two children. Here is how she makes it work.

"[My husband] and I have been together for twenty years. Anyone who knows us well can attest to the fact that we have had our share of ups and downs. I will explain. It is pure commitment. We are totally committed to our marriage for the sake of us, as well as for the sake of the kids. We want a "whole" family — a complete one and not one that is broken up. Even though we have had problems, we are grateful that we have always made it work. We are definitely a team. I have my "chores" such as being a good mother and doing the typical mother things, and I do all the cooking, laundry, cleaning, paying the bills, etc..

He has his "chores," which are tending to the yard, the vehicles, doing all the food shopping for me (which I really appreciate), as well as carting the kids around to sports, etc. I always have candles lit so when [he] comes home from a hard day's work, the house smells nice. It is always clean and picked up and dinner is usually made. I know he really appreciates the way I keep the house because he has told me so. We are both hard workers and we thank each other every time we have to put in extra hours.

We also give each other a lot of space. He has a Harley Davidson motorcycle and loves to ride. He visits with his brother and his best friend. I have my friends that I see whenever I want. There is never any question when we want to do something without the other. There is total 100% trust... and neither one of us are jealous people at all. We also like to travel together with the kids.

Okay, here is the one (I repeat <u>one</u>) reason why we have problems. We are total opposites. I never shut up, I love to laugh, I am extremely outgoing, try to always be cheerful and am perpetually optimistic. He, on the other hand, is extremely quiet and reserved and rarely laughs! I know it doesn't sound like much, and some other couples might not be affected by this, but to me it can definitely be an issue at times. But like I said, the good most certainly outweighs the bad. He is a wonderful person so it would be pretty unfair of me to break up the family and get a divorce simply because he's quiet! Marriage is a commitment, and it is very, very hard work, but it is something to be proud of to know that we have been together for twenty years, through good and bad, and we will remain husband and wife until death do us part!"

<u>Gayle:</u>

Gayle is an impressionable thirty-four-year-old woman. She is cute, intelligent, sweet and has a great sense of humor. Prior to her marriage, she was in a long relationship with another man whom she realized she did not want to marry and left him. Here is her advice:

"Couples need to realize that there will be difference(S!) of opinions and it's not about "being right." Listen to each other and if the agreement is to disagree, that's okay. You and your significant other don't need to change your opinion.

"We tend not to dwell on something for a long time. If we have a

disagreement, we discuss it and never yell or name-call ever. And sometimes, you just don't see eye to eye... that's okay! If it's something that calls for a decision, then we will discuss and see if we can agree, again listen to each other and see if there is a compromise. Never be disrespectful and once the discussion is over, move on and... don't hold grudges.

We truly enjoy each other's company, whether that's running errands, sitting in front of the TV watching our favorite shows, or doing construction on my mom's house — we like being together. We are affectionate people and it's important to show each other affection regardless of where we are or what we're doing, even if it's an occasional flirty wink, holding hands, love tap on the rear... etc.. [Also], don't forget to thank each other — even for the small stuff — everyone likes to feel appreciated."

<u>Sarah:</u>

Sarah is fifty-years-old. She has been with one man for almost thirty years! She is attractive, very intelligent with a wry sense of humor. Here is her take on her relationship.

"We've been together for twenty-eight years — and we just got married two years ago! He is twenty-one years older than me and one day I realized that we weren't going anywhere; we were definitely committed to one another and why go through the hassles of when one of us gets sick or worse, having to explain to people at the hospital who we were to one another.

Since married, I know he feels very secure (he thought I would never marry him because of the age difference), and I feel secure as well. It's like we both relaxed and knew for absolute sure that the other person wasn't going away. You think before you're married that you're secure, but then you feel the difference afterwards and realize how insecure you really were.

I can say proudly that we have never ever fought about money. We are both "savers" and know that we both like to "live within our means" so that has never been an issue. When most couples fight about money... it really puts a strain on the relationship. I know that he holds things in and when he gets mad, I can see his mood change but he won't say anything. Then he'll act funny and sometimes we don't talk, but now I'll say "OK how long is this [tantrum] going to last?" and he stops. It's very frustrating. Sometimes when I see his mood coming on or hear a remark, I tease him before it gets too far and say something like "Oh what's the matter, feeling sorry for yourself?" and I make a baby voice and then we start laughing because he knows how ridiculous he's being.

He drives me crazy. He's not an emotional man. If I cry over a movie or something, he'll say "You did this to yourself," which aggravates me. He's only sensitive to animals. Other than that, he hates to show emotion — I think he feels it is a weakness. [For the most part,] we get along fine though. We both don't like the other's family though — for different reasons but we still stay loyal to one another. I think couples these days give up too soon. It's harder to stay together than it is to leave. People are just too willing to say "Oh forget it" and move on. And lots of times they're sorry afterwards. A few months ago, he had a heart attack which opened both our eyes to how fragile life is. We changed our diets and take better care of ourselves and try and remember how much we mean to each other."

THE SEVEN KEYS TO A SUCCESSFUL RELATIONSHIP

From the testimonies above, can you see some of the common denominators that make relationships work? Aside from your most sought after qualities like honesty, fidelity, and respect (of course!), here are my top picks for what makes couples stay together:

1. *Commitment* to keep working at the relationship.
2. *Communication* and *Listening* to one another.
3. *Affection* and *Playfulness.*
4. *Meeting* one another's *Needs.*
5. Allowing for disagreements but *Setting Limits.*
6. *Accepting One Another* for who you are.
7. *Gratitude* and *Showing Appreciation.*

Remember, listening and being able to satisfy each other, while still maintaining your own identity and set of values, is key to your happiness as a couple.

Chapter 10:
Some Things That May Surprise You about Men

In this section, you will see examples of some of the most common behaviors exhibited by men. You may be surprised to know that his "Y" chromosome has a lot to do with "Y" he does the things he does...

He is Who He is

You fell for him the way he is, and now you want to change him? Wrong. There are some things that may change about each of us when we fall in love, but the basic make-up of who we are, for the most part, stays the same. So many women are under the impression that they — being *the* love of his life — will be the exception to the rule and he won't do that *awful* thing anymore (like being friendly and talking endlessly to the neighbors or fussing over his beloved sports car). Oh, he'll try to go along for a while — to keep the peace. But if you try to change him, especially by using ultimatums or threats of withholding sex, you are only going to cause problems in the relationship and set yourself up for disappointment. If he's naturally gabby and has a passion for cars, let him be.

Some men interviewed for this book gave examples of things that they were doing in the beginning of their relationships that didn't seem to bother their partners until about six months down the road (one of the men said it was his one night a week out with the guys; another man said it was the way he dressed). Then, the complaining and arguing began.

When you think about it, all that time you devote to trying to change your man can be better spent improving your own life. By focusing so completely on someone else, you can become blind to your own faults and lose focus of your own goals. And anyway, nobody can change unless he/she really wants to.

Remember that some things are just not worth fighting about. Compromise when you can and accept him for his good and his other, rather *unique* qualities, as he should accept you.

> *"Men marry women with the hope they will never change. Women marry men with the hope they will change. Invariably they are both disappointed." ~ Albert Einstein*

He'll Never Understand PMS

What drives all women crazy? When a guy says "You must be saying this/acting this way because you have your period." UGH! Unfortunately, one thing you can't change is the fact that most men don't understand PMS (and some don't believe it even exists!). If your man actually leaves you alone, as one woman put it, "when Aunt Mary visits," consider yourself one of the lucky ones. I've heard men say "She's just crazy," or "It's just an excuse to be bitchy." All you can do is give him fair warning each month that it's no time to mess with you and do what you have to in order to get through it. (I never have to say anything; my range of emotions is like a neon sign blinking: "She's a Mess. Stay Away!"). After talks and mood swings and warnings, if your man still doesn't understand, don't try to explain again; don't try to persuade him — save your breath. Just try to resist the urge to smother him in his sleep.

Your Man = Caveman

Now I'm not saying that he picks at a wedgie in front of guests or pees on the front lawn, but there are certain other things men do that drive women crazy. According to humorist Dave Barry, men are not, in fact, acting inappropriately when they do certain things like lounge on the couch and channel surf, stopping only at football games, fights or sexy women. They are merely following the *instinctive behavior* that is generated from their male brains, like the urge to compete in sports, their inclination to gawk at women and their utter refusal to ask for directions! Also, according to *Making Sense of Sex: How Genes and Gender Influence Our Relationships* authors David P. Barash (an evolutionary biologist) and Judith Eve Lipton (a psychiatrist) draw upon science and case studies to explain to readers how "men and women are fundamentally, inalterably different" in terms of hormones, genes and evolutionary cultures. They examine studies relating to courtship, male aggression, violence and motherhood, but trace the gender gap to the basic, defining difference between males and females: one makes sperm, the other, eggs.

In today's society, we know that our lovable cavemen like to gather together and brag about their hunting and mating skills (commonly known as *a night out with the guys*). When around his peers, the caveman likes to relax, jump around and pound his chest for a while. A lot of men with whom I spoke could identify with this observation. I am told that men feel most like who they *really* are when they are in a group comprised solely of men. They feel comfortable enough to think, talk and act more instinctively then. The men whom I interviewed admitted to acting a bit juvenile when there were no women around (or at least none with whom they were acquainted). One man said it was "...a chance to be more irresponsible than we normally would." Men will also talk about women more openly and, shall we say, *descriptively* than they would if they thought a woman was listening. Ever sit in a bar or restaurant and *overhear* a bunch of guys talking? The conversation can get pretty vicious! They don't worry about hurting each other's feelings or acting inappropriately like they do when women are present. They enjoy rough-housing with one another and "breaking the other guy's balls." If someone does happen to go too far, it is responded to with a jab or a series of four-letter words — none of which is usually taken too seriously. But are all males (and male species) instinctively the same? Some *amusing* research says yes.

One report I read explained that it is quite common for male baboons to fight with one another when it comes to females and food (like trying to take French fries away from a teenage boy!). Wolf Hollow in Ipswich, Massachusetts, an organization designed to inform people of the importance of wolves in the wild, teaches us that families of wolves (called packs) behave like human families. There are mothers and fathers and even misbehaving teenagers. In order to discipline a young wolf who dares to challenge the daddy (the alpha male) or disrespect the mommy (the alpha female), he is chased away from camp to spend time alone until he learns to behave! Lastly, canine behaviorist "Dave the Dogman" tells us in his article entitled, "Sexual and Behavior Tendencies," that male dogs have an instinctive urge to leave their homes for periods of anywhere from hours to weeks. He goes on to say studies show that male dogs that are kept inside all the time experience frustration and want to mate with anything nearby! Ahem... draw your own conclusions, please.

In truth, it is actually important for men to spend time together to blow off steam and let that "little boy" out — the one we women are always trying to make grow up and be responsible. Rest assured, however, that when they are done hollering and swearing and drinking and making unflattering noises from various parts of their bodies, the cavemen will usually put their alter egos away and settle down into the sane, caring, serious men we have grown to love, honor and dare I say... *respect? And speaking of prehistoric behavior...*

He Masturbates
It's a fact. They all do it. Knock before you open a door... any door.

He's Competitive
Another characteristic of our cavemen is that they are born competitors. Whether it's running a road race, playing football or shopping for cars, men can't help but want to "one up" each other. Research done by the University of Chicago Graduate School of Business concluded that the need to compete begins in early childhood when, unlike little girls who are primarily interested in establishing relationships, boys will challenge one another to find out who is bigger or better at something (i.e., by building blocks higher, running faster), or who is strong enough to keep up with the others. And this competitiveness can last a lifetime.

One man whom I interviewed fondly remembered one family reunion when all the relatives got together — cousins, aunts, uncles and everyone else. He said that, before long, the older men noticed the younger ones playing football in the backyard and began to criticize their (lack of) expertise on the field. The younger men then issued a challenge to the older sportsmen, which got everyone on their feet. He said they played football for a couple of hours laughing (cheating!) and falling all over one another until the food was served (and *real* sports came on television). Once seated around the table, however, the senior players began to get stiff and sore and some of them began to moan. As everyone noticed their growing discomfort, the young men claimed victory and that was the first and last time that ever happened!

Your man will usually display his competitive nature when he is around other men; however, he may even compete with *you* on occasion. A woman named Denise told me about how she consistently defeats her husband in tennis. It's a standing joke among their friends. Every time she wins a match, it drives him crazy, though he can't resist coming back again — each time even *more* driven to succeed!

Here's an idea. You can always use his competitive nature for productive purposes around the house. Challenge him to a contest to see who can paint the spare room the fastest or who can put their closet in the best order. It's not like he'd see through *that* plan! Whatever the case, let him enjoy getting excited over the challenge — just keep the hydrogen peroxide, aspirin and bandages handy.

> *"And while the law [of competition] may be sometimes hard for the individual, it is best for the race, because it ensures the survival of the fittest in every department." ~ Andrew Carnegie*

He Thinks He's in Charge

Once I had a disagreement with my fiancé over a rather large credit card charge he made (for a relative) without telling me. I felt that because we were both paying the bills, we should both have a say in major purchases. As we were (ahem) "discussing" it, he got frustrated and said, "I don't have to report to you. I'm a grown man and I can do what I want." As you can imagine, that didn't go over very well with me at all. I crossed my arms, looked at him in amazement and calmly said, "You're kidding me, right? Do you hear how ridiculous you sound?"

And then I realized that he truly believed he had the last say over everything. Years earlier, during a discussion we had about "head of the household" he said, "Well I know two people may have differing opinions, but one person has to hold forty-nine percent of the vote and one has to have fifty-one percent or nothing would ever get decided." I guess he thought he was the fifty-one percent vote holder!

I went into the bedroom to cool off for a while and then began to laugh. It was really funny to think about him standing in the kitchen, eyebrows tensed and roaring like the king of the jungle. All that was missing was him beating his chest! The truth was that I cooked the food in that jungle, cleaned up that jungle and put money in the jungle's bank account and gave good lovin' to the head lion, so there was no way that mathematically I held only forty-nine percent of the vote... no way! After being in separate rooms for a while, he wandered into the bedroom and sheepishly said, "I'm sorry. I am just used to handling everything myself. I know you're right. We should discuss large credit charges since we are both paying the bills..." I smiled and accepted his apology because I knew my caveman would grumble for a while and eventually come to his senses... and for that he got a belly scratch and a big kiss!

He Takes His Job Seriously

As you help him to improve his decision-making abilities, you should support him in his work as well. Most women have friends to confide in about their work worries, but men really don't talk to one another about their problems when it comes to business (I think it's the whole competitive thing) — that's where you come in. Be interested in what's going on. As you talk openly about your job, ask about his too. Sometimes, just being there to listen or offer suggestions will help him see things from another perspective and can make all the difference.

One woman told me that, at her husband's request, she tries to stay involved in her husband's business and help out by throwing pool parties in the summer. She says it helps to keep communication going among all levels of employees. Another woman said she stays connected to her husband's business associates by making sure that they regularly attend events at their local boat club. She said that this kind of networking often results in some great business opportunities for both of them.

If he asks, welcome his boss or co-workers over for dinner. Help him plan an event. Assist him with advertising ideas. Remember, his work (as yours) benefits the both of you, whether financially or psychologically. If your man feels successful, he will treat you like the valued partner that you are.

He Has Limitations

Just as women evolve and learn to prioritize their lives, it can be said too that men try to be all things to women (breadwinner, handyman and expert lover), which of course we understand is not always possible. He may attempt to do the food shopping and fix the garbage disposal or build that closet you've been wanting, but at some point after dropping the kids off at the mall and then sitting in a two-hour traffic jam, he's going to want to take the Superman tights *off!* (Some signs that he has pretty much had it are grumpiness, scratching his head, rubbing his eyes and screaming.) At that point, he cannot possibly be asked to go pick up the Chinese food or rub your shoulders. Sorry. Just can't.

> *"People throw away what they could have by insisting on perfection, which they cannot have, and looking for it where they will never find it." ~ Edith Schaeffer*

He's a Nice Guy

Maybe your man *is* a little overwhelmed or nervous or clumsy — but that doesn't mean he's a wimp. So many of us are drawn to the "bad boys" that we *know* are no good for us. Any man — the man you have right now — could potentially be your *forever-and-ever* man. Nancy Campbell tells us in her article entitled "Can nice men be sexy?" that it may take a certain amount of maturity and self-confidence before our tastes in men evolve. I spoke with many women who admitted to being attracted to the dangerous and unpredictable types, like the handsome loner in high school or the cute guy who was always in trouble with the principal. One said that she thought a lot of women were attracted to the "boys in the band" (the whole sex, drugs and rock-n-roll temptation). As women get older, however, they grow tired of trying to figure out their rebels' next moves and begin to crave stable, dependable, loving companions. One woman reminisced, "I remember Anthony... he was so cool. He smoked and cut school and drove that gorgeous, shiny, black Trans Am. We were all nuts about him... we were so *stupid!*").

It may surprise you to know that there is a website called

Niceguys.org whose mission is to "reaffirm the fact to nice guys that you are not alone and to tell women that there are still nice guys out there." The site created by "Mr. Nice Guy" and a few of his friends offers programs, dating advice, articles, links and recipes! On a blog entitled "Nice Guys Finish Last" one contributor writes "To all the girls out there with boyfriends that don't treat you with respect, that don't listen to you and that don't care about you I say… look next to you. The guy that has been standing next to you the whole time is the guy you have been looking for. He is what you want… He knows more about you than you know about yourself… because he has listened to it all."

It's important to remember that nice men are often self-conscious about their lack of machismo and may even hesitate to approach an attractive woman because they anticipate rejection. I say, unless you hear circus music when you look at him, give the guy a chance. Appreciate being treated nicely by a sweet man and, I guarantee, you'll get used to it and you won't go back to the jerk-offs.

I Beg Your Pardon! Is Chivalry Dead?

The other day I thanked a well-dressed, older man for holding the door open for me and he replied, "You sound so surprised. It's my pleasure." Evidently, after so frequently having doors close in my face, my voice revealed my enthusiasm along with my disbelief! We then began chatting about men and women and manners, and he told me that a few weeks ago he opened the door for a woman who made a point of telling him she was perfectly capable of doing it herself. To her comment, in my opinion, he gave a fabulous reply. He said, "I didn't hold the door for you because you're a lady, I did it because I'm a gentleman."

So what gives? Is it now considered degrading for a woman to be on the receiving end of a kind gesture by a man? And do men feel this change and react accordingly? Are these acts really "gentlemanly" or just good manners, and whom do they actually benefit? As a child, I was taught to be polite and help out whenever possible by, say, holding the door for the person behind me, giving up my seat on the bus to a pregnant woman or the elderly, assisting people who drop their bundles and saying "please" and "thank you." Those simple gestures became part of me, and I felt a boost in my self-esteem as a result.

Today, I still enjoy exhibiting courteousness and having the same extended to me, even though those occasions seem to be verging on extinction! I continue to jump up for expecting mothers and the handicapped, but I also have no problem helping out a grown man, a child, or an animal in need. I think most of us notice when the "good" folks offer their help to others, and those who don't reciprocate these usual and customary kindnesses are silently scorned by the members of the Good Manners Club and labeled as "rude" and "selfish."

Although years ago it was more expected that a man assist a woman, these days I think we need to go beyond those boundaries and establish a new, revolutionary, state-of-the-art guideline that will be acceptable to both men and women, despite their individual philosophies, expectations and capabilities. Every able body should be considerate of and helpful to one another despite age, gender, physicality and occupation. How's that for radical?

Kindness to one another — a brief respite from the harshness of the human condition. And something that I believe could go a long way in helping solve a lot of the world's problems.

His Space Can't be Too Feminine

Even if your man is the sensitive type, be sure not to smother your man in flowers and lace when you decorate your living space. Your surroundings should be comfortable for *both* of you. If the place is too masculine or too feminine, one of you may feel uncomfortable. If you live in clutter or disrepair, your lives may feel out of sorts when you're at home. Also, the colors you choose can affect both your moods and outlook on your life together. Remember, his design preferences are probably different from yours (and hopefully don't include a giant moose head). If there's a real standoff about certain items, try blending the common or family rooms into a mixture of the two of you (and save the "five foot, framed poster of King Kong" for his office or the TV room). If you want your dainty, little porcelain ballerina on your nightstand, then he may want his black gargoyle statue on his. When blending male and female tastes, it's best to find out your man's favorite colors and match them up with yours (try using earth colors), go for an uncluttered, minimal look with comfortable wood furniture pieces, and where you can, use sturdy fabrics like leather and wool.

If your attempts at a solution fail, consult a design magazine, HGTV, or agree to hire a professional to combine your tastes. The goal is to create a wonderful *retreat* you both will enjoy.

He Thinks Farts are Funny

One thing you'll have to get used to sooner or later in that house you now share is the smell of unidentifiable and *hilarious* gaseous fumes. I heard one story about a newly married man who tried to light his farts on fire with a lighter. 'Nough said?

He Hates to be Told How to Drive

In 1994, Hal Rubenstein in the *New York Times* wrote: *"MEN AND CARS — TRUE ROMANCE: It goes anywhere he wants, never expects a phone call, or commitment, and lets him dress as he pleases. No wonder he's in love."*

Remember that the next time you try and tell your man how to drive. I am so guilty of this; I do it all the time (*unintentionally*, of course). It's something that I have really tried to change. Don't tell him where the turn-off is or which car to pass in traffic. Unless you are reading directions aloud to him, stop. Chew gum. Look out the window. Talk on your cell phone. Do anything but co-pilot the vehicle!

My fiance actually solved this problem on his own for us. After asking me many times to stop insisting that he look for a parking spot near the *front* of the mall (he used to immediately drive to the farthest end of the lot and park there, which infuriated me!), he took matters into his own hands and just began dropping me off at the front entrance and then parking the car himself. Works for me!

> *"Any man who can drive safely while kissing a pretty girl is simply not giving the kiss the attention it deserves."* ~ Helen Rowland

He May Sometimes Have Performance Problems

Although he may be able to handle a variety of issues with ease, impotency may not be one of them. Impotency is a man's inability to achieve and maintain an erection. The causes for this condition may vary from psychological reasons, such as anxiety or depression, to medical problems, such as clogged arteries or high blood pressure. Interestingly, none of the men I spoke with admitted to *ever* having a problem "in that area." When I asked some women if they had ever experienced the problem with their partners, however, they replied casually, "Oh, yeah, it happens to all of them now and then."

So if he's been "bouncing the check of love," there are some things you can do to help. Check to see if he is feeling ill or if he is taking a medication that may be causing the problem. Make sure he is exercising and eating well. Next, if he is stressed from work or a personal problem, encourage him to talk about it or seek professional help. Diet can play a role in how your man feels as well and can especially affect his energy level. You may also want to check his alcohol intake. Too much can negatively affect him. Of course, there are drugs on the market now that may help him if his doctor thinks such treatment is appropriate. Not all men are able to take these medications, so make sure he gets a professional opinion from a *physician*. Also, according to the University of Pennsylvania, nitric oxide, which is naturally found in the body, may be the answer to treating the problem for those who can't take the current pharmaceutical drugs.

If you find yourself in this predicament, be sure to tell your man that you are perfectly satisfied with him as a lover and that you love him very much. Reassure him that you know this is only a *temporary* situation and that you are there for him if he needs you. Also, act as if there is no urgency to have sex — *whenever* he feels better is fine with you. The best thing you can do is not to make a big deal; the less pressure on the *little guy*, the better!

He May Have a Mid-life Meltdown

A more serious problem affecting him sexually can occur when he gets to a point (usually between age forty and fifty) when he questions his life choices and wonders about what to do with the remainder of his days. Some men reach a point when it suddenly hits them that they no longer have their whole lives ahead of them like when they were kids. They may suddenly feel the weight of their responsibilities and realize that not all (if any) of their dreams have come true. This *psychological* realization usually happens simultaneously with certain *physical* changes, such as a diminished sex drive, moodiness, lethargy, loss of strength and a decrease in work performance — it's commonly referred to as *male* menopause. Such changes can also trigger feelings of panic or depression, which can add to the anguish and confusion. Some people question whether the equivalent of menopause really happens to men. However, Harvey Sternbach, M.D., a clinical professor of psychiatry at UCLA's Neuropsychiatric Institute in Los Angeles who originally published a review on the topic in 1998, says that more and more studies are pointing to a concern that the reduction in the supply of the male hormone testosterone (caused by aging, stress and some medications) could be the cause, although it is not entirely to blame. Dr. Sternbach is also looking at a link between testosterone levels and "psychiatric manifestations." He goes on to say that "depression lowers testosterone, as does obesity" (so watch the heavy pasta and French fries).

A man in such a state may feel an urgent need to rectify or change significant areas of his life, including his job, friends and even marital status. Are you picturing the stereotypical older man in the sports car with the twenty-year-old babe with the big boobs? But not all men react this way to *the change*. One woman told me that it really "hit" her husband when he retired. However, after getting used to his new, "freer" lifestyle, she said he became more helpful to her and *much* more easygoing!

Again, experts say the best way to help your man during this time is to be understanding and help him to find new ways to alleviate the pressure. Ask him what things on his life's "To Do List" he would like to finally achieve, and then assist him in achieving those goals (make the skydiving appointment, book the trip to the Congo or go with him to buy that new, more stylish wardrobe). Tell him that he is still vital and *desirable*. Reassure him that you love him and remind him of all the good in his (and your) life. If he has a sympathetic partner and an *outlet* for the stress, maybe he'll refrain from getting the hair plugs and the Corvette!

> *"Male menopause is a lot more fun than female menopause. With female menopause you gain weight and get hot flashes. Male menopause - you get to date young girls and drive motorcycles."*
> *~ John Wayne*

You Gotta Love 'Em!
His Adorable Little Habits.

Let's see, there's:

☺farting, ☺scratching, ☺snoring, ☺monopolizing the clicker, ☺adjusting his balls, ☺gawking at women, ☺putting his feet on the coffee table, ☺leaving the toilet seat up, ☺leaving the cap off the toothpaste, ☺spilling pee around the toilet, ☺talking too loud, ☺cracking his knuckles, ☺clearing his throat, ☺breathing…!

I have to admit that this was a fun topic of conversation in my interviews with women. Most of them were more than willing to *volunteer* this information. They shared stories involving things like tapping his feet and/or shaking his leg when he sits and blowing his nose in the shower! Still, others reported some even more "unique" habits. One woman said that her husband leaves the trimmings from his nose hair all over the bathroom sink, while another woman (I'll call her Jean) told me that her boyfriend bites his own *toenails* while watching television! So the next time your Prince Charming begins to get on your nerves with one of his annoying habits, look on the bright side — you could be Jean!

MUCH ADO ABOUT LOVE

Can you believe these are the same creatures who can melt our hearts? It's true, however, some at times do have a bit of trouble with the crossover… like on Valentine's Day. Most men dread the day. Most believe it to be a holiday concocted by big business to guilt people into spending money. They have anxiety about what to buy for their girlfriends or wives — struggling to find the appropriate gift. And their stress is well-founded because a lot of women believe that is her man's perfect opportunity to show her (and the world) how he feels about her! Well, to help clear up any confusion for next year, I wanted to find out exactly what women really want from their paramours on that special night. I sent a little survey around which included a list of the usual and customary ingredients thought to make up a wonderfully memorable evening. Here's what I found out.

♥ Even though it seems to be a romantic cliché, most women indicated their top choice to be a fairytale evening of candlelight, a pouring out of emotion and a proposal of marriage (that is, if it's appropriate). I guess nothing can beat a man on his knees begging you to accept his love and a diamond ring!

♥ The second highest choice was receiving a gift of jewelry and a romantic dinner. A lot of women liked imagining their boyfriends or husbands going out and purchasing a surprise just for them; the combination of thoughtfulness, time spent and value made them feel special.

♥ The third most popular choice was a relaxed evening including flowers and dinner, although one controversial point was the flowers. Most women rated them very to moderately important, while some women didn't care either way. (The tricky part here is to know which category your lover falls into!)

♥ Interestingly, a big whoop-dee-doo of a night including a limousine, dinner, flowers and a gift was not rated very high among most women, nor was an evening at the theater.

♥ When it came to a "sexy night alone with your man," women were split fifty-fifty. After I did a bit of investigation, it seemed that the results related to age and frequency of sex during the rest of the year — a lot of older, divorced women rated it a top choice, while younger, more active women did not.

♥ One of the options I put on the survey was "a shopping spree, which surprisingly was only a moderate choice for women!

♥ And last but not least was the card. Let me put these results to you in the carefully-chosen words of one woman, "It's the most important thing. If you don't have that, don't come near me."

Please, women, tell your husbands, brothers, friends — tell them all for women everywhere: *Take your time picking out the card. If you grab the wrong one (or the last one), you could end up in the doghouse. Women talk. They compare stories. They prepare your meals, for heaven's sake, so please, for your own health and mental well-being, if you follow one piece of advice in this column, let it be this. Don't forget to buy her a card!*

Here is a true story to help you understand the weight of this simple, thoughtful gesture.

On a crisp February 15th morning several years back, I was at the office getting coffee in the kitchen when a newly-married woman with whom I worked asked me about my Valentine's Day. Since nothing very eventful happened, I gave her the usual, "it was nice," and asked about her evening. She gestured with her finger for me to follow her to her desk as if there was a big secret she was about to share with me. The look on her face, however, was not one of joy, but one of bewilderment. With a furrowed brow and a low voice, she handed me an envelope and said, "Look at the card my husband gave me. I'm so upset. I don't know what to think. I knew my husband was not the smartest guy in the world, but I'm beginning to think he can't even read." Now confused myself, I opened the envelope and pulled out the card. At first glance, it was a lovely card. It was larger than most cards, had pretty roses on it and in large, sparkly script read, *"Happy Valentine's Day To My Uncle."* (I almost wet my pants.)

Think of it this way: when it's all said and done, wouldn't you rather have performed an act of love and kindness than pissed off the person whom you have to trust not to shave your eyebrows while you sleep?

Being a woman myself, I know that women are very aware of that particular holiday and usually don't forget their mates, so I will only remind them that men like to be appreciated too! And whatever special (or unusual) effort your man makes for you, give him a break and acknowledge his gesture of love. (Baby steps… Rome wasn't built in a day!)

Friendliness or Flirting?

Although it's true that everyone likes to feel that they are attractive to the opposite sex, men, especially, like to (and need to) feel desired by women. But when you're in a committed relationship, what kind of flirting, if any, is acceptable? *Is* there such a thing as "harmless" flirting?

A conversation at a dinner party and a glance across a bar are ways of flirting that are non-threatening to your relationship. It is important to know how to enjoy the company of others while still being respectful of your partner. There is definitely an *invisible line*, however, that if crossed can lead to hurt feelings and an interruption in or termination of trust. One woman named Jen confessed that when she was out with her ex-boyfriend, he would stare at other women (and flirt with them *more* after getting their attention). Finally, one night while at a restaurant as he was staring at a woman at the next table, Jen got up, walked over and told the woman that her boyfriend was obviously interested in her, pointing out his rude behavior. The boyfriend was stunned and embarrassed when *both* women told him to get lost.

Max, one man to whom I talked, told me how he and his ex-wife were "born flirts" (notice I said ex-wife). He said it seemed as though at every party or event they attended, one or the other of them went too far and soon their social life was about who-can-do-what-to-whom first. Of course, their relationship eventually ended in divorce.

So where is the line? Well, if you have to wonder whether you are upsetting your date while you are "socializing" with someone else, you've probably crossed it. Some things to avoid when engaging with the opposite sex are being too close physically, too aggressive or mentioning specific parts of the body (quickly *glancing* at breasts and *commenting* on them to their *owner* are two *entirely* different things!). I think talking and laughing with other people in a group is quite alright, but don't go off by yourselves, don't talk about sex and absolutely no touching!

Another more recent problem is "on-line" flirting (dating?). A report published by the University of Florida said that there is an enormous amount of married men who go into chatrooms and talk to thousands of women because, they admit, it's easy, anonymous and exciting. I'm sure it is. Yet most women believe that if you are having an intimate relationship behind the back of your loved one, then it's cheating! Eighty-three percent of the men questioned in their interviews, however, didn't feel as though they were doing anything wrong because there was no physical contact. The report went on to say, "The Internet will soon become the most common form of infidelity, if it isn't already."

Don't be someone who watches her man like a hawk; allow some room for his friendly banter with other women. If, however, your partner is pushing things a bit too far, sit him down and tell him exactly what you find uncomfortable or insulting. If you establish limits with one another, you will spend a lot less time examining each other's behavior and have a lot more fun.

"God created the flirt as soon as he made the fool." ~ Victor Hugo

Rites of Men

Another exasperating practice of men — one that our society has made a rite of passage — is going to a strip club. It is a usual and customary destination for bachelor parties and also a place where our cavemen may go to let loose once in a while. A woman may view this type of field trip as a threat to the relationship — and understandably so. She may analyze the activity, blaming herself for lacking something that would otherwise keep her man at home. A woman may also get upset and secretly feel insulted when her man goes to a strip club, asking herself, "Why does he have to go look at other women when he has me?" or "Doesn't he find me attractive anymore?"

I was told by many of the men with whom I spoke that the reason men visit such places is not because they've become disinterested in their partners, but rather, it's a chance to *visually* experience something new and *different* and to get close to what is forbidden, which is fun and exciting (and as I said earlier, one of the caveman's instincts is to roam and hunt and explore, remember?). If you are a woman who does not condone such behavior, you are not alone. But like it or not, these clubs *do* exist and men *are* curious about them.

If your man goes to strip clubs, tell him how you feel. More importantly, figure out to what degree he is interested in them. If he's visiting these places in a habitual manner and it makes you uncomfortable, you should find out whether or not there is a problem in the relationship or with your partner sexually and address it accordingly. In most cases, men in committed relationships outgrow (or at least have learned to ignore) the desire to visit strip clubs very often. Hmmm. I wonder where strippers' boyfriends go for something *different* — a PTA meeting?

How Men Are Like Women

Haven't heard that one before? Well it's true. Both women and men have strengths and weaknesses and some basic human needs. Like women,

(1) *Men need proper care and pampering*. If it appears that your man has "hit a wall," it may be that he needs a day to himself. If a Saturday comes along and he decides to hop on the sofa and stay there all day — let him. We all need some downtime once in a while to just "veg out." (If

you don't take some, that's your fault!) Indulge him in his belly-scratching, television-watching, eating-everything-in-sight behavior for a day. Let him enjoy doing nothing at all or something special to pamper himself. Some men mentioned that "a day golfing" was their favorite past-time.

Forbes.com recently reported an increase in male clientele at major spas around the country. It seems that with all the focus in the media on toned bodies and better skin, a lot of men who travel for business are now taking advantage of a little pampering time. Not only are they utilizing the gyms more regularly, they are scheduling massages, manicures, facials and even seaweed wraps!

(2) *Men need recognition and appreciation.* Men love to be told by women that they are wanted and needed in all areas of the relationship. Whether it's a discussion about finances or the children or projects around the house, make sure your man knows he plays a vital role in your life. Make a point to always show respect and admiration towards the person with whom you share your life. He will appreciate feeling as though what he does for you is important and matters. Don't you like to feel as though your love can't live without you and what you do for him? Just like we were told as toddlers, the words "thank you" are magic!

> **"Courtesies of a small and trivial character are the ones which strike deepest in the gratefully and appreciating heart."** ~
> **Henry Clay**

(3) *Men have fat days.* If your man seems distant or agitated or acts as though *his* interest in having sex with you has waned, there may be a simple, *familiar* reason. Occasionally, men (some more often than others) may be dissatisfied with themselves in some way, which could be preventing them from wanting to expose themselves to women in an intimate way. They may feel unsuccessful, self-conscious and/or unattractive — like women when they're having a "fat" day!

(4) *Men are looking for love.* You may think your gruff, stinky, old man doesn't care about the mushy stuff, but he does. Of course men like sex, but they also need to feel the security of your loyalty and know that they are loved and accepted for who they are, as they are. Most men want

to have that special chemistry with a woman. They want to feel the butterflies in their bellies, and when they do fall in love, they usually fall hard! Often times, though, they can't show how they feel unless they know that a woman feels the same first. But once a man knows that he is being given the support he needs, he will feel more eager to give a woman what *she* needs. You know when you need a hug or to hear that you're beautiful even with that awful new haircut? Same thing.

(5) *Men are insecure.* You know what it feels like when he looks at an underwear-clad Victoria's Secret model or comments on his buddy's new girlfriend, right? Well, men can feel the same way. They don't always like to admit it, but when a big *strapping* dude gives you the eye, or a handsome man asks you out while he's in the men's room, it shakes them up! Men can be just as insecure and jealous as women. Insecurity in men can also be triggered by problems at work, the place from which they draw their feelings of success and worthiness, unlike women who seek security from relationships. In both cases, however, each person needs reassurance, support and comfort from the other.

> *"Too often we underestimate the power of a touch, a smile, a kind word, a listening ear, an honest compliment, or the smallest act of caring, all of which have the potential to turn a life around."* ~ *Leo Buscaglia*

MYTH BUSTERS		
Most women said they thought men were self-assured and narcissistic.	→	Most men confessed to feeling *insecure* in relationships!
A lot of women perceived men to be "only interested in one thing."	→	A lot of men said that they were looking for the right woman so they could *settle down* and have a family — but admitted to enjoying sex with most any women *if it was offered*!
Quite a number of women accused men of lying — and most men admitted that they	→	For two reasons: because they *didn't* know how a woman would react to their honest comments or

do lie. Why?		because they *did* — to them, either way was a losing battle!
Many women think that when they meet a guy they should always be helpful, upbeat and agreeable.	→	However most men said they aren't attracted to a woman who appears "too eager" and prefer those who are a bit mysterious and *reasonably* disagreeable!
Some women think that men will do whatever they want no matter what.	→	But most men told me that they take their cues from women – a man will pretty much follow the standards and pace the woman sets!
More than a few women think that if they miss a phone call or an opportunity to be with a man that he will lose interest.	→	However, all the men I talked to agreed that if a guy is *really* interested in a woman, he will continue to pursue her despite an unanswered phone call or an incomplete pass!
A large number of women think that men believe they are superior to women.	→	The truth is, most men are intimidated by women because of their ability to express themselves and their strong wills.
Many women think that if they stay loyal to men and put up with their intolerable behavior, it shows that they really love them.	→	However, most men admit that they would not tolerate the kind of heartache they themselves put women through!

Amusing Things to Consider
From the Minds of Men... Are You Scaring Him Away?

Only a small fraction of women may qualify for this man's list of the "Top 10 Signs She's Crazy" on AskMen.com — and thank goodness! Do you see yourself in *any* of these statements?

10. She calls you endlessly.

9. She's been in weird relationships.

8. She infiltrates your family and circle of friends
    (without you knowing).
7. She argues in public/instigates confrontation in front of others.
6. She's unpredictable; has wild mood swings.
5. She lies for no reason.
4. She interrogates you.
3. She snoops around your apartment; invades your privacy.
2. She freaks out over other women.
1. She stalks you.

The following list of "The Top Ten Kinds of Women to Avoid" (also written by a man and published on AskMen.com) gives us a glimpse into things of which men are fearful. Again, this list probably represents only a small percentage of women, but do you recognize yourself in any of these?

10. The woman who is obsessed with getting married.
 9. The woman who is always looking for a fight.
 8. The woman who needs to be handled with kid gloves
     (everything in life hurts her).
 7. The woman who really needs to cover up/dresses too young for
     her age.
 6. The woman who is a constant drag/negative and complaining.
 5. The woman who can't shut up (always makes a comment about
     everything).
 4. The woman who takes and takes and takes (money hungry).
 3. The woman who has nothing to say (talks constantly but says
     nothing of interest).
 2. The woman who is one big freak show (impatient/complete
     mess in her life).
 1. The woman who is all out evil (could send you to prison on false
     charges).

Twelve Things Women Do To Sabotage Relationships
(According to Men)

1. Giving up their passions.
2. Too soon ask "where is this going?
3. Think they can, and try to change him.
4. Put down his friends.
5. Become clingy.
6. Become too compliant.
7. Live only for the future.
8. Insist their man meet all the criteria of their "perfect man" list.
9. Sleep with him too soon.
10. Over romanticize the relationship.
11. Do too much for him.
12. Expect too much, then give up too soon.

☺   ☺   ☺   ☺   ☺   ☺   ☺   ☺   ☺

Okay ladies, pay attention! Here's one last tidbit I received from a man that I thought was very telling and worth sharing.

IF A MAN WANTS YOU
If a man wants you, nothing can keep him away.
If he doesn't want you, nothing can make him stay.
Stop making excuses for a man and his behavior.
Allow your intuition (or spirit) to save you from heartache.
Stop trying to change yourselves for a relationship that's not meant to be.
Slower is better.

Never live your life for a man before you find what makes you truly happy.
If a relationship ends because the man was not treating you as you deserve, then heck no, you can't "be friends." A friend wouldn't mistreat a friend.

Don't settle. If you feel like he is stringing you along, then he probably is. Don't stay because you think "it will get better." You'll be mad at yourself a year later for staying when things are not better.

The only person you can control in a relationship is you.
Avoid men who've got a bunch of children by a bunch
of different women.
He didn't marry them when he got them pregnant, why would he treat
you any differently?
Always have your own set of friends separate from his.
Maintain boundaries in how a guy treats you.

If something bothers you, speak up.
Never let a man know everything. He will use it against you later.
You cannot change a man's behavior. Change comes from within.

Don't EVER make him feel he is more important than you
are… even if he has more education or a better job.
Do not make him into a quasi-god.
He is a man, nothing more, nothing less.

Never let a man define who you are.
Never borrow someone else's man.
Oh Lord! If he cheated with you, he'll cheat on you.
A man will only treat you the way you ALLOW him to treat you.
All men are NOT dogs.

You should not be the one doing all the bending... compromise is a
two-way street.
You need time to heal between relationships... there is nothing cute
about baggage... deal with your issues before pursuing a new
relationship.

You should never look for someone to COMPLETE you... a
relationship consists of two WHOLE individuals... look for someone
complimentary... not supplementary.

Dating is fun... even if he doesn't turn out to be Mr. Right.
Make him miss you sometimes... when a man always know where you
are, and you're always readily available to him, he takes it for granted.

>Don't fully commit to a man who doesn't give you
>everything that you need.
>Keep him in your radar but get to know others.

Makes you think, huh?

The Dance

Armed with this knowledge, it would be wise to think about how to handle a budding new relationship. Ladies, you already know that I would never *ever* encourage you to play games in a relationship. However, there is a sort of "dance" that is done when it comes to dating a new man that can leave him wanting more!

Here is a list of dos and don'ts that you should remember in the *beginning* of the relationship — for your good as well as his. As men have told me, they usually follow the lead of the woman, so you may as well start things off right. Besides, men love the mystery and the romance and the chase — so give it all to them!

Top 10 DON'Ts
1. Don't ask *him* out.
2. Don't invite him over to your home (to sit or fool around).
3. Don't do anything sexual on the first date.
4. Don't divulge *everything* about yourself.
5. Don't make yourself available to him at *all* times.
6. Don't call him (too much).
7. Don't give him too many compliments.
8. Don't offer to do his errands/favors.
9. Don't let him know when you have nothing to do.
10. Don't introduce him to your family/friends too soon.

Top 10 DOs
1. Do look your best when you see him.
2. Do talk respectfully of others.
3. Do say thank you when he compliments you.
4. Do offer a handshake or quick kiss on the cheek on the first (few) dates.

5. Do be the one to end phone conversations and dates.
6. Do be upbeat when you see him.
7. Do be nice to his friends/family.
8. Do return phone calls/e-mails — eventually!
9. Do watch your language (no cursing or talking dirty too soon).
10. Do be honest about who you are, what you want and expect.

Chapter 11:
Three Days in a Life

Here is a behind-the-scenes look at some of the most common day-to-day problems experienced by people just like *you* — all crammed into *three days* for the benefit of your rapid education! You probably won't experience all of these things every day, however, you will surely see yourself in some of these examples. And keep in mind that, as you discover how to see the bigger picture, you will learn to pick your battles and just let go of the little things!

Day One: Spaghetti as a Weapon

6:00 A.M. "Good morning, dearest."

It's early and you're still asleep. You're dreaming that you, your friends, Jim Carrey and your cute dentist are sitting on the beach under tall palm trees, drinking pina coladas and having a great time. But wait. That's not island music you hear. It's your husband singing "Zoom, Zoom Zoom..." — the theme from the Mazda commercial. As you open one eye, you see him standing there in your bedroom shaking his jacket at you. "Honey, here, my button fell off and I need you to fix it." He then adds, "Oh, and I need you to get me our dentist's number. I think I cracked a tooth." As you roll over and pull the covers over your head, you reply, "He's not there. He's on vacation."

There are times when a man and a woman just need space — for example, in the morning. My fiancé wakes up in a good mood almost everyday. He is usually energetic, happy and talkative (poor me!). He comes out of the bedroom smiling and says "Good morning family" (I swear), and I could just kill him. So as you can see, I am, well let's say, *not a morning person!* I need to be left alone to wake up slowly and begin my morning routine in *peace* and *quiet*. If he comes at me with too much conversation or freakin' cheerfulness, I can react like a tiger that is being poked with a stick. But what would that solve? It would only begin the day on a sour note, cause unnecessary anxiety, and probably make us both late for work. Instead, we've learned to understand that we are different (he grew up in the "Loud Family" and my house was like a morgue), and we allow each other a little space in the morning hours. Then, once we have had a chance to wake up in our own ways, we get back into our normal routines, talking and laughing and smooching up a storm. It's all about understanding and allowing one another room to breathe.

S P A C E

Unfortunately, for one reason or another, it seems that most couples become attached at the hip. They begin to do everything together and eventually start to smother one another, and that's not good. Consistently giving each other room to be who you are can do wonders for a relationship.

For example, when my fiancé and I moved in together, I came from owning my own two-story townhouse (that's almost 1500 square feet all to myself) and was concerned about having some privacy (I was also going to be living with his two teenage sons). As we talked about how things were going to be once I moved in, I mentioned having separate bedrooms. At first he was a bit insulted (thinking that I didn't want to sleep with him) and was resistant to the idea. As we discussed it further I explained that, of course we would both be welcome in one another's room at any time, but for storing our things (I had so much stuff!) and sleeping we could finally retire for the night in our own rooms. Well, he agreed to try my idea and was soon thrilled at having his own bedroom! He decorated it the way he wanted, put up (ugly) pictures, was able to watch late night television, sleep with the windows open and snore up a storm — whatever he wanted — without me complaining!

Once he dropped his stereotypical ideas of what a husband and wife should do, he discovered a wonderful sense of independence while still having me close by. He also woke up missing me and looking forward to seeing me in the morning again. He has since mentioned to me many times that it's nice to be able to be close to someone, but also to not be on top of one another all the time. He expressed his notion that the conventional way of living seemed to be the reason why many couples got on each other's nerves and thought we should tell everyone we know about this! I agree!

There is something to be said for being able to care for and live with someone you love while still maintaining your individuality, allowing yourself the space to enjoy your own private thoughts and fall off to sleep in the comfort of your own bed, all spread out, covers untucked and pillows everywhere. And again, there's that "missing you" feeling that makes you look forward to seeing each other — kind of like when you were dating, remember?

7:00 A.M. "You want me to do what?"

You get up and tell him to choose another jacket because you're not gonna sew anything at this ungodly hour. You jump in the shower and then go downstairs. As you are walking around the kitchen in your stocking feet, skirt and blouse, he looks up from his newspaper and asks, "Where did you get that outfit?" in a not-so-flattering tone. You think: He's one to talk — he looks like he's wearing police caution tape in that stupid, yellow-striped shirt. As you leave for work — now feeling ever so beautiful — you hand him a list of things to pick up on his way home from work.

The fact is that men sometimes talk before they think things through. They get images and information in their heads, and before it all makes sense and is in the "proper packaging" it comes falling out of their mouths in great need of repair. Try to understand that he didn't mean it *if he says he didn't* and give him a chance to reformulate what he truly meant to say. He may not even know that he hurt your feelings or insulted you — then again, it may be painfully obvious.

As I listened to the stories of men and women, it became evident that this was a common misunderstanding (more than one man confessed to putting his foot in his mouth quite often!). One woman said her boyfriend was "brutally honest" when she asked him (and even when she *didn't* ask him) his opinion on her outfits and jewelry. She said sometimes, no matter where they were, he would all of a sudden point at her and say, "I hate that... it's ugly" (despite your level of self-esteem, sometimes these comments *hurt!*). His defense was that he *thought* she wanted him to be truthful with her at all times (evidently, at the expense of discretion and good manners). Another woman said that her careless, impulsive boyfriend habitually invited people over and accepted invitations for them *both* without checking with her, which often resulted in awkward social situations.

Another reason for his "premature annunciation" could be insecurity or nervousness. Case in point: A friend of mine told me that upon breaking up with her boyfriend of eight months, he persisted in calling her to talk things out (again and again). She ignored his calls as best she could and was fine until she heard a message he left where he seemed to be crying and apologizing for his apparently grotesque behavior. She felt badly for him (it was near Christmas) and agreed to go to dinner to talk things over. You'd think he'd be on his best behavior right? Wrong. On the night of the big reunion, he was late meeting her, insulted her apartment (again) and commented later that because dinner cost him so much that evening she should consider it was to be their "holiday" dinner out together! Now, does a man who wants to get back into a woman's pants say such stupid things? Yes, he can't help it!

And yes, even *I*, the Accidental Expert, have been the victim of a silver-tongued-devil's perplexing remarks. One night, my fiancé and I were having dinner with some friends of ours. It was a lovely evening and the four of us were eating at an outside café. All of a sudden, my fiancé looked at me and said, "Honey, you look so beautiful now that it's getting dark." Of course, the other couple began laughing. I just stared at him with that "thanks a lot" look on my face as he tried to explain (in fact, he's still trying to explain) what he really meant... he was commenting on how pretty I looked in the soft light of the sunset. Smooth, isn't he?

5:30 P.M. "Welcome home, dear."

You come home with some groceries and put them away. You begin to take the clean dishes out of the dishwasher so you can set the table, but instead you find them looking horribly crusty — again. He wouldn't let you call a professional repair person and promised you that he had fixed it. You're feeling frustrated. Right on cue, he comes through the door with a newspaper and a smile, but no prescriptions or dry cleaning. He never read the list.

I'm not saying to greet him at the door with pearls on and martini in hand, I'm just saying that if something is bothering you, you don't have to yell at him the *minute* he walks through the door. It's very off-putting and it's not fair. You never know what kind of afternoon he's had or what traffic was like (or if he has a present for you!), so give the guy a chance to come in and get settled. Additionally, if you immediately fly off the handle, you may lose credibility because of your erratic behavior, even when you have a perfectly valid reason to be upset. And if he reacts to you in anger, you may never get heard and the issue may not get resolved. Remember that once anger is introduced into a situation, it overshadows logic and prevents both parties from being heard and understood and the essence of what you are *really* saying is gone. Reacting to anger only makes people say things they don't mean and find themselves way off the original subject, which if handled without losing your cool would most likely be settled quickly and without spent emotion. I know it may be difficult to hold in your emotions when you're upset (I know it is for me!), but stop and take a deep breath while he's taking off his coat. Remember, you're in control. Give him a kiss and a hug to start things off right. Then *calmly* tell him why he's sleeping with the dog.

6:00 P.M. "What's for dinner?"

You shrug it off, hope you don't pass away in the night due to your missed medication and start dinner. You've had a tough day and you're exhausted. You put the water on to boil and grab a jar of sauce. You wonder whether anyone will notice that it's not homemade. As you rewash the dishes, you think: I'm worried about kids who eat paste and a guy who once mistakenly ate a dog treat?! He said it tasted like a Slim Jim.

If he's a man, he loves to eat. Unless he has a health issue, you should indulge him in nutritious food as well as the occasional treat (chocolate-covered strawberries and whipped cream — *ooh la la!*). If it's your turn to cook (yes, you should be taking turns!), mix it up when it comes to planning or preparing (or sending out for) meals. He'll just love to come home to his favorite meal of steak and mashed potatoes or your delicious lasagna, and it will leave him feeling satisfied and cared for. Furthermore, did you know that his diet can affect his mood? Too much sugar or caffeine can make him irritable, and not enough protein can make him feel weak. In most cases, as long as he doesn't have to cook it, he'll eat anything.

When I am in the *rare* mood to stand at the stove, here is a quick, delicious meal I love to make. I cook my favorite pasta and make this light sauce to go on top.

<u>Audrey's Easy & Delectable Light Pasta Topping</u>
In a small saucepan, put 2-3 tablespoons of olive oil.
Then crush 6-8 average, very sweet, very ripe tomatoes and add
    them to the pan, stirring and mashing them with a fork.
Next cut up into tiny pieces 1-2 small garlic cloves (depending
    on taste).
Add a small handful of chopped fresh basil (and/or spinach).
Heat and stir on a medium flame until everything is liquidy but
    still lumpy.
Then cut the flame and let simmer for about 12-15 minutes.
Spoon it over the top of the pasta (cooked al dente) and enjoy.
    Deliziosa!
(These portions serve 2-3 people.)

Even though I don't cook very often, I make sure we are both well fed... and I *never* forget dessert!

6:15 P.M. "Are you listening to me?"
During dinner you talk to the kids about school and their homework and they respond back about cool sneakers and where they want to go on vacation (they say, "Disney World," you think, "Summer camp for a month"). After a while, you begin talking to your man about your day

at work. You tell him about an ongoing problem and as you're saying, "Yeah, she did it again. Margaret took credit for all my hard work even after I told her…" you suddenly stop. Why is he staring out the window?

You've heard of SHD (selective hearing disorder), right? It's found in men who don't listen, as diagnosed by women who want to *kill* them. Most of the women with whom I spoke expressed frustration about the lack of attention they get from men while trying to engage in ordinary, everyday conversations. It's an argumentative issue, for sure, but to tell you the truth I don't think men *naturally* hear the way we do.

Women, who are instinctual multi-taskers, can take in everything around them — the phone ringing, the baby crying and the television blaring in the background. Men, instead, focus on the task at hand, which means that if they are reading the sports page or watching television, they are concentrating on that one thing and block out all other "noise" around them. If a woman happens to talk to a man while he is involved in something, his ears automatically knock the sound back and away, deflecting it as though an invisible force field surrounds his head.

Perhaps it's the pitch of a woman's voice that can't penetrate that force field. Is it possible that men only hear what they *want* to hear and certain phrases like "could you," "would you," or "when you get a chance," trigger the switch? I remember when I was growing up I would visit my aunt and uncle. She would be in the kitchen and call to him in the living room, "Could you help me for a minute?" to which he would reply, "Yeah, coffee sounds good." One day I think he sat there for two hours before he realized he wasn't getting any coffee!

New information released by the Indiana University School of Medicine reports that after conducting research trials involving MRIs (magnetic resonance imaging), scans showed that men listen with the left side of the brain — the part that interprets language and speech, while women used the left side *as well as* the right side of the brain, which deals with auditory functions. What that means is that a woman's ears are programmed by the brain to grab the sound that comes to them and interpret it, while a man will interpret and respond to sounds that somehow manage to get through to his brain! Whatever the reason for this mystifying phenomenon, it seems to cause problems for couples everywhere! Many women believe that no matter what comes out of their mouths at *any* given time, all a man hears is blah, blah, blah — regardless of what he is doing! All I can say is, try talking slowly and loudly. Otherwise, wait for a feminine hygiene or pharmaceutical commercial to get his attention, and then speak. If all else fails, walk by naked.

6:45 P.M. "I told you about this three times."
After dinner, the kids go upstairs and you begin to clear the dishes. You ask him what he was planning on wearing to your parents' house for dinner the following evening so you can make sure it's clean (or hidden — in case he wants to wear those old acid-washed jeans). He looks at you with a blank stare (like when you asked him who ate all the Doritos). He doesn't know <u>what</u> you're talking about. "Hello. Anybody home in there?"

Isn't it amazing? You look at them, and they're nodding their heads as you're talking, but nothing is gonna stick. And after spending a considerable amount of time with one man, you'll know when this is happening... almost always.

One night, my fiancé and I were talking about when we met and the beginning of our relationship. He shared his memory of the first time he told me he loved me. As he looked into my eyes and started to speak, I could see the love he felt that night come back to him. Once he began the story, however, I knew immediately that it was completely inaccurate. When he finished, he noticed the subtle look of surprise on my face (all right, my mouth was hanging open). I told him that, in fact, was *not* how it happened and that I knew he would agree with me once I told him my (the true) version. When I finished, he smiled and nodded. Then he said the most amazing thing. He said, "Well, I don't know about that, but I remember the first time *I* remember." And that was when I realized how functionally different his memory was from mine.

You see, most women try to keep track of everything for everyone (birthdays, keys, socks) and can remember things by cataloguing events in their minds (much like recipes or diaries). Men, on the other hand, tend to remember mostly what *inspires* them. I realized that my fiancé remembered *his* version of that first time because it *moved* him and made him feel special. While talking to me, in actuality what came back to him was the moment that produced the most emotion.

According to a study done in June 2004 by Duke University, researchers found that the brain's emotional center interacts with the part of the brain that deals with memories during the formation of *emotionally-charged memories*. This was determined by testing the memories of human subjects after viewing highly emotional pictures and then re-testing them after viewing more neutral ones. These tests resulted in the subjects being able to recall the emotional scenes much more easily.

Other experts say that women are *biologically* equipped to remember things better than men. A study conducted solely with men showed that those with higher levels of testosterone outperformed those with low amounts (remember what I said earlier about stress, alcohol and medication affecting testosterone levels?) What's more, another study in which men were given high doses of *estrogen* in place of a loss of testosterone (from treating prostate cancer, for example), showed that their memories improved. And of course, women are full of the stuff, so that may explain why our memories are better!

I have to say that a man's "selective memory" was a very common complaint among the women with whom I spoke. Whatever the situation, my advice to you is to document everything and maybe put him in an *escalated emotional state* before discussing the important stuff!

7:00 P.M. "@*&%$#!"

As you clean the kitchen, he insists you didn't tell him about dinner at your parents; you know you did. He's being a complete jerk, now talking about not going at all (so what if your brother-in-law tries to sell insurance to everyone,) and you're getting upset because your whole family will be there and are expecting all of you to come. As he goes on and on, you just want him to shut his big yap. Then, out of the corner of your eye, you notice the leftover pasta.

When you're angry or upset, be sure to monitor your actions and your language as best you can. Some cursing is understandable, but don't allow swearing to become part of your every &%$# sentence! You're too classy for that. And *don't* go for the jugular. Certain subjects should be off limits like bald spots, his mother and the size of his penis. (You wouldn't want him to call you "fat" when he's upset, now would you?) Frankly, the more in control you are, the easier it will be for you to state your case and make your point. When arguing with your partner, experts say it's wise to (i) stop and listen to one another, (ii) be prepared to accept your part in what happened, (iii) think about what can be learned from the experience and (iv) be prepared to make up, forgive one another and let it go.

Also, *never* lash out at each other physically. When things are getting heated, it's a good idea to let everyone involved cool down a bit before proceeding. There is a line that, once crossed, can change your interaction with one another and begin to wear away at the level of respect you have for one other — so don't go there.

Anger in Relationships

Anger, of course, is a natural, human emotion. Both men and women can and will experience anger throughout their lives, which can be triggered for many reasons. Expressing anger can be a healthy outlet for feelings of sadness, hurt, guilt, frustration, disappointment or rage. However, how, when and in what context that anger is expressed are the deciding factors in whether it is beneficial or detrimental to your relationship.

Some of us have been raised to hold in our anger, keep our feelings to ourselves and deal with it on our own. Unexpressed anger can lead to passive aggressive behavior, which means that the angry person will criticize and be hostile to their target, rather than just deal with their emotions. Others have grown up to the sudden explosions of our fathers who yelled and screamed because dinner wasn't ready on time. This type of "surprise attack" due to the smallest disappointments can put a lot of stress on your body and mind, as well as on those around you. I think between these two extremes, there is a medium, which is probably the healthier of all the choices.

Men seem to be prone to anger when something is done to them or they feel insulted or disrespected. According to *Science Daily* which featured details of a report published in the January/February 2003 issue of *Psychosomatic Medicine*, it has been proven that it is healthy for men to outwardly express their anger. It stated, that the "occasional anger expression is associated with decreased risk of stroke and coronary heart disease." Some things men can do is to exercise, play a sport, read the newspaper or watch television. Their main concern needs to be to calm down first before expressing themselves through words.

Women, on the other hand, may get angry for additional reasons, like when children are disobedient, pressures at work, relationship problems, overwhelming feelings of responsibility or hormones! Regardless of the reason, a woman also has to find an outlet for her anger even when it doesn't necessarily require a confrontation. Talking with friends, writing in a journal, meditating and taking a walk can help relieve the pressure for women, as does a good laugh or cry now and then.

Whichever way you choose to handle your anger at a person or situation, it is important to remember to (i) allow yourself to feel your anger, (ii) express it in a non-violent, assertive way and (iii) move on.

"Temper is a weapon that we hold by the blade." ~ *James Matthew Barrie*

7:10 P.M. *"Not in front of the children."*
All of a sudden, you notice that the kids have wandered in and are standing in the doorway. They stare at the two of you because you're both yelling, and there's spaghetti on dad's head.

If it has to do with relatives, money, sex or the children, most experts say that it's best to hash out your differences in private. According to an ABCNews Primetime Thursday report in April 2002 entitled "Inside Two Marriages — Kids Caught by Couples at Crossroads," there are *physical* side effects for children who witness their parents fighting, such as increased heart rates resulting from fear, anxiety and stress. Additionally, very young children may mistakenly believe that *they* are the cause of your arguments. Alternatively, CBSNews.com in a story from October 2001 called "Let The Kids See You Argue" reports that if your children *do* see you argue, you should stay calm, show them that you are listening to one another, that you can compromise, and that you ultimately resolve the issue. Psychologist Brad Sachs says, "Children of parents who have regular and resolved fights have higher levels of interpersonal poise and self-esteem than those whose parents have chronic unresolved fights or those whose parents appear not to fight at all." Children should see the *whole* process. This will teach them how to have civilized disagreements and allow them to observe responsible adults whom they can talk to and trust.

7:20 P.M. "It's only money."

As you and your man become quiet, your youngest suddenly remembers to tell you that he has to sign up for hockey in the morning and that he needs $500 right away. "...you know," he explains "for registration and new skates, a uniform and a stick and stuff." You glance over at the rest of the spaghetti. Your husband runs.

Don't avoid conversations about spending, but at the same time don't fight about money to the extent that it hurts the relationship. The Consumer Credit Counseling Service reports that more than half of couples surveyed said that they had problems in this area. The CCC advises us to be clear and honest about our finances and to make the time to discuss the details *before* the problems become overwhelming. I spoke to people who admitted to arguing with their partners about big purchases (new cars, big-screen televisions), as well as mortgage payments and clothes shopping expenses. In *How to Stop Fighting About Money and Make Some: A Couple's Guide to Financial Success*, author Adriane G. Berg says that because couples usually have "conflicting styles of spending and saving money" they will usually argue over *how* to spend money whether they have a little or a lot. And it's normal. Usually, men see money as a "scorecard" (you know, whoever has the most toys when they die, wins!) while women view it as security — something to accumulate in case of an emergency. So therein lies the conflict. But don't avoid the subject because you're afraid of a confrontation. As a couple, both of you need to be involved in your finances. It's important to discuss these matters with patience and an open mind and agree on how to spend, save and invest your money. So talk calmly about the bills and expenses, set some limits and agree to check with one another on the big stuff.

7:40 P.M. "I never said any such thing."

"Fine," you say after your husband's quick departure. "I'll handle this alone like everything else around here!" As you're slamming down pots and pans you announce that there's no need to worry, you'll just pick cash off the money tree out back. With that, the kids groan and take off upstairs, and then the phone rings. It's your friend from work. She can hear that you're upset and asks what's wrong. You spew, "We're going to the poorhouse, my husband has Alzheimer's and there's pasta everywhere!"

Venting to a friend is understandable; however, keep the more delicate matters between you and your man and try not to say anything you'll regret. Don't embarrass him by telling your private stories or broadcasting your arguments to friends and family (unless, of course, there is some kind of abuse going on or you are seeking help). One man named Jim told me how his ex-girlfriend used to embarrass him by calling up her family and telling them about an argument they were in the *middle* of having (her version, of course) in an effort to "prove" to him that everyone agreed with her. Her sisters and girlfriends would get caught up in the fight which usually resulted in humiliating him and causing hard feelings. Another man told me that if he and his girlfriend began to get into an argument, she would immediately turn to whichever friends they were with and involve them in the disagreement. She'd say, "What do you think? Isn't he wrong?" That type of behavior seems a bit insecure to me; why would you need to look for the validation of others? Think about what's happening and if you're that upset, then excuse yourself and leave. Otherwise, be discreet and wait until you are alone with your partner to settle things. In the end, you will most likely patch things up, so why drag others into the disagreement or give people a wrong impression of you or your relationship?

> *"Nothing is more dangerous than a friend without discretion; even a prudent enemy is preferable." ~ Jean de La Fontaine*

8:00 P.M. "Hello in there."

Everything is finally clean and put away. You walk into the living room and your man gives you that "Is the fight over?" look. You smile and remove one last piece of spaghetti from his head, then sit down to join him watching a movie. After a while, you happen to look over and notice that his face is all pinched and he's staring into space. You ask, "What's the matter?" He replies, "Nothing." You smile and continue to watch the movie. Again, you notice his thirty-yard stare. You don't want to say anything, but you can't help it. "What are you thinking?" you ask, a question dreaded by every man on earth!

If he told you he was thinking about "nothing" when you asked, it could be true, but it also could be that he doesn't want to "share" at that moment or get himself in trouble. Most men will tell you that, for the most part, they don't analyze their relationships or look for "signs" of how things are progressing in relationships the way women do. They think about sex (with you), food, sex (with other women), sports, sex (with themselves) and sex! Sometimes they just sit and let their minds wander and think about "nothing" (sex).

One man recently told me, "If a man doesn't want to answer you, he's going to lie." He described a situation to better clarify his point. "If a man was honest with a woman a week ago when she asked him if he liked her outfit — and he said *no* and she got *upset* — the next time she asks him, he's going to lie to her because he doesn't want a repeat of the last time." He added, "And women know the answers to the questions before they even ask!"

What do women think about when their minds wander? Unfortunately, women think less in terms of "What would please me to think about right now?" and more in terms of "What have I forgotten to worry about?"! So don't let your insecurities get the best of you and don't create problems where there are none. Let him think about "nothing." You should think about "nothing" sometimes too!

> *"I have often regretted my speech, never my silence."* ~ Xenocrates

8:30 P.M. "Don't I always?"
After a while, you go downstairs to grab the towels from the clothes dryer and notice his stack of dirty work clothes on top of the washer. He must have just put them down here. You know that if you don't

wash them, he'll have nothing to wear tomorrow... what a pain in the ass. You're aggravated and tired and feel like everyone's slave. You look around for something you can use as a noose.

Don't take on a responsibility at the beginning of the relationship that *he* will come to expect you to do and which, after a while, *you* will come to regret. You may want to impress him by showing off your domestic capabilities, but more often than not your incredible talent at something could bring you "ownership" of it. For example, one woman I know continues to complain that she has to do "everything" for her husband such as cleaning up after him in the kitchen (and bathroom) and ironing his clothes. (She used to iron their towels, pillowcases and even his socks!) I asked her how long she had been doing those things for him and she said that she began even *before* they were married. That was *her* mistake. Another woman who had just begun dating a man would brag to him during their phone conversations that she was a great cook and always preparing delicious meals for herself and her son (probably as part of her efforts to "woo" him). Well, he showed up for their next date asking her to cook something and carrying his own Tupperware container hoping to take home leftovers — I swear! You may want to appear to be the *perfect* woman, but if you don't want to be in charge of a certain task for the rest of your life, then don't make a habit of taking charge of it! My fiancé teases me about my "limited" cooking. (I usually cook about twice a week. Other than that, we eat dinner out or get take-out food.) When I do cook, it's a big deal to him and he's very appreciative — and you better believe he helps me clean up!

So whatever the task may be, be sure to start things off (or *re-start* things) reasonably. There is no law against mixing up the responsibilities of the conventional "Her Jobs" and "His Jobs" rosters. You set the rules. You make the lists.

<u>Setting Precedents: The Roles of the Man and the Woman</u>

During your "getting to know you" sessions, it's a good idea to discuss what you believe your roles will be when combining your lives. Are you someone who believes that women are in charge of the cooking and men are in charge of taking out the garbage?

When you've gotten to a point in your relationship where you begin sharing household chores and responsibilities, it may be a good idea to discuss what each of you is willing to do to help out, as well as what each of you really despises and wants nothing to do with. If you like to cook but hate to deal with vacuuming, make the deal. If you hate the kitchen but don't mind cleaning and taking out the trash, then say so. If you both hate doing something, then agree to take turns or find another way to get the job done.

It's important to get what's expected of you out in the open so that no one feels too much responsibility is being dumped on them and that the other is not pulling his or her weight. That anxiety can lead to built-up resentments which can come spouting out when least expected.

In my experience, I sat with my fiancé and put my cards on the table. I told him that I didn't mind cooking a few times a week, but asked if in exchange he would be in charge of the trash. He agreed. He then asked that I take care of the food shopping each week, which I agreed to do in exchange for him dealing with all car repairs and helping to keep things in order around the house. We also gave a few chores to one of his sons, in exchange for an allowance each week. By discussing what needs to be done and what is expected of one another, we eliminated the surprise, disappointment and resentment that could build by unfulfilled and mistaken expectations.

9:00 P.M. "Told you so."
You come back up from the basement and notice that he's drinking a beer and eating from a jar of pistachio nuts. Later as you pass through the living room again, you see the once full jar of nuts half empty. You remind him about his stomach problems and he grumbles that he's fine — but you know better. You go into the bathroom to make sure he has all he needs when Mt. Vesuvius finally erupts.

There are times when you try to tell a man something that you know to be true, and he is just as sure of the opposite. Something bad's gonna happen if he doesn't listen, but you know *him*. There's really no stopping that train once it leaves the station. All you can do is share the information; the rest is up to him. After all is said and done, when he comes back to you looking upset and defeated (or ill) over that bad decision, chances are he is expecting to hear a big, fat "I told you so." But, as tempting as it is, try not to do it. He may *seem* not to care about what happened — however, that is not usually the case. The truth is he's a little embarrassed and cares *a great deal* about what you think of him (his self-esteem at that moment may be several thousand feet lower than yours). One woman I discussed this with told me that when she gets even a *little* upset with her partner about something he does, he gets "all flustered" and defensive. Your man wants you to think of him as strong and capable, and he can feel threatened and inferior if he thinks you don't. Sometimes, what means the most is what is *not* said.

Debbie, a woman with whom I talked, told me about the time she was invited to go on a date to a twelve o'clock showing of *The Nutcracker*. It was a very cold night in December, but she got all dressed up in a sequin dress and high heels in an effort to impress her escort. They met at eight o'clock and went out for dinner and drinks before the show. Later, as they arrived at the theatre, to their surprise they found the place dark. After helping to check the tickets, Debbie noticed that the show was scheduled to begin at twelve noon, not twelve midnight. Her date's expression of complete embarrassment turned to relief as Debbie suggested they go for coffee and plan another evening. Believe me, your man will greatly appreciate your restrained behavior at the very moment when you'd have every *right* to let him have it. You may also help to ease the situation by pointing out the positive aspects of the situation ("At least we're together"). Then again, depending on the circumstances, ignoring the whole thing might be an even better idea (like when an appliance doesn't fit because he didn't measure the area properly — oops).

Another woman told me that, since her husband has no sense of smell and bad eyesight, it was not surprising that one day he used the BENGAY® that was on the sink to brush his teeth — she said it took every ounce of strength inside her not to point at him and laugh as he was jumping around in *hot* disgust!

Whatever the situation, allow him to vent (or confess) without criticism from you. Wouldn't you want the same? Hold him and comfort him (and feed him antacids). Gloat and giggle *after* he leaves the room!

9:30 P.M. "Anything I can do?"
About a half hour later, he rushes to the bathroom and slams the door. He's in there for a while. As you pass by the door, you ask if he is alright and if he needs anything. Though difficult to speak, he tells you to go away. You can almost hear him sweating.

He loves being cared for, but don't overdo it. He already has a mother and has a real fear you'll become *your* mother. Make sure you look out for him, but also recognize he's a grown man and can do (most) things for himself. A couple of men confessed to me that when doing ordinary household chores, they didn't like it when their wives would explain how to do them each time *in detail* (e.g., "If you're going to microwave that, make sure you take it out of the box first."). Diana Boxer, a professor at the University of Florida said in the February 2002 issue of *The Journal of Pragmatics* that "the 'cleaning boss,' the one in charge of the household chores," will want to monitor what others are doing to make sure things go smoothly. That usually means *you*, so try not to get carried away.

On the other hand, some men may appear as though they are looking for you to take care of everything for them. They may feign helplessness and even ask you for unnecessary things, but you need to resist this temptation to coddle them. Deep down men don't really want their partners to become their mothers because in the natural evolution of things, don't men ultimately grow up and assert their independence and leave their mothers? Yes. Don't let this happen to your relationship.

Part of having a healthy self-image is knowing that you are capable of doing things on your own and so should you allow others the chance. One man told me that each time he goes into the kitchen, his wife calls from the other room (in that *sing-song* voice), "What are you doing?" I'll leave you to imagine how he responds!

> *"All women become like their mothers. That is their tragedy. No man does. That's his." ~ Oscar Wilde*

9:35 P.M. "Perfect timing."
Then his mother calls. She asks how you are and then inquires about her son. You tell her he's in the bathroom with a stomach ache from

eating a whole jar of pistachio nuts. She asks why <u>you</u> let him eat so many!

You have to accept and tolerate those he loves. It's sometimes difficult to deal with his meddling mother, his lazy brother or his obnoxious friends, but you have to make the best of it. You must understand that these people mean something to him (even if you can't figure out *why*). Remember, we can't choose our families.

One woman I'll call Laura told me about her strained relationship with her future mother-in-law. Laura said that when her fiancé's mother comes to visit for a few days, she competes with Laura for her precious son's attention. Most evenings, when Laura and her fiancé Bob have finished with work and chores, they routinely change into pajamas and settle in to watch a little television. One night, just as Laura entered the living room after changing her clothes, Bob's mother raced by her and over to the spot on the couch next to her son. Laura told me that his mother does this often and, although it drives her crazy, she tries to be understanding. When she is finally alone with her fiancé, however, the Little Prince gets an earful!

Another woman told me about how uncomfortable she felt around her father-in-law when her husband's family gathers together. After a few cocktails, her father-in-law had a habit of expressing his rude and *prejudicial* views about the world and usually ended up insulting her ethnic background as well. She said that on several occasions she tried to ignore it and walk away so as not to cause problems between her husband and his dad. After awhile, however, she could no longer hide her feelings and told her husband how she felt. Now when the family is together and her father-in-law begins one of his toxic monologues (which *have* become less frequent), her husband quickly reminds his father to be respectful of his wife's and others' ethnicity.

Try to let the *little* things go, but if a situation becomes intolerable, take your partner aside and tell him about it. "Honey, I didn't want to say anything before, but this has really got me upset." Make sure to ask for his advice and suggest your own solutions to the problem. Begin by saying, "This kind of behavior is upsetting to me…" Then add, "Tell me what you think of handling it this way" and suggest a solution, then ask for his ideas as well. Be sure not to turn the situation into "It's them or me" because that's not fair. With honest communication, you should be able to come up with a way to deal with the problem.

10:00 P.M. "Didn't I tell you?"
You've finally finished the laundry and can sit down again for awhile. He comes out of the bathroom slowly, leaning on the wall, and panting. You tell him to call his mother back. He sees that you have his clean shirts in the laundry basket beside you and says, "Oh, I meant to tell you. I'm not working tomorrow..." Great. You rushed to do his laundry for nothing. You say, "Here, honey... have some more pistachios."

In their leisure time, most men usually aren't concerned about what they're doing from one minute to the next and may *forget* to give you a heads up about a change in plans. So if you've got something coming up, it's worth double checking with your partner. For example, if you're supposed to go to dinner together one evening, be sure to confirm the details. He may decide at the last possible milli-second that he'd rather go to a movie or attend a basketball game and show up wearing sweatpants and sneakers. He doesn't know that women have a "thing" about planning. He doesn't realize that we will structure our wardrobes, accessories and even attitudes around the plan for the evening. For him, the plan doesn't have the same impact. As long as he has a clean pair of underwear, he's ready to go! As frustrated as you may feel, if it's just a casual evening, try to be as flexible as possible (as should he!) — women are always being accused of being too rigid, when the truth is we just like to plan our outfits and hairdos! To be on the safe side, understand that things are never definite until you are actually *doing* what was planned, and be prepared as best you can (throw a t-shirt, a pair of jeans and a baseball cap in a bag — *I* do). Last but not least, remember this: if he does change your plans at the last minute, you can always say "No, thank you." And if you find that one evening as plans change you are not wearing the right kind of shoes, make him stop and *buy you a pair!*

10:15 P.M. "Maybe next time."
After you fling his clean laundry across the room, he decides to call it a night and go to bed. As he starts to leave the room, you ask him to please take his empty beer bottle and pistachio container into the

kitchen. He turns and informs you that he is not going to the kitchen
— he's going up to bed. You stand there and watch him as he passes
right by the kitchen on his way upstairs.

Last year, a speaker at a wonderful *Women in Leadership* conference talked about how men and women are different when it comes to their approach to errand-running and getting things done. She said that women are more likely to do a long list of chores that are related or "on the way" to one another. Men, on the other hand, are more likely to do one thing at a time. For instance, a woman will go to the bank, then stop at the grocery store, then go next door to the video store and, finally, to the post office on the way back. A man will say, "I'm going to the Home Depot," and that's where he goes. If asked to do *another* errand (even if it's "on the way"), he may get agitated.

Additionally, a man's lifestyle (before living with you) may also shed some light on his approach to chores. Research suggests that men who have lived on their own, or who have been divorced and remarried, are more likely to be more conscious of what needs to be done in terms of chores because they have had to fend for themselves for a period of time.

One woman named Terry, clearly tired of her husband's thoughtless behavior, decided one night that enough was enough. She said that as she was standing at the kitchen counter preparing dinner, she noticed that her husband got the milk from the refrigerator, filled *his* glass and then put the milk away. Upset at his obvious lack of concern for her thirst-quenching needs (they both drink milk *every* evening with their meals), she piled food on *her* plate, sat down at the table and began to eat. Sitting there watching her, he looked over and said, "Where's my plate? Aren't I getting any food?" to which she replied, "Well, aren't I getting any *milk*, you selfish son-of-a-bitch?"

When something like this happens, address it right away so that things don't build up. If words continue to fail, do what Terry did — take care of *your* own needs and let him fend for himself. He'll eventually get the message.

You decide to call it a night too, 10:30 PM. As you head upstairs,
you can hear him already snoring in the distance. He only went to bed
five minutes ago.

Lessons of the Day

♥ *Give each other space.*
♥ *Pick your battles.*
♥ *Be his partner, not
   his mother.*
♥ *Discuss finances; don't.
   fight over money*
♥ *Always have a Plan B.*
♥ *Get his attention, and then talk.*
♥ *Kindly tolerate his family
   and friends.*

♥ *Think before you speak.*
♥ *Don't take on everything yourself.*
♥ *Protect the kids from unnecessary
   stress.*
♥ *Let him have his private thoughts.*
♥ *Avoid saying "I told you so."*
♥ *Watch what you say when
   you're angry.*
♥ *Forgive and forget.*

Day Two: Footsies with your Brother-in-Law

2:00 P.M. "I miss you."

You wake up on your own (the death threat from yesterday morning must have worked!) and wander into the shower. Your morning routines begin and end, and as you leave for work you remind everyone about going to your parents' house for dinner — and there is no mention of your outfit this morning (better silence than cruelty!). Soon you're at the office and by your second cup of coffee, you begin to feel badly about arguing with your man last night. You start to miss his cute, sweet, exasperating face.

In order to keep your relationship healthy, it's not a good idea to leave things on a sour note. Try not to go to bed angry. Whenever possible, settle your differences so you can concentrate on your daily responsibilities and won't be preoccupied with nagging worries. If that's not possible, at least find a way to put things on hold and send one another out into the world with love and support. Remember, your man needs to feel accepted and loved by you, even in your absence.

When things are back to normal, there are ways of making sure that you are on his mind in a *good* way. Leave a love letter in his briefcase or coat pocket. He'll know you were thinking of him when he sees your handwriting and smells your perfume on a lovely sealed, white envelope. Every so often, I make sure to send my fiancé a card in the mail — sometimes funny, sometimes romantic — just to let him know that he is loved. Make an impromptu phone call to him during the day. He will love to hear your sweet voice calling *just* to say you love him (and that's all — no "pick up milk on your way home" allowed!). I can remember sitting near two co-workers and hearing the way each of them talked to their husbands on the phone. One usually spoke harshly to her husband saying things like, "Jim, I don't know where your %$#*@ socks are… for crying out loud!" while the other spoke softly to her husband, answering his questions and hanging up only after saying, "I love you."

Men love to be reminded that you care whether it is in little, spontaneous, romantic gestures or by the tone of your voice. He will be touched by the fact that the woman he loves was thinking about him and misses him… and you know what he'll think of next!

5:30 P.M. "Thanks, anyway."
You hurry home to find your man sitting on the couch all dressed and ready to go to dinner at your parents' house, but the kids are not — they are horsing around on the floor still dressed in their school clothes. You look at him and then back at the kids, thinking: Why aren't the kids ready? He smiles proudly and points to his clean, button-down shirt, oblivious to the sloppy, screaming children.

In his defense, when a man really wants to do something that a woman has asked him to do, he tries to follow her directions *to the letter* so as not to screw up. He may not do exactly what she *meant* (letter of the law versus spirit of the law), but she must understand that he tries. During one interview, Beth told me about how much her husband really does try to help out at home but sometimes falls a little short. One evening, as she was exercising on her treadmill, she asked her husband to go into the kitchen and help start dinner. She instructed him to get out the big pot, fill it halfway with water and put it on the stove. Twenty minutes later, she went into the kitchen and found that he had followed her instructions *precisely*. It was the correct pot, filled exactly halfway with water and placed on top of the stove… except the burner was not turned on!

What women have to understand is that men communicate with just the necessary facts — like using bullet points. Women seem to put more importance on the meaning behind the words and feel as though a man "should know already" how to interpret her words without a long explanation. If your man seems to be responsive to your requests and messes up — the answer is just to make your responses a little clearer! I mean, if he's willing to help out, that's more than half the battle right there! With a little coaching and praise, your man will appreciate the direction and feel as though he is contributing as well. If and when something does go wrong, don't make the mistake of getting upset and retorting with anger, "I'll just do it myself!" because then you'll be back owning that job all over again. On the other hand, rumor has it that there are *some* men who will do something wrong *on purpose* so that they won't be asked to do it again — but *I* find that really hard to believe!

> *"When you're self-absorbed, every day is a celebration"* ~ *Anonymous*

7:30 P.M. "Please take out your number two pencils."
You made it to your parents' house without any (serious) physical injuries. Over dinner, in her most concerned voice, your mother asks your man how his stomach is feeling (<u>his</u> mother must have told <u>your</u> mother about the pistachios), so you decide to change the subject. You notice your sister is wearing her gorgeous diamond bracelet (is there a time when she doesn't wear it?). You comment (lie) about its (lack of) beauty and say offhandedly (on purpose) that <u>your</u> husband would never think of surprising you with something like that. Across the table, you see his cheeks turn red. Oops.

No one likes to be put on the spot and chances are if you test him, he may fail. If you go making things up to see how he feels or how he would react, you might not like the results. When testing her boyfriend's fidelity, one woman told me that she asked a friend of hers from work (whom her boyfriend had never met) to try and "pick him up" at a bar one evening when he was scheduled to be there with his friends. What happened? Well, when her friend went to the bar and learned how nice the guy was, she immediately confessed the whole plan to him and he dumped his girlfriend like a hot potato!

I've also heard some women admit to sending themselves flowers or pretending to have the interest of another man in order to provoke jealousy or even elicit a *proposal* from their boyfriends. This is very old, impractical advice. Only desperate, insecure women would even think of doing this and that is not you! Those who play games in relationships are fine as long as they are winning. Once they lose, however, it may be too late to make things right, especially if the one you start playing with doesn't want to play with you. And even if the game *does* go on for a while, where and when will it end?

Timing is everything. Trust that what you need will come to you when you're ready. Let things happen naturally in your life and don't test him — you're just asking for trouble.

7:45 P.M. "You're special... let's get out of here."

You know you shouldn't have said that in front of everyone and now you're sorry. As the conversation around the table picks up, you try to get his attention. He finally looks at you and you wink. No response. You get his attention again and make "kissy" lips. He looks confused. You try to touch him under the table with your foot but get your brother-in-law instead. At least someone's smiling at you.

It's fun to have private gestures or words that only the two of you understand that mean "I love you" or "I want you" — signals you use when you are at a social event or otherwise can't speak openly to one another. It's also another form of intimacy. One woman named Stacey showed me a gesture with her hand that means "I love you" which is known only to her and her boyfriend — and now, of course, to me! All forms of intimate communication include touching, facial expressions, eye contact, and sounds (not words) and make up a non-verbal language of love that can build secure and exciting relationships! As I always say, "Actions speak louder than words."

And then there is that pair of red boxer shorts that I bought for my fiancé one Valentine's Day. They are red and have the word "Love" and little white hearts all over them — so cute! After wearing them for a while, they became known as the "Love Underwear." Not because of the design, but because when he wore them it became his signal to me that he wanted to make love. It was so funny, each time watching him undress and looking out for the Love Underwear! And that worked fine until one day he told me that the Love Underwear was in the laundry and then asked for suggestions on how he could signal me that evening that he was feeling frisky! (I told him actually *saying* the words works well, too.)

8:00 P.M. "You're so immature."
Dinner is over and you and your two sisters head into the kitchen to wash the plates and put the food away. Someone turns on the radio and out comes one of your favorite '80s tunes, "Livin' on a Prayer" by Bon Jovi. You all squeal and dance around the kitchen while the rest of the family gathers in the doorway to watch the show. Your mother, however, is worried someone will fall and your children are shocked and embarrassed.

Remember what it was like to be a kid (all those years ago)? Well, your partner sure does — his mind still works that way. Men naturally hang on to more "childlike behavior" than women (tactfully put, huh?). A woman usually gets so caught up in taking care of those around her that she buries her more frivolous side until the occasional friend's birthday bash or bachelorette party. (We are sooo grown up, aren't we?) So does being responsible mean we can't have fun? Through younger eyes we looked at a food fight and laughed; today we get angry because all we see is a mess that *we* have to clean up. True? As children, we jumped up and down on the bed — when was the last time you did that? Stop and remember about how you *used to* have fun and work it into your *adult* routine. Learn to think young again.

Some people (like me) believe that by concentrating on or anticipating something negative, you feed it your energy — projecting the power of your thoughts onto it — which can help to make it happen. The same is true for bringing things to yourself *physically*, like premature aging, illness and perhaps even death. If that's true, then why not think about running and playing and laughing and learning — all the things that you associate with young people. Don't you think that kind of positive meditation and visualization can have a similar effect on your life as well?

It's a little harder for women to let go when they lack confidence or feel self-conscious due to low self-esteem. But life is *waiting* for you to feel it so start with simple, little things. Stretch out on the floor with a bunch of cushions in front of the television. Impulsively wiggle at the sweet sound of your favorite song. Swoon over an actor you admire. Have a pillow fight. Wear an offbeat item of clothing. Change your accent when talking to someone (I do it all the time!). Don't be afraid to *entertain* your inner child and scream with delight when something makes you happy!

A Sense of Humor

Life will be full of disappointments, emergencies and tragedies so try to stay positive when *minor* calamities occur. Humor can defuse a stressful or awkward situation and make a negative one seem less intense. When a child spills something, it's not the end of the world. Just like when your man brings home the wrong brand of ice cream or you show up at the doctor's office on the wrong day — if you don't laugh some things off, you will be repeatedly upset and miserable. Everyone I interviewed agreed that a good sense of humor is crucial to any healthy relationship. I found that in my surveys, it was consistently rated by both women and men as one of the most important characteristics a person could possess.

And did you know that laughter is not only fun, it has been said to have healing powers as well? Researchers in California reported in the *Humor and Health Journal* that laughter can reduce pain and also stimulate the immune system to fight off infection by activating T cells. Some cardiologists also believe that laughter can help prevent heart disease by protecting some layers of the heart from the effects of stress. Dr. Trisha Mcnair further explains that when we laugh, endorphins are released into our bodies, which act as natural painkillers. Don't quite feel like laughing? Begin with a smile. Smiling pulls our facial muscles upward which, as a result, sends a message to our brains that we are happy, which, in turn, makes us *feel* a little happier. Try it.

Loretta LaRoche, a terrific, internationally known consultant, author and performer says that most people walk around "squeezing a quarter between their cheeks" and really need to lighten up. Like we talked about a, so many of us let the pressure of everyday problems build up, until we finally blow up at something insignificant. In her book, *Life is Short-Wear Your Party Pants*, LaRoche teaches us how to bounce back every day with humor and sound psychological advice — along with making sure that we don't forget to wear our party pants - meaning don't save the good china or new clothes for that special occasion, which may not ever come!

Take my test. In order to tell if you are taking life too seriously, look in the mirror and check the following.

☺ Is your reflection smiling back at you?

☺ Do you see a crazy hairdo and runny makeup?

☺ Is there any type of food on your clothes?

If you answered "no" to these questions, then you gotta loosen up! Now we'll examine your experiences.

☺ Do you laugh *out loud* at funny movies?

☺ Does aggravating the kids entertain you?

☺ When somebody trips or falls in front of you, do you laugh?

☺ Do you derive pleasure out of playing tricks on people (scaring them, hiding their keys, giving them shocks from the static electricity in the carpet)?

If not, then you simply have to try some of these things! When you laugh you give your mind and your body a break from the stress, fending off the million and one responsibilities that bog us down in our daily lives. Lastly, as I said before, one secret fear men have is that the fun will eventually go out of the relationship — so don't let that happen! Men love to share relaxed, funny moments with the women they love. Communication with your man does not only have to be about bringing home the groceries or what to have for dinner. Ask him, "Do you remember what happened on our first date?" to spark some sweet conversation or share a funny story with your partner. "While I was in the ladies' room at a restaurant today, a little girl came in and stood right outside the stall door, talking to me and asking me questions the whole time…" (true story). Find the humor in something he says ("Honey, can we have sex tonight?" — just kidding) or something he does (makes that cute expression when he combs his hair) and laugh at yourself as well.

> *"Nobody grows old merely by living a number of years. We grow old by deserting our ideals. Years may wrinkle the skin, but to give up enthusiasm wrinkles the soul." ~ Samuel Ullman*

10:30 P.M. "I'm sorry!"
As soon as you get home, you take your man aside and apologize for the comment about the bracelet. He gives you a sheepish nod and a kiss on the forehead, and walks upstairs. You figure it'll take a while for him to get over that remark and you playing footsies with your brother-in-law.

Admittedly, men aren't as outwardly emotional as women and most can only hint at how they would like things to be in their relationships. The truth is that most men don't like confrontation or long, heart-rending talks involving herbal tea and tissues. But under all that muscle and hair is a person with feelings and emotions, who really does want to know that you are proud of him.

There are also things that we wouldn't necessarily think bother men because they don't readily show their feelings. This kind of emotional control makes it easy for women to assume that men are not affected by offhand remarks or criticism — but they are. For instance, a comment about a sexy rock star may bruise his delicate ego, while making fun of a gift he picked out for you could hurt him deeply. You may not even realize it, but if his words don't tell you (he probably won't come right out and say, "Honey, you really hurt my feelings") his behavior will — he may be oddly quiet or seem agitated for no apparent reason. If you suspect he is upset, and ask him about it, most times he may not admit it. But try anyway. Don't say, "Okay. What did I do now?" But in a gentle voice say, "I can tell that you are upset by something I said. Please tell me what it was because I didn't mean to hurt your feelings, and I'd really like to clear up any confusion." Part of having a healthy self-image is being able to accept when you've made a mistake, acknowledging its consequences and making amends. If you already know what you said, explain what you meant in better terms, or take it back if it was thoughtless and apologize.

Basically, your man wants you to think of him as the be-all and end-all of the male species! A study entitled "Men, too, are sensitive to media body ideals" in the *Journal of Social and Clinical Psychology* says research shows that some men feel inferior when they see pictures of perfect male bodies as portrayed in ads and on television, just as *women* do when they view tall, gorgeous supermodels!

Another study published in May 2002 in *The Journal of Nervous and Mental Disease* reported that men were just as likely to suffer from Body Dysmorphic Disorder (BDD) as women, although their concerns were more about body build, hair loss and the size of their genitals. So even though he may grunt his answers at you or scratch his butt while drinking his morning coffee, remember that under it all, your man has a heart that is gold… (plated).

Lessons of the Day

♥ *Take the time to show you care.*

♥ *Don't test one another.*

♥ *Be spontaneous; remember to have fun.*

♥ *Have patience and understanding; don't assume anything.*

♥ *No one's perfect.*

♥ *Don't go to bed angry.*

♥ *Everyone wants to feel wanted.*

♥ *Show your appreciation for one another.*

♥ *Apologize when you're wrong.*

♥ *Be sensitive to and aware of each other's feelings.*

♥ *Remember, the little things can mean a lot.*

♥ *Hold on to your sense of humor.*

Day Three: Furry Ears and Flopping Breasts

11:00 A.M. "At last it's the weekend and I can relax."

It's finally Saturday. You get up by nine and feed the kids breakfast. Then you clean up the kitchen, pour some more coffee and read the paper while you wait (as usual) for your biggest child (your man) to come downstairs. Around quarter of eleven you hear a noise and see "it" come around the corner. The cat doesn't recognize this tangled mess of hair, pillow-face and robe and gets so scared she hisses and darts out of the room. He sits down expecting you to jump up and fetch him something to eat. When you don't, he asks "Well, can you give me something?" to which you think: Sure, how about a divorce?

We all have a friend or co-worker who just bitches and moans about everything, right? Don't be the person who constantly complains and does nothing to change an unpleasant situation. Your negativity will affect the mood of your man and of others around you. If something is upsetting you, don't use sarcasm to get your point across. State the facts succinctly, "Honey, I've already made breakfast and cleaned up and now

I'm relaxing…" And above all, don't whine.

Another problem women sometimes have is that they *anticipate* a bad reaction from their man (and from others, as well) even *before* a discussion has taken place, which can bring out a defensive tone in your voice. (Later we'll talk about how this kind of anticipation may actually give rise to a bad situation.) There is no reason why things should result in conflict if you state your feelings and ideas calmly, clearly and honestly. If it turns out that he is, in fact, upset by something you told him, allow him to react accordingly and give him enough time to feel what he is feeling and get over it. You can't control anyone's feelings but your own so have confidence in your words and actions and let others take responsibility for theirs as well.

One woman told me that she knows exactly the kinds of things that will upset her husband (like a dent in the car or running out of his favorite ice cream), and she said she gets a stomach ache every time she has to "break the news" to him. My response to her was, "Don't get yourself upset over what his reaction might be. If you get into a fender bender, tell him that accidents happen and to be thankful that you were not hurt — then walk away from his ranting and raving. Don't stand there and be abused." If your man is like hers and gets upset when he runs out of his favorite ice cream, that's too bad. I suggest holding up a mirror and the car keys. Let him choose to either stop eating or go get it himself.

Getting to the Root of the Problem

Many times, when you blow up over something stupid, you know deep down that what happened at that moment was merely the trigger point of something far bigger which is bothering you. Apparently, you suppressed your anger and chose not to deal with it at the proper time. So you kept it inside and as it festers, you feel irritable and, as you simmer, you know it's just a matter of time before you lose your temper. So why did you let things get this way?

You were avoiding the problem for some reason. Could it be because you feared the outcome? You avoided dealing with a problem because it felt overwhelming? Did you avoid beginning to work on an issue because it seemed like it would take forever to resolve? Maybe you thought the issue was something your partner would think was petty and you didn't want to appear like a nit-picker. Whatever the reason for your inaction, the results of your eruption usually end up being worse than had you discussed the problem with your partner when it happened — and, if you continue this kind of ineffective behavior, it can be detrimental to your relationship. So if you are someone who is in the habit of holding things in and then blowing a gasket, how can you change that behavior?

Well, first of all, it takes more energy to hold your tongue and your feelings in than to just utter a simple sentence in the proper moment. Next, it's not healthy to suppress what's bothering you or to hold in anger. Lastly, when you finally do allow yourself to be upset, as you flip out over the burned toast, your loved one is looking at you like you're nuts. And then the explaining comes along with lots of pent up emotion and reflections on a past event which your partner may not even remember!

When something upsets you, face your fears. Address it immediately by expressing your confusion or hurt feelings or whatever honest emotions are present inside you at the time. You have to learn to stick up for yourself (which, as you know, builds self-esteem) and trust in your partner that he loves you and will work through the problem with you.

> *"Life is so constructed, that the event does not, cannot, will not, match the expectation."* ~ *Charlotte Bronte*

2:00 P.M. "That smarts!"
After doing a few more chores, you dash out to do some errands. Soon you're back home and sitting on the porch alone with your man (the kids have gone to his parents' house for the night.) As you look over at the expression on his face, you think "He's looking a bit philosophical..." or did he just eat more pistachio nuts?

Besides physical stimulation, most men like to be intellectually engaged as well. He already thinks you are wonderfully talented, sweet and beautiful — now show him you're brainy as well. Let him know your thoughts on an important political issue. Discuss what's in the newspaper that day. Don't be too shy to talk about how you would solve some of the problems facing society, like homelessness, health insurance coverage or rising taxes. And don't be afraid to disagree. Did you know that Mary Matalin, a no-nonsense Republican commentator and author, and James Carville (a/k/a "The Ragin' Cajun"), a Democratic strategist, talk show host and author, are married and constantly express their opposing views in the press? Carville was once quoted as saying, "I'll give you two bets to make — Hillary doesn't run for president in 2004 and Mary Matalin does not want or will not get Karen's [Hughes] job ... Because if she gets that job, she'll have to get a new husband." Imagine their *private* conversations!

A healthy exchange of ideas is fun, interesting and shows passion. Just remember to stick to the issue and don't get personal. Also, remember you can listen to your partner and respect his opinion without necessarily agreeing with it. By talking together about world events, you will grow to learn more about each other and how you each view certain issues. Expressing your beliefs about things outside your own backyard also gives him a look at your individual, *spirited* side. He will be impressed by your independent thinking and enjoy your interest in *his* opinion on current events as well.

2:30 P.M. "That's okay."
As you're sitting together talking you realize that he's ending each sentence with the phrase "but that's just me." You think: That's new. Then, still listening to his story, you notice that hair has begun growing out of his ears. You wonder when that started. As your eyes search his body for additional mutations, you notice one long, pointy fingernail on his left hand, and you lose it, jumping up and screaming, "That's disgusting!"

Expressing your opinion when engaged in a discussion is admirable, but don't overdo it by constantly picking apart your partner's *minor* imperfections. Choose to concentrate on and appreciate the positive side of your man and those around you. Constantly focusing on the negative and criticizing your partner is unfair, uncool and unattractive! Don't flip out over the little things or blow things way out of proportion (unless you're pre-menstrual, and in that case, who could blame you?). Go through his "home inventor" phase with patience and eye goggles. Help him through his body-builder period with protein drinks and buy him a new hat when he comes home with a shaved head (because, as one young newly-married man put it, "… all my friends did it"). As you watch his waistline expand and his hair recede, try to concentrate on his positive attributes, like his eyes — focus on his eyes!

3:00 P.M. "You're the greatest."
After a while your man goes into the kitchen and brings back some lemonade for the two of you. It's in the big pitcher, mixed with just the right amount of water and sugar and tastes delicious. You're suddenly overcome with suspicion. He did this all by himself — but why?

In case you still don't know it, men are always hoping we'll notice when they look particularly handsome or when they've done good deeds — they secretly want to be thought of as our heroes. So make a point to commend your man when he does something nice for you. Believe me, his ego really longs for your acceptance and recognition. I actually witnessed one woman make a really big deal out of a very small task performed by her husband. As he walked away grinning and proud, she looked at me, smiled and rolled her eyes! See? She knew the importance of praise.

Joyce and Barry Vissell, a nurse and doctor who counsel couples on relationships, say it's important to thank each other for taking on responsibilities and doing good deeds, and also for being your friend, a good parent and a loving partner. Joyce gave an example of this kind of positive reinforcement in an interview to writer Melissa West in 2002. She said, "For instance, if [a] wife was changing the diapers, the husband could thank her and appreciate her for the love she was showing in that task. Even in this very active stage of having young children, they [can] find a way to reach out and show gratitude, so that each [knows] they [are] being noticed and appreciated."

I try to remember to do this often for my boyfriend. When he's especially thoughtful or does something as I requested, I take a moment to thank him for the effort and let him know that I really appreciate his help. When I do this, his face lights up and he gets so excited — if he were a puppy, he'd pee on the rug!

There are plenty of things that your man will do that you will be quick to criticize, so it's only fair to let him know when he's doing the right thing, too (as rare as those times may seem)! Remember, no one likes to be taken for granted. You've got to show him that you *absolutely live* for the sweet little things he does — and you will!

> *"The glory of friendship is not the outstretched hand, nor the kindly smile...it's the spiritual inspiration that comes to one when he discovers that someone else believes in him and is willing to trust him with his friendship." ~ Ralph Waldo Emerson*

3:15 P.M. "Teach me."
You suddenly remember that on your lunch hour the other day (God forbid you actually eat!), you picked up a jazz CD that he's been wanting. You think: He can use that pointy fingernail to slice open the plastic package.

Show some interest in his treasure trove of old comic books. Help him look for those vintage t-shirts or baseball cards he collects. Ask questions about his favorite musician. If you do, he will get to share his passion with you and show off a little by teaching you something you may not know. That will allow you to explore something outside of your comfort zone and make him feel good as well. After that he'll look forward to sharing even more of his favorite things with you. And who knows? Over time you may wind up enjoying this wonderful obsession together.

One woman told me that when she met her fiancé, he was hooked on watching NASCAR racing. In the beginning, she would watch all of the races on television with him in order to appear interested and involve herself in his life. After a while, she became a huge fan of Rusty Wallace and now watches racing even when her new *husband* isn't around.

3:20 P.M. "Oh, really? I had no idea."
He looks at his gift and then looks back at you with wide eyes. He thanks you and begins to tell you for the hundredth time about how he and his father used to sit and listen to jazz for hours and hours.... You think: Oh no. What have I done?

We've all experienced it — sat there, patiently listening, while our brains screamed, "You've told me this story a thousand times!" To keep the peace, there have been many, many times I've *ignored* the fact that I can recite that same story, word for word, awake or in my sleep and, instead, sat there smiling and nodding. But I must admit, I learned that the hard way. For instance, each time we pass a certain building downtown, my fiancé tells me all about how he used to work there years ago, the people he knew, and how much fun they used to have, yada, yada, yada. One day I couldn't stand to hear it yet again and, without thinking, I shouted, "Please, stop. I've heard this already!" He was surprised and a little hurt by my sour reaction to his *wonderful* and *interesting* tale. A lot of the women I spoke with related to this experience, while most men I talked to refused to admit that they were ever such an offender.

So as much as you want to yell, pull your hair out, or jump from the moving car as he points out for the millionth time the location where he and his friends got drunk and "mooned" passing traffic, try to resist the temptation. You *could* try asking a question about the event, which may lead to some *new* information and would keep from hurting his feelings. If that doesn't work, just smile, laugh — or maybe think of shopping instead.

> *"Between repetition and forgetting, it is a marvel that a new thought ever struggles into existence."* ~ *Mason Cooley*

3: 25 P.M. "Ah ha!"
While telling you his stories, he mentions something about how you wouldn't know anything about <u>real</u> music because you only listened to crappy <u>disco</u> music, and then he continues on about how wonderfully knowledgeable he is about jazz…

Don't assume that when he hurts your feelings it is on purpose. In most cases, it will turn out to have been completely accidental. (You'll get used to this after a while — we all do!) Bring his attention to the remark and tell him how you feel. Ask him what his intentions were. Let him explain his objective in acting as he did (which may include stuttering and words like, "huh," "eh," and *occasionally*, "sorry").

One man told me that when a certain friend of his came over, his wife suddenly got very quiet. At first he assumed she was just "in a mood" but then noticed it happened each time that particular friend visited. One day, he finally asked her about it. She confessed, to his astonishment, that she did, in fact, feel uncomfortable and self-conscious because the first time she met his friend, her husband made a remark about the way she looked in front of him that really hurt her feelings. He apologized, explained that it was only a joke (agreeing it *was* one of bad taste) and promised to be more aware of her feelings in the future.

In most cases, you should trust that someone you love would not intentionally do you harm or cause you grief. Think about whether your reaction is a real result of something that happened or a case of fear or insecurity on your part. Then, discuss what's bothering you with an open mind and forgiving heart.

3:45 P.M. "Forget about it."
He soon notices your wounded expression, and you explain to him that what he said about your "disco days" and lack of music savvy really hurt your feelings. He says that he didn't even realize what he said and that he was sorry. You think: Liar. He adds, "It was just a careless slip of the tongue." You say, "So what else is new?"

Accept his apology (and his explanation for what happened) if he is *truly* sorry and forget about it. Keep in mind that no one is perfect and, being human, he will make mistakes as will you. Louise Hay in her book *You Can Heal Your Life* talks about the importance of forgiveness and writes that forgiving others and then *letting go* (of the incident or the person who hurt you) helps you to heal yourself by freeing you of resentments and bringing you closer to inner peace and joy. Research says that many women tend to keep things bottled up until something happens and then it *all* comes spewing out — what he did last week, last month and last year! I personally witnessed a friend get so upset with her boyfriend that she began rattling off a whole list of things he'd done to upset her — going back a few years (I happened to be in the car with them when all *heck* broke loose)! Dr. Fred Luskin, the director and cofounder of the Stanford University Forgiveness Project, says that holding in resentments can lead to physical ailments such as high blood pressure, muscle tension and stress-related diseases. So don't bring up past mistakes every time you have a disagreement. It's unhealthy, ineffective and it drives men crazy. Deal with the problem at hand and get on with life.

> *"Hanging onto resentment is letting someone you despise live rent-free in your head." ~ Ann Landers*

4:00 P.M. "Shake it, baby."
It's getting a bit chilly now so you both go inside. He turns on the television and flips through the channels. On one channel, he pauses. Of course, you think, he stopped here because he sees attractive women strutting around in sexy dresses with high slits on the sides. Then you realize it's an international dance contest and the finalists are competing Salsa-style. You laugh thinking: He's probably hoping he'll see a breast flop out. He continues to watch, then smiles and shakes his head. You get an idea.

You will have to attend parties and social occasions all of your life and, of course, at these events there may be music and dancing. A lot of men don't actually know how to dance. Some won't even try, while others just seem to get out on the floor and move around awkwardly. Here's where you can help. Find the right time and place, without the presence of onlookers (or even shoes), and *teach that man to dance*! (If he balks, tell him there will be lots of *touching* involved!) Show him some easy steps and let him practice moving in a comfortable way. Or join a couple's dance class. I knew of one couple that met at a dance class, fell in love and got married. To this day, they continue to wow everyone at weddings and parties with their sassy, swing dancing!

Dancing is fun, great exercise and can be an intimate experience for both of you as well. Can't you just picture swaying across the floor in each other's arms? Show him enough moves to make him look and feel confident and somewhat skilled on the dance floor. And then, when the time comes for him to move his body to music in front of others (now known as *dancing*), he will hold his head high and won't embarrass himself or you (not to mention step on your toes or drop you on the floor).

5:00 P.M. "You're gonna give me a heart attack!"
For the first time in weeks there are no children in the house. You're

feeling relaxed and a bit silly now after dancing, and he does look cute sitting over there with his messy hair and misbuttoned shirt. You slink off the couch and onto the floor. He looks excited. You crawl over to him; he begins to squeal with delight. You are on all fours kneeling before him now, and you begin to unzip him with your mouth. It's been so long since your mouth has been near his pants, he faints!

<u>Lessons of the Day</u>

♥ *Exhibit all your wonderful qualities.*

♥ *Share your interests with one another.*

♥ *Don't judge.*

♥ *Maintain intimacy.*

♥ *Don't just complain, do something about the problem.*

♥ *Don't nit-pick; cut each other some slack.*

♥ *Recognize one another's efforts.*

♥ *Forgive and forget (you know it!)*

♥ *Make time for you as a couple to have fun.*

♥ *Have a conversation about something other than kids, money or errands.*

Once he regains consciousness and realizes exactly what you're trying to do, it'll be time for the two of you to rekindle your romance. Read on for the sexy, tantalizing secrets to keeping your love life sizzling!

Chapter 12:
Men and Women and Sex

Men love sex. It is a scientific fact that they think about sex every few seconds throughout the day. They get flashes of it in their brains continuously while they are walking down the street, eating lunch with friends or sitting in a business meeting. They interpret everything as having a sexual connotation. Poor things.

Before we continue, I must tell you that almost all of the men with whom I spoke said they were not getting enough sex (and not *nearly* enough *oral* sex)! So what is enough? What are we supposed to do — let them take us from behind while we do the dishes? Hide them under our desks at work? Will they ever be satisfied?

It is important to men that they feel satisfied sexually. They need the physical connection and release in order to feel strong, confident and healthy. Women are a different story. Of course, they like to have satisfying sex lives, too; however, it's only been in the last few decades that women have focused more on their own sexuality. It wasn't so long ago that sex was thought of as "just for the men" as one woman's grandmother used to say. Most of the women with whom I spoke said they were generally comfortable with their sex lives, whether they had sex two times a week or five times a month (with a few exceptions, of course). They usually didn't keep a strict count, unless there were underlying problems in the relationship. But believe me, men do.

In my conversations with men, I realized something that most women don't truly understand: not only is sex important to a man's overall physical state, *sex is vital to his mental and emotional health as well*. Basically, men equate love with a physical connection and see love as expressed through physical contact and satisfaction — and it's not a choice for them; it's a reality. Women, on the other hand, feel and interpret love by more symbolic gestures, like attention and thoughtful words and actions. However, despite how each gender defines and comprehends love, couples *can* have a mutually fulfilling relationship, both sexually and non-sexually, as long as communication on both fronts is flourishing — and that takes time, patience, education and understanding. Interestingly, in my interviews, both men and women said they desperately wanted the other to understand, respect and comply with *their* sexual natures.

One contributing factor, I think, is that men don't understand the whole "process" that goes on inside women when it comes to sex. Women have that whole mental/physical connection to deal with. Our minds and hearts definitely have a strong impact on our bodies and, unfortunately, our sex drives are different than men. As a woman, I know there are times when, if we are feeling worried, neglected, fat, stressed or agitated, our ability to *feel* sexy and *be* sexual can be greatly impaired. The demands of family and work responsibilities can also put pressure on women. Managing a home, a family and a job can zap the energy out of the best of us. A lot of the time, it takes knowing the chores are done for our minds and bodies to relax and for us to feel more comfortable with and *entitled to* intimacy. On the other hand, on a day when we are able to fit into our skinny pants (score!) or we are feeling particularly confident because of a job well done or a successful shopping trip, we feel more at ease, more beautiful and much sexier.

A research team (including professors from the University of New Mexico School of Medicine and U.C.L.A.) working for Pfizer in an effort to develop a "Viagra for women" found solid evidence of the sexually instinctive differences between men and women. Mitra Boolel, leader of Pfizer's sex research team said, "There's a disconnect in many women between genital changes and mental changes. This disconnect does not exist in men. Men consistently get erections in the presence of naked women and want to have sex." Recently, after eight years of tests involving 3,000 women, Pfizer decided to abandon their efforts to prove that a similar drug will work for females. Their report said "[Our] exhaustive research has concluded that men and women have a fundamentally different relationship between arousal and desire. A women's arousal is triggered by a network of emotional, intellectual and relationship-based factors rather than the simple physical response required by a man." Their conclusion: "In women, the brain is the crucial sexual organ."

What the problem boils down to is this: *Men get aroused easily as a result of visual, physical or mental stimulation, and when women don't respond in the same way, men feel rejected and women don't realize that!*

Another influence on a woman's desire is how her man treats her on a daily basis. Is he sweet and respectful? Is he patient and romantic? Is he paying attention to her outside the bedroom? Sometimes a nice word or gesture from your partner can help to override the weight of the day's responsibilities, and spark your desire for intimacy. According to MarsVenus.com, *most men don't realize how much romance and attention mean to women.* If you think you know the reason, let your man know what has caused your diminished interest in sex. For example, when my man acts stubborn or insensitive, I can feel myself shrink away from him. When he takes a moment to listen to me talk about my day at work or goes out of his way to pick me up at the office (or hides my favorite cookies from the kids), I get so crazy about him that I could eat him up! And, after a tough day, when he looks into my eyes and talks *softly* to me, he drives me wild!

Lastly, if you very rarely feel like having sex with the man you love, check with your doctor. There could be a number of medical or biological reasons for your diminished sex drive, like changes in hormone levels, infection, kidney disease or thyroid disorders. Also, according to an article entitled "The Chemistry of Desire" which appeared in the January 2004 issue of *Time*, our bodies contain chemicals (namely, oxytocin and dopamine) and hormones (testosterone and estrogen) which send messages throughout our bodies to create and contribute to our feelings of desire, attraction and orgasm, and if these become low or depleted, therein lies the problem. Unfortunately, this happens to a lot of women after a certain age and it can be a difficult situation to handle. So check it out with your doctor, and talk to your man. You deserve to have a wonderful and satisfying love life.

<u>Get in the Mood: How to Do It Yourself</u>

So after a hard day at the office or wiping runny noses and dodging flying oatmeal, how does a woman prepare — in body and mind — for an intimate encounter with the man she loves (and enjoy it)? Well, it may not be that easy, but it can be PROVED. It takes Preparation, Relaxation, Oral (stimulation), Visual (stimulation), Excitement-builders and Direction.

Step 1: When you look in the mirror what do you see? No wonder you don't feel sexy. Take a hot shower, put on something pretty, clip your hair up, add a little lipstick and strut your stuff! Looking sexy can make you feel sexy.

Step 2: Your muscles are probably tight from your laps around the playground, so ask for a little massage around your neck and shoulders. Most men jump at the chance to caress a women, so let the first touch start the relaxation process and stimulate your imagination.

Step 3: You know when you rush out the door, you kiss him quickly, which is okay for the busy, daylight hours, but not for an intimate occasion like this. In the dimly lit room (which of course you chose for your rendezvous), stop and look at this man, whom you love and who loves you, then close your eyes and kiss him like you mean it.

Step 4: Think about what you want — what would make you feel good. Let your mind, your hands and your mouth wander. Subtly guide his body to do the same for you.

Step 5: Now take control and lead your partner to do what you want. Experiment with new ideas or stick with the tried-and-true stuff. Either way — lie back guiltlessly allowing him to pleasure you the way you desire.

The Seduction

Visual Mastery:

One thing to remember is that men are visual creatures, which means they are more easily stimulated by what they see than are women. Your man will appreciate your attention to detail if you make the environment sexy and intimate. This mood-setting may include subtle lighting, a sexy scent and, of course, lots of skin.

Men love to look at women's bodies. (Why do you think *Playboy* magazine has been around for so long?) Chances are he loves to look at yours too. Remember when you first started dating? How did you dress? Wasn't it in a way that you hoped was pleasing to him? So what's stopping you now? Tease him with a little leg. Show some cleavage. Sophia Loren, the sexy Italian movie star, once said, "Sex appeal is fifty percent what you've got and fifty percent what people think you've got," so have fun getting dressed and play up your positives!

Dressing a little seductively for an evening out is a turn-on for a man. He will love looking at your exposed neck, shoulders and legs in a skirt — just a glimpse of your skin will cause his heart to skip a beat. (A man once told me that the sight of the back of a woman's neck when she wore her hair pulled up was one of the sexiest things he had ever seen.) When at home, drop the robe and give him a peek every now and then — accidentally, of course. Or better yet — do your own striptease. Did you know that *stripper* classes (as a form of exercise) are becoming very popular? And when you're done, you could put on one of *his* shirts — with nothing on underneath. Most men find that *very* sexy!

So pretend you're getting ready for a love scene with your leading man. Shed that business suit and enjoy some *uninhibited* behavior for a change.

Touching and Massage:

Men love it when women touch them in subtle, playful ways throughout the day or night. As a matter of fact, we all, as human beings, have a fundamental *need* to be touched. According to Dr. Tiffany Field, director of the Touch Research Institute at the University of Miami Medical School, touch has a profound effect on newborn babies in that it helps them to gain weight and grow faster. Studies showed that it also decreased stress levels in children and increased serotonin levels (a natural anti-depressant). Other research suggests that touching also enhances learning abilities in school-age children and can even improve an adult's mathematical calculations!

Sharing impulsive, thoughtful caresses will keep him feeling loved and secure. A squeeze from behind or a quick cuddle will warm his heart. A gentle touch on his arm or leg when you are sitting together or driving in the car will make him feel special. Hold his hand when you walk, nibble his neck at the movies like you used to or put your hand on his back as you pass by him. Touch his face when you kiss him goodbye or stroke his hair as you watch television. All of these ways of touching convey that you care as well as an underlying sexual message that will captivate and excite him.

And who doesn't love a massage? It's an ancient technique believed to promote healing through human touch. In adults, massage can lower blood pressure, increase blood circulation and give relief from certain injuries. It also relaxes tired, tight muscles and initiates a physical interaction between you and your man. So go ahead. Get some beautifully scented oil, light a candle and gently rub his body. Touch him slowly. Begin with him lying on his stomach and rub him with deep, long strokes from his shoulders all the way to his hips. But be careful not to touch him too lightly; instead of turning him on you could make him ticklish and jumpy. Massage the small of his back slowly and with medium pressure. Show him that you enjoy touching him. Rub the length of his strong legs and work your way back up to the top of his head (my fiancé *purrrrs* like a kitten when I run my fingernails through his scalp). Then, turn him on his back and blindfold him for a more *erotic* experience. Rub his chest, shoulders, and arms using both hands to touch each spot. Knead out the knots and stretch his muscles. He'll be excited to find out where your loving hands will move next. Then, take one of his hands and put it on *your* body. Moan a little. Rub up against him with *other* parts of your body and take your time. I know a woman who told me that she once gave her boyfriend a two-hour, full-body massage — a night he *still* talks about! Let him see how gentle touching and massage can relax his muscles while stimulating his desire for you.

UFOs: Undisclosed Fun Occasions:

When you've planned a surprise for someone, that person knows it involved careful planning and a lot of imagination. It can be very ego-boosting. Men also love being surprised by their partners also because they find it sexy for a woman to take control of things occasionally. According to an article in *Redbook* entitled "Keeping Romance in Your Marriage" men fear that once they settle down with someone, after a while all the mystery and fun will disappear. Show him that is not so!

Let him find rose petals and little notes all over the house leading him to the bedroom where he finds you already in bed, with the candles lit and the wine poured. If you want to go out, be all dressed up when he comes home and take him out to an intimate dinner, or arrange a romantic rendezvous in a new place. How about a bubble bath for two?

A woman named Andrea told me how she surprised her boyfriend for his birthday. She hired a limousine and instructed the driver to her boyfriend's house. When the limo pulled up to his house, she asked the driver to go to the door, ring the bell, and escort her boyfriend back to the car. Then, as the door opened and her boyfriend stepped inside, he found his beautiful, sexy girlfriend sitting inside wearing *nothing* but a fur coat! (Needless to say, they had a very late dinner.)

Keep in mind, also, that a surprise doesn't necessarily have to do with sex (although it may lead to it!). Cut out an article you think he may be interested in or grab the new CD by his favorite artist. One man, John, told me that his live-in girlfriend used to surprise him by doing a lot of little "extras" for him, like reorganizing his clothes closet or having his favorite take-out there for him after a tough day. He said *all* of her surprises turned him on. A surprise every now and then re-charges our batteries and makes our tough, daily responsibilities a little easier to bear.

Erotic Tête-à-Tête:

Men love to be told that they are wanted and needed sexually by women. Your man longs to feel that only *he* can satisfy you. Tell him often that you think he is sexy and that you *crave* him. He'll strut around proudly and continually try to live up to your accolades. Call him up at work in the afternoon and tell him you can't wait to see him. Always try to get the message across that he is your special guy, your one and only, your paramour!

Men also want to be thought of as *expert* lovers, and if you are routinely silent he may wonder if he is pleasing you at all. Now don't get me wrong, I'm not telling you to *shout out* directions, but praise in the right place at the right time can go a long way. Whisper to him in detail what you enjoy about his lovemaking techniques. One "*Oh, yeah*" will give him confidence to know that he is doing something right (for a change!). A sweet, low moan will send the message that you are enjoying yourself, and a "Honey, you are *soooo* good…" will have him prancing around for days! Tell him often that you think he is *sexy* and that you *crave* him. He'll strut around proudly and continually try to live up to your accolades.

Alternatively, if there is something he is doing that you *don't* like, you should let him know as well — but be careful. When you are too critical of your partner, sex can become more of a performance than a sharing of genuine feelings and love. Make sure to be gentle and tactful when talking with him or he may get "stage fright," becoming self-conscious and feeling as if his every move is being judged. Also, find the right time to discuss it (not when you are in the middle of lovemaking) and choose your words carefully. Don't begin with "I hate it when you…" but instead say, "What I would really like is if you would …"

Kissing Like a Connoisseur:

As you know, depending on the circumstances, there are different kinds of kisses. He's not your brother (hopefully), so let your kiss show him how you feel. Softly kiss his lips and all over his face. A man's ears are very sensitive too, so run your tongue lightly along the edges and just *barely* inside, then softly sigh in his ear. Next, nibble at his neck, making sure to touch on both sides and the front *and* back. Kiss his mouth gently with your wet lips partly open. Kiss him again when both your mouths are open; let your tongue explore his mouth and let his explore yours. Then stop, hold his face in your hands and look into his eyes. After a moment, press your lips together. Mash your mouth onto his closed lips, staying perfectly still for a minute. Finally, as you pull away, suck and tug a little at his bottom lip. Then take his hands in yours and kiss his fingers. Lightly lick them and then suck on each fingertip. Tickle his palm by wiggling your tongue on it as well.

Next, kiss his chest. Allow your fingers to follow the curves of his muscles. Sex expert Jane Greer, Ph.D., points out that men's breasts are also a sensitive area. Trace circles around his breasts and suck on his nipples and play with them. Then head south towards his lower abdomen, kissing him along the way. Caress him softly, tugging on some of his pubic hairs as you go, but don't pull hard. Rub your wet lips gently across his skin and kiss him all the way along his inner thighs, slowly increasing his hunger for you.

Lovemaking

There's nothing more intimate than giving your whole self to someone, letting him know you inside and out and allowing him to see you at your most vulnerable. Making love usually comes pretty naturally to two people *in love*, but perfecting it takes practice as you both learn how to fulfill the desires of your bodies.

> "I love to feel her wrapped around me."
> "I love to *hear* that I'm giving her pleasure."
> "I enjoy seeing her body. I don't like always doing it in the dark."
> "I like her to tease me... a little dancing... or talking dirty."
> "I like it when she takes the lead."
> "I enjoy just having "sex" sometimes [as opposed to lovemaking]."
> "I love it when she lets herself go."

Begin by letting your bodies move naturally. Your goal is to achieve an erotic rhythm with your partner. That rhythm along with relaxation, kissing, touching and heat all work together to achieve orgasm. As I indicated earlier, guide your man and let him guide you to what feels good.

According to an article by Stacey Grenrock Woods published the August 2004 issue of *Esquire* magazine, another erogenous zone on your man is around his anus. Believe it or not, a lot of men secretly love this kind of stimulation. You can lightly touch it, lick it or insert the tip of your finger if you (and he) desire. Also, the patch of skin between his testicles and his anus (called the perineum) is very sensitive. Stroking him there during sex is *sure* to heighten his pleasure.

Another source of arousal for men is to watch a woman touch her own body. Start by caressing yourself all over, then just follow your instincts. Moan or talk softly to him as you go — he'll love to hear you. If you are a little shy, do it in a dimly lit room so you feel more comfortable. Also, games and role-playing may interest both of you and can also increase intimacy and desire.

Lovemaking can include a variety of positions. You can *spice up* the "woman lying on her back" position by elevating your hips while meeting his thrusts or moving to the end of the bed forming the [legs] "over the edge" position. Take charge with the "woman on top" position which enables the *woman* to set the speed and depth of penetration. "Doggie style" where the woman is balanced on all fours, gives the *man* a sexy view and control of penetration. And for an added boost, she can reach under with one hand and touch him as he moves into her. The "side by side" position is the one for *cuddlers* because partners can kiss and touch while making love. The "cross position" where the woman lies flat on her back and the man lies on top and slightly across (forming an "X") doesn't allow for much cuddling but allows for an alternate and flatter angle of penetration.

Remember, while making love try to incorporate *all* of the things that will stimulate yourself and your partner. Most importantly, be sure that *you* are comfortable with what you are doing — whether it's fast and passionate or slow and luxurious. Just relax, explore and love each other's bodies.

Tantric Sex:

I don't dare address this without help from the experts. Tantra is said to be the "total surrender of all mental, emotional and cultural conditioning." According to Tantra.com, here is a lovemaking technique through which you learn to "prolong the act of making love and to channel, rather than dissipate, potent orgasmic energies moving through you…" Tantric sex encourages participants to maintain eye contact and touch one another with all parts of the body. It is also said that there is no stopping point with this technique, only "the present moment of an ideal, harmonious union."

How to achieve this and other types of intense sexual pleasure is described in an ancient text called the *Kama Sutra*. The *Kama Sutra* is considered by many to be the ultimate sex manual. Way back in the fourth century, the ancient Hindus believed that life had three equal purposes: religious piety (dharma), material success (artha) and sexual pleasure (kama). The seven volumes of the *Kama Sutra* were written by a man named Vatsyayana Mallanaga as a guide to help men seduce women as well as to teach women how to attract men and keep them sexually happy.

Book 2 (the sex manual) teaches men the fine points of foreplay and other kinds of touching which are designed to heighten arousal. There are ten methods of kissing described in the *Kama Sutra*. As translated, one section reads, "The following are the places for kissing: the forehead, the eyes, the cheeks, the throat, the bosom, the breasts, the lips, and the interior of the mouth." There are also sixty-four sexual positions having interesting names like the *hammock*, the *arm chair*, the *wheelbarrow*, the *tiger* and the *mill vanes*. (What does your mind conjure up when you say these words?) For example, when describing some of the various positions, the *Kama Sutra* reads, "When the legs of both the male and the female are stretched straight out over each other, it is called the 'clasping position'... and after congress has begun in the clasping position... when the woman presses her lover with her thighs, it is called the 'pressing position'..."

It also discusses biting, scratching and shrieking, using sex toys and having sex while bathing. It reads, "The places that are to be pressed with the nails are as follows: the arm pit, the throat, the breasts, the lips, the... middle parts of the body and the thighs." It is said that these techniques produce "confident" arousal, prolongs and strengthens orgasms, calms the body and improves your personal relationship. The book also condones infidelity and multiple partners.

As outrageous as some of these suggestions might seem, the message here I think is to allow yourself to enjoy sex in an uninhibited way, doing whatever feels good. Your personal mix of what excites you should be your main objective.

His Most Private Wish Granted

Intercourse is important to men but oral sex is appreciated on a whole other level! A lot of women admit that they do not particularly enjoy performing this intimate act (although they are all for receiving it!). If you can't or don't want to do it — that's fine, but I'm telling you right here and now girls, men fantasize about getting it from you, your sister, your friends, the check-out girl at the store and the lady at the lunch counter! Get it? They love it! And *that*, as I've been informed by many men, is an understatement! In fact, some of their exact words were "I love getting a blow job."; "I wish she'd just unzip my pants and attack me."; "I get really cranky when I haven't had one."; "It relaxes me... relieves all the tension and puts me to sleep." If you can, try to do it often for him. If you want to find out what your partner likes, ask him some questions. If you really don't know how — learn. He will be at your mercy!

Begin by *building his anticipation.* Before you make any real contact, close your eyes and let your face, your hands and your hair brush over his abdomen and his genitals. Look as though you are going to take him in your mouth, but at the last minute, stop and look up at him; then, pull away. After doing this a few times (and intermittently *just barely* kissing him there), you will begin to see steam coming out of his ears! Now, lightly close your mouth around him and wiggle your tongue all around. Then, move him side to side inside your mouth with your tongue. Next, lick him from the base to the tip like an ice cream cone. A lot of men also love it when you kiss the tip of the penis lightly and *ever so gently* nibble and tickle the head, swirling it around with your tongue. His moans will tell you what he likes best.

Now, begin to use suction and movement (friction). Find out what kind of pressure and speed your man likes best — you'll be able to tell by his breathing, moaning, and movements. Some men like it when you softly lick and suck them; others prefer harder suction (either way, make sure his skin is well-lubricated, and watch those teeth). Be sure to find and maintain the rhythm he likes; some like a fast motion, others prefer it a little slower with an even pace. Also, you may want to try softly humming as you do this. Humming creates a vibration he can feel. Ultimately, he will guide you with his pelvis (and maybe his hands) to let you know what is bringing him the most pleasure. Follow his lead and you will drive him out of his mind!

So here's a wrap-up. To give your man the best oral sex *ever*, remember to:

♥ Be enthusiastic! If you don't enjoy it, *pretend to*. Men like to know that you *enjoy* pleasing them.

♥ Include a little teasing at the beginning to build up his anticipation — until he's squirming.

♥ Use your hands, hair, face and other body parts to touch him there.

♥ Let your tongue touch, tickle and move him around in your mouth.

♥ Pretend he's an ice cream cone; lick up and down the shaft.

♥ Use the "hands free" method (a lot of men like that).

♥ Try humming to create a vibration that excites him.

♥ Move yourself around. Don't stay in one position too long. You can kneel in front of him, lay beside him, lean over him or even lightly sit on his legs or belly. Let him feel as though you are anxious to please him from *all* angles.

♥ Mix it up. Do a variety of things. Don't just maintain one motion constantly; go from licking to nibbling to sucking until he's almost there.

♥ Don't forget his testicles and his perineum. Lightly tickle or stroke him with your tongue and/or fingers while you continue exciting him.

When sex is finished, remember that cuddling and talking afterwards about how great you feel or how much you enjoyed a certain *something* is another way to continue the intimacy. This transition is important because it conveys that there is much more to lovemaking than just the physical part. You connect with your partner on a deeper level and reinforce the love you expressed with your bodies with soft spoken words or *just being present*. These still and quiet moments together can strengthen and intensify the precious bond between you.

Chapter 13:
Eyes Wide Open

The Big Talk Every Couple
Should Have Before Marriage

Before getting married, Catholics who marry in the church have to go to "Pre-Cana Marriage Preparation" classes. There they are given counseling by priests and in preparation for the sacrament they are encouraged to discuss all aspects of the marriage. Some of the questions to be answered by couples in the sessions are: How many children do we want? What religion are we going to raise our children? Where are we going to live? How are we going to divide household chores?

Although some people may not agree with this mandatory concept, I respect its goal which is to get out in the open all of the issues that may come up in a marriage and on which couples should be compatible or at least know where each other stands. Considering that between forty percent and fifty percent of marriages end in divorce, I think knowing as much about one another makes perfect sense. I mean, think about it. We have to get a driver's license to drive a car and take boards to get certified at our professions, but before combining lives and raising children there is no set assessment or standard guidelines in place to determine competency and compatibility. And considering that most of us came from an *assortment of dysfunction*, why shouldn't we do all we can so we don't make the same mistakes our parents did?

If you are wise, you will schedule your own pre-wedding conference session with your partner and go over all of the what-ifs and
potentially problematic situations which may arise after you are married.
Your efforts will result in both of you having some idea of how each of
you views certain issues and your individual approaches to solving
problems. Topics should include: family; children; sex; careers;
relatives; housework; finances; friends; religion; vacations; hobbies;
traveling; politics; ethical beliefs; diet; medical history; past
relationships and death and dying.

Wake Up and Smell the Dysfunction

As we finish discussing ways to improve yourself and your
relationship, I think it's important to also review some other more
serious issues which can exist in any relationship so you can spot them
before it's too late.

Some people just cannot be monogamous. According to
Askmen.com, some men cheat to prove to themselves that they are still
attractive to women. Others can't resist finding out if the "grass is
greener" someplace else. Still others will use the excuse that they feel
unappreciated at home or that they don't deserve their "saintly" mate.
(There's also that good, old standby "my wife doesn't understand me.")
Experts agree that some signs that he may be cheating are his frequent
traveling, hiding of financial details, lack of interest in sex, moodiness,
and *your* limited access to his cell phone or e-mail. One woman admitted
to being "very naïve" when her ex-husband cheated on her years ago.
She said now she realizes that his incessant drinking, his lame excuses
for coming home late, and the phone call from his nineteen-year-old
girlfriend should have tipped her off! Of course, when you're young and
in love, you make yourself believe even the most *ridiculous* explanations
because sometimes the truth is too monstrous to handle. And remember
what I said before? When we fall in love our brains generate certain
chemicals that give us that euphoric feeling — making people in love
temporarily *blind* to the reality of a bad situation.

If something like this does happen, it's up to you to decide if you can
continue with the relationship. The bottom line is, whether you take him
back or move on, you have to figure out why it happened. Have you been
intimate with one another? Was it a one-time mistake for sex, is he just

a cheater or did he fall for someone else? Is he truly sorry and willing to change, and realistically, can you forgive him and put the whole thing behind you? With your new and improved self-image, you may no longer be able to stay with someone who showed you such disrespect. Ultimately, the decision is up to you — there is no right or wrong choice — you have to live with whatever you decide.

So what can you do if you suspect infidelity? Well, don't jump to conclusions but *listen to your gut instinct*. If you really feel as though something is going on, have a talk with your partner and tell him how and why you feel as you do. If you find your suspicions are confirmed, you should figure out why this happened. Then review your choices, and decide what's best for you. Whatever you decide to do, it won't be easy.

To move on is one choice and will certainly involve a lot of self-analysis and the whole painful process of getting over a loved one. But to forgive can be just as, if not more, difficult. You must truly believe that your partner is sorry for the indiscretion and believe it will not happen again. Then in order to get back to a healthy, functioning relationship, you must correct whatever went wrong, and return to trusting your partner and making yourself vulnerable again, which takes time and a whole lotta love. During this process, your partner must be willing to live with your suspicious nature and endless questioning for a long time (until you feel comfortable). He must also be forthcoming with the truth without anger or resentment. And, after checking out his story more than a few times, you should eventually believe what he tells you... although sometimes this is simply not the case and trust is never regained.

Next, there are some men who will just take from you until you are drained, never giving of themselves in return. Then, when you're empty (or fed up), they will leave you and begin taking from someone else. Other men need to be in constant control and simply do not know *how* to share or be *vulnerable* to someone in a loving relationship (maybe because they have never experienced that level of love). If you are always giving of yourself and what you have, and never having *your* needs met, you may want to set some boundaries and goals in the relationship. Remember, that *little girl in your pocket* is counting on you!

There are some men who abuse drugs or alcohol, both of which can set off negative and destructive behavior. Some may have a propensity towards violence and obscenity. This is just degrading and not something you should *ever* allow into your life. There are doctors, private agencies and groups who specialize in these things and whose jobs it is to listen to you and help you to sort things out. You don't deserve this and you are *not* alone.

These situations *are* out there. If you are with someone who has serious problems, try to identify what's going on. Be truthful with yourself. Don't hide your eyes from seeing the reality of how things really are between you and *don't make excuses for him* (so many women do that!). If discussing your concerns with your partner is futile, you may have to be the one to alter your situation if things don't improve or your partner is unwilling to (or simply can't) change.

Can You Recognize Emotional Abuse?

Another important thing to understand is that there is a difference between having disagreements with your partner and emotional abuse. If your partner is emotionally abusive to you, he may:

- Refuse to acknowledge the value or self-worth of others.
- Not listen.
- Humiliate others.
- Ignore logic.
- Not take responsibility for hurting others.
- Be jealous and possessive.
- Often see himself as a martyr or victim.
- Make you feel guilty for no reason.

This type of behavior by your partner can leave you feeling out of control, weak and/or humiliated. You may feel like you have to walk on egg shells to avoid confrontation and must anticipate his moods in order to keep the relationship at peace. You may also feel pressured into having sex, or be confused as to where you stand in the relationship. Basically, you may feel as though you are on a roller-coaster ride of good and bad times, and often you may even feel afraid and isolated from others. Emotional abuse usually happens slowly as a relationship progresses until one day you realize what's happening and have to deal with it.

Alicia, one single mother told me that while contemplating a divorce from her verbally abusive husband, her friends (at the time) told her she was crazy. They would say, "you're gonna give up that nice vehicle… you won't be able to have a house on your own." She said that she realized that her number one responsibility was to raise her son well and "everything else was secondary." She said that today, although they live in a small apartment and she struggles with a busy schedule, she has a great job, good friends and is much happier than before. She says, "I had to go it alone. It's so much more important that [my son] sees me happy and that I teach him that material things don't matter as much." As you can see in this example, as hard as we try to improve our awareness and self-image, when you love someone, it's easy to be blind to the existence and effects of emotional abuse.

It is important to remember that emotional abuse can also be traumatizing. When something bad happens to you, if you can't resolve it in your mind or convey its intensity to others in order to get help, it probably caused you some sort of emotional damage. Emotional abuse is also harmful to a woman's self-esteem. According to the website, Thisisawar.com (an educational resource which helps people deal with illness, grief, pregnancy, debt and other personal issues), emotional abuse can have "serious physical and psychological consequences for women, including severe depression, anxiety, persistent headaches, back and stomach problems." Other symptoms include panic attacks, irritability, emotional numbness, eating irregularities and insomnia. So how can you determine how much damage was done to you and how can you fix it?

Scientists now have the technology to examine the brain and read the damage caused by emotional abuse through brain scans. According to recent research, these scans reveal such a trauma actually "changes the structure and function of the brain, at the point where the frontal cortex, the emotional brain and the survival brain converge." One of their major findings was that scans of people who had experienced emotional abuse were similar in "structural and functional irregularities" to people diagnosed with Post Traumatic Stress Disorder.

If you feel you are or have been a victim of emotional abuse, there is help. First, if possible, remove yourself from the abusive situation. If you can't, then you should surround yourself with a network of people — family and friends — who can help you cope in such an unhealthy and often dangerous situation. You should also *talk to a professional* who will know how to help you through analysis and counseling. Under these circumstances, a professional will help you decide the best course of action for you. Couples therapy may be an answer or you may discover that it's time for you to leave.

This brings up an interesting point. It's very difficult for a lot of women to move on. I know several women who have stayed for years with partners who were abusive, neglectful and unfaithful. Women who say they can't leave (besides having very low self-images) usually have long-standing erroneous beliefs that keep them tied to these undeserving men. Some of these women believe that they cannot abandon their dysfunctional partners; that these men somehow need them in order to survive. Oh, really? If those men really needed them, they would fear losing them and smarten up! Some women tell themselves that their partners will change and eventually recognize their value and love. Wrong. That outlook puts off happiness and fulfillment until "someday," which is when exactly? And deep down, do they believe it will ever really happen with this man? Other women believe that they will never find another man to love them so they stay with their abusers even though they are extremely unhappy. Why? Classic low self-esteem — even if this were true, I believe that a woman can be alone and happy (I was), which is far better than feeling miserable sharing your life with a sadistic man! Don't make these mistakes. Acknowledge your value as a person who deserves love and respect. Recognize when something is really over.

One important thing to keep in mind is that the people in your life whom you love should make your life easier and *add* to your joy, *not* take away from it. Ask yourself: are you more often upset and confused than you are peaceful and happy? If so, then something is not right, and you should remedy the situation. If world events of the last few years have taught us anything, it's not to waste a moment of life. Do what it takes to make yourself happy. Above all, be true to yourself. If you follow your heart, and you love honestly and openly, you will at the very least know that you gave your all and will have no regrets.

Men and Control

In my interviews and on my website, women have often complained that they find men to be "controlling." Do you know what that means? Can you distinguish between a man who is controlling and a man who is behaving like a bully or is overprotective?

Some characteristics of a "controlling" man may be that he is manipulative, arrogant, clever, and has a need for constant stimulation. He may be a liar, inconsiderate, aggressive and have been in a lot of short-term relationships. He is basically only concerned about fulfilling *his* needs and attaining *his* goals. Experts say that most controlling men are "sociopaths" or as they are now more commonly referred to as having antisocial personality disorder. They appear charming at first and "normal" to everyone around them, but inside they have a real need for control.

According to the criminal profile given at Wesleyan College, the official list of common sociopathic traits include:

- Egocentricity
- Callousness
- Impulsivity
- Conscience defect
- Exaggerated sexuality
- Excessive boasting
- Risk taking
- Inability to resist temptation
- Antagonizing
- Deprecating attitude towards the opposite sex
- Lack of interest in bonding with a mate

Usually when around such a man, a woman's self-esteem takes a nose-dive. His inappropriate and abusive behavior makes her feel uneasy, badly about herself and anxious about what his next move may be at any given moment. She may also feel alone, not realizing that he has isolated her from her friends and family. She is often confused by his actions and "logic" and will see him get angry when criticized or scolded.

Other reasons a man may be controlling could be that he was spoiled as a child or has simply gotten used to being in charge of everything, like a single father with children who has grown accustomed to barking out orders in an effort to keep things peaceful and on schedule. When a woman enters into a situation such as this, she may be viewed by that man as another one of his underlings who needs his supervision and for whom he is responsible. Usually this is an unintentional impulse on his part, and a discussion and some practice will make him view and treat you as an equal partner and even seek out your opinion and help with responsibilities.

RESOURCES
National Domestic Violence Hotline, 1-800-799-SAFE (7233)
www.youarenotcrazy.com (An interactive tool designed to help
women recognize abuse)
www.feminist.org (Provides state-by-state telephone help lines)
www.ncadv.org/resources/resources.htm (National Coalition
Against Domestic Violence)
www.vaw.umn.edu/(Violence Against Women)
www.4woman.gov/violence (Resource for help from various
kinds of abuse)

The Toughest Call of All:
Knowing When Not to Leave Too Soon or Stay Too Long

If you've been hurt in the past by boyfriends or lovers, you tend to
be on the look-out for the signs you may have overlooked in past
relationships that mean you should go. As a result of this *offensive*
attitude, you may be hyper-sensitive to the mistakes of others and prone
to having one foot out the door most of the time. Alternatively, you may
be the type of woman who believes in riding out the bad times (which is
good) but uncertain about when enough is enough (which is not so
good). Here are some guidelines that may help you navigate through
these troubled and confusing waters.

Is it too soon to leave?

What has he done to make you consider leaving? Is there any pattern
of neglectful or hurtful behavior? How many times has he made the same
mistake? Does he apologize and, if so, does he mean it (i.e., does he try
not to do it again)? Is he open to discussing problems and
compromising? Is he respectful of you? Is your level of intimacy
satisfactory to you? Basically, what you're trying to determine is, "Is his
behavior *wrong enough* for me to leave?"

Is my leave overdue?

Are you always upset or confused or miserable? Is he abusive
(verbally or physically)? Have you discussed all the issues with him and
you are sure that he knows how you feel? Have you set standards and
established limits which he does not respect? Does he cheat? Do you not
desire him sexually? Do the bad times outweigh the good? Do you stay

because *every so often* you still have fun? *You must consider if you have not suppressed your own feelings of unhappiness and begun to live with things as unacceptable as they are just to avoid the pain or upheaval that comes with changing your life.*

In my contact with my website visitors requesting advice, I hear horrible stories about disrespectful, cheating mates and miserable situations and yet, the last question is almost always, should I leave him? I know that because that is a big step for my clients, all they really need is some reinforcement and support because, really, their decisions have already been made. And like them, no matter what *you* might say out loud to your friends about your relationship, you know in your heart and in your gut what is right and what is wrong, (and when you should stay and when you should go). It's just that, when you're deeply immersed in such an emotionally-charged situation, it doesn't always feel as completely "right" or as completely "wrong" as you'd like it to — you know, you say, "If he does that one more time…" and when he does, you still hesitate. What stops most people are the uncomfortable feelings associated with such a move like change, being alone, a fear of an unknown future and, of course, the fear that they will leave their dysfunctional partner and *then* he will miraculously become Prince Charming. In the end your decision to leave may be based on your belief that you are just not right for one another.

A Size Eight Foot in a Size Seven Shoe

When a relationship ends, it may not be because someone cheated or was truly awful to the other. It may just be that the two people weren't designed for one another or "meant to be." I talked to so many women who asked, "Why couldn't he just love me?" to which I responded, "He just couldn't. He wasn't the right one for you." It's like shoes. You may be able to squeeze your foot into a few pretty pairs that appear to be your size (especially if they're the last ones of their kind on the shelf), but if they're not exactly the right size, they're gonna hurt you. It's better to put those back and look for ones that fit. Eventually, you will find a pair you're happy with and that are comfortable and durable.

For a while, you may not meet your Mr. Right but instead meet a slew of Mr. Right-Nows. Those are people who come into your life for a short time and are meant to help you in some way or teach you something, and visa versa. I believe that during that time, you are in the process of learning some lessons and experiencing certain things in life, all in preparation for the "you" who is ready to have a relationship with that person whom you are destined to meet. In short, timing is everything.

So if you find that you are having trouble finding the right man, have patience. You've got to meet the right person at the right time in both your lives. Have faith and believe that you will find someone to love and who will love you.

Be Open To Compromise

I feel that in order to make a relationship work, we must *show* the other person that we are willing to work at it and really care — not just say it. We must *listen* in order to know what the other needs and desires and then fulfill *those* needs (not do only what we *think* is appropriate or convenient for ourselves). However, with that comes respecting each other's uniqueness even when sparks fly. For example, when your evening at the theater conflicts with his playoff championship is *precisely* the time to respect the other's passion, and try to work around what's important to the both of you (although, this does not excuse a person from keeping a promise). Can you go to the ballet a different night? Can he tape the game? Can you enjoy your evenings separately? Are you *respectful* enough of one another to *understand* and *accept* the outcome? As I said, your contentment as a couple depends on this type of give-and-take and you should not have to morph into one another simply to get along.

One situation presented to me by a friend of mine was when her boyfriend of ten years asked her to wear sexy lingerie for him at night because he was "bored" seeing her in sweatpants and t-shirts over and over again. At first she was insulted and upset. She said she kept putting off doing this because she didn't want to "look like a hooker" — totally understandable, right? I suggested that she take her time and shop for some sexy, *elegant* lingerie (maybe a tasteful teddy, a slinky slip, or an ensemble with a sheer cover up); something that would spark *his* interest and make *her* still feel comfortable. She agreed and, as it turned out, when she asked him for the money to fund this excursion he was more than willing to fork over enough to purchase some very beautiful bedtime attire (and, of course, there were still nights when flannel was just fine)! See, you don't have to give up who you are in order to get along, but trying something your partner suggests once in a while (with, perhaps, some modifications) can only deepen your understanding of one another.

Another example could be when the two of you have different sleep habits. You are used to total silence when going to sleep and he likes to fall asleep with the television on. In this case, you may choose to compromise by leaving the television on for, say, fifteen minutes after you get into bed and then turn it off. If that doesn't work, you may decide to try something else; you could go to bed first and shut the door so that you have the quiet you require, and he can watch television in another room until he gets sleepy and then comes into bed.

It's important to understand that you and your man come together from different backgrounds, with your own unique tastes and preferences. When a situation arises that puts you at opposite ends of the spectrum, you should talk about it. Discuss what each of you requires and acknowledge that some decision needs to be reached that will somewhat satisfy both of you. Remember to respect your differences, keep the stubbornness in check, and listen. Be open to at least *trying* something new. Another suggestion may be to take turns; this time you do it his way, next time he does it your way. And as time moves on, who knows? One of you may get used to the other's way of doing something and even prefer it. Compromise *should* work in *most* situations (except perhaps where religion or allergies are concerned). Remember, there is really no right or wrong when it comes to preferences. Each time someone compromises for the other, it is a loving and unselfish gesture that should be acknowledged, appreciated *and* reciprocated.

The Tingles

Of course, every couple experiences lulls in their relationship; times when it feels like there seems to be no excitement left between you. Before you panic or do something you'll regret, start with an examination of yourself.

Most busy people are creatures of habit. It helps the day to flow more easily when you keep things structured and familiar. With that convenience sometimes comes boredom. When this happens, make some changes — not necessarily big ones — just some changes that will make things feel new and different for you. Adjust your schedule; get up earlier in the morning. Take a different route to work. Exercise at lunch or go for a walk. Move the furniture around in your rooms (I love this one!). Vary your hairstyles. Begin a new hobby or take up a new sport (tennis, swimming, or painting). Start a project, maybe a renovation or something creative. Anything out of the ordinary or challenging might be just the thing to put that spring back into your step and improve your outlook.

If what you're feeling has more to do with a relationship issue between you and your partner, then you may be interested to know that it's *not* a sign that the love affair is over. Earlier I informed you that when we fall in love our brains generate chemicals like dopamine and norepinephrine which give us a euphoric-like feeling. After a time, however, our bodies generate smaller amounts of those chemicals, which leads to a decline in what I call the "tingles." Fortunately, however, as things happen in our lives that excite us, similar chemicals get released once again in our bodies temporarily giving us back that elevated feeling!

So, when you lose the tingles, instead of assuming that the relationship is over or that you have to begin looking elsewhere for someone new, make an effort to spark things up with the one you love. Rekindle your connection in the bedroom; take time to just kiss and hold each other like you used to. Begin by reminiscing about how you met, and remember all of the things that you love about one another. Take a vacation together (without the kids). Turn off the television and tell stories about your childhood or read together. More importantly, go have some fun! Visit new places together, join a group of some kind (something charitable or that will benefit the community) or take lessons in an activity you've always wanted to learn (how about ballroom dancing, wine tasting or skiing?). Set some new goals (in business or during free time) and make them happen. One couple I know bought a weekend cabin and are making it into their own *special* retreat. Another couple began buying and renovating old houses together. Not only were they able to be creative and have fun *together*, they made a bundle of money! Whatever you do, just don't give up. Stop and think about how much you mean to one another and you'll be able to get through this rough patch *together*.

So there you have it. I have shared with you my personal experiences, research and survey findings, feedback from clients, data and statistics, and sample situations and dialogue... all of the information and tools you need (and to which you can continually refer) to begin a more loving and satisfying relationship with yourself and an exciting and fulfilling journey through the rest of your life! Let's do a quick review.

If you're feeling down, take the time to figure out why. Investigate your feelings. Ignore the old, unproductive *toxic imprints* and concentrate on positive, constructive, motivating thoughts. With your new confident attitude, get back out there and actively pursue your goals and dreams and don't settle for less than what you believe you deserve! Accept the beauty of your uniqueness and be proud of who you are and who you will become. Communicate clearly and treat others with respect and kindness and expect no less in return. Remember to express your appreciation and gratitude to the people you love and drop the drama when it comes to the little things! Allow yourself a bad day occasionally and during those times, let your emotions out so that you can release the tension and resentment, and then return to your newfound state of grace.

Allow yourself to be vulnerable, to love others and to feel every emotion fully. Open yourself up to the vast possibilities that are trying to seek you out to bring to you all that you need to succeed and be happy. And above all, take risks, slow down enough to savor every moment, and listen to your instincts!

As you put down this book, you're probably praising my brilliance and picturing me relaxing on a lounge chair on an island in the Caribbean, sipping some kind of tropical drink and fanning myself with all my money. But fear not, for there is still much work to be done. In truth, I will be at home trying to cook a meal for my family, while one stepson continuously pokes me with his finger, the other plays his rap music so loud the furniture shakes, my fiancé humps my leg and the cat drags her poopie butt on the rug... yes, *this* is paradise!

From Me to You

Try this. In order to get in touch with that "little girl in your pocket,"
try carrying a picture of yourself around with you. Find one that shows

you as a child full of sweetness and beauty. Then, when you are feeling hopeless or angry or lost, take out that picture and look at it for a moment. Look at her innocent little face and hands. I guarantee if you do this, it will change how you feel; it will melt your heart. I still carry a little picture of myself in my purse just in case — it works every time!

Here are some of my philosophies, which I truly believe have helped change and enrich my life.

I am grateful for everything I am and everything I have.

I feel blessed.

Respect means everything to me.

I feed and nurture my spirit by listening to inspirational people and reading positive material.

I love and respect animals.

I stopped caring about what other people think a long time ago.

I always try to do what I think is right.

I'm learning that almost everything I need I can find within myself.

I stopped trying to fit in. I now embrace being a unique woman.

I try to learn from my mistakes. I've stopped berating myself for making them.

I no longer lose myself in my partner. I am my own person and now make myself a priority.

I am kind and generous to others, and I am learning to be more forgiving.

I try to get the absolute most out of every day.

I have learned how to feel joyful and would not trade that for anything.

I try to love everyone to the best of my ability — and show them as well.

I help myself and others the best I can, but then I let go and trust fate to figure out what's best.

Finally, contemplate this: What if you had only a week to live? Would you feel a sense of panic? Urgency? Anger? Would you be at peace? Ask yourself the following questions: What would you do with your last remaining days? Who would you want to be with? Would you be grateful for the people you have in your life? Would you have regrets? Would you be satisfied with how you've lived your life, treated people, done things? Would there be things that you wished you had made time to do? In the grand scheme of things, a life is short. So what are you waiting for?

Chapter 14:
TheAccidentalExpert.com

Here is a sneak peek into some of the issues I've helped clients resolve on my website.

DEAR ACCIDENTAL EXPERT: I am very much in love with my longtime girlfriend, but there are security issues with her that I fear will be our demise. She gets defensive and shuts me off. Her self-esteem is almost non-existent. She accuses me of cheating, and checking other women out and I'm not. Please help.

DEAR FRIEND: Unfortunately, there is really nothing one person can do to change the self-image of another, except to continue to speak positively and support her. She must want to change how she feels and realize the consequences if she does not (e.g., damage to her relationships, her happiness, the rest of her life!) and examine her self-esteem and then work on improving it. I suggest you again try talking to her, tell her the truth about how you feel and point her in the direction of counseling, self-help books and, of course, this website so she can begin to solve her problems.

DEAR ACCIDENTAL EXPERT: My boyfriend and I have a long distance relationship and my parents think he is using me for a long distance "booty call" when he's in town. He recently just lost his job but

I don't care because he doesn't buy me things or send money… at the same time I don't ask. Am I being played or what?

DEAR FRIEND: If you are happy the way things are, then nothing is wrong, right? If you want more and you are not getting it then you may want to look at this arrangement and consider how one-sided it is. Ask yourself if you want something different than you have or have feelings for him that he may not have for you. I believe you know deep down what's going on, even if you don't want to give it up because it's nice to have a guy come around once in a while. Just don't sell yourself short. You deserve much more.

DEAR ACCIDENTAL EXPERT: When you have broken trust, how can you get your mate to trust you again?

DEAR FRIEND: Broken trust is very difficult to regain, but not impossible. You more or less have to take your punishment from your mate — meaning answer his or her questions, clear up suspicions, verify where you've been, etc. over and over again for an unknown period of time (until your mate feels comfortable again). Once you have been consistently honest for a length of time, your mate should relax a little and slowly believe what you are telling him/her. During this delicate time, do not, under any circumstances, hold anything back or lie about anything, because if he/she learns about something you didn't tell them, you may never be trusted again. So if one partner is willing to give the other a chance, what is expected of them must be discussed. The one who was hurt has to tell the other one that they will have to answer any and all questions without complaining until the trust is back — and like I said there is really no telling how long that could be — but if you want the relationship, you gotta do the work!

DEAR ACCIDENTAL EXPERT: I am dating a man who has told me from the beginning he isn't looking for anything serious, he wants someone to hang out with from time to time and if it goes any further than that, that is fine, but he isn't looking for something serious. I'm just curious to know what your thoughts are.

DEAR FRIEND: I've found that a lot of women are having relation-ships with men who say they just want to have fun — or who aren't look-ing for something serious, etc. These women say "okay" and spend time with these men, but inside are really hoping the guy will fall in love/change his mind meanwhile are feeling hurt, confused and used. This may happen, but if it doesn't the woman is always hurt because she wanted more (right from the start) and, as long as he was honest about his feelings, it's really not the man's fault. I think women should be honest with men as well. You deserve a nice man who treats you right, who you have fun with, who respects you, and who loves you back. If this guy doesn't want that and you do, then move on. You'd be amazed at how good it will feel to take control of your life even if for a while you feel sad.

DEAR ACCIDENTAL EXPERT: How do you let the past go, his past relationships, and mine so they don't get into the present (ours)?

DEAR FRIEND: I think the first thing you have to do is trust each other. You have to know — in your heart — that the other person is not going back to anyone, no matter what. Without trust you don't have anything. And if you don't feel that then you better work on that issue. Secondly, as much as possible, eliminate the people from the past from your daily conversation (unless there are children involved and someone has to speak to an ex with regard to them). Once that's done, forget-about-it! Who cares about those people — obviously those were not the right people for either of you or else you would still be with them. Try to think of those people as "practice" relationships and yours as "the real thing." If you go to a place one of you has been before - keep it to yourself — and just enjoy this new experience with your partner. Also, you may want to make one another feel secure in the relationship by showing support — remind each other how you feel and that you are glad to be together here and now, and not with those other people. One thing I always say to my fiancé is that "I would not be the person I am today if I hadn't gone through all of the experiences I did in the past. I was not the same person years ago, so I was not ready for you — and we probably wouldn't have made it." Lastly, I think you need to set some goals together and make some history. As time passes, you will have your own memories and pictures together and little by little, I believe those reminders of other people will fade away.

DEAR ACCIDENTAL EXPERT: I've recently gotten myself involved with a newly-divorced man and he seems to already be rushing things by telling me how he feels and wanting to see me constantly, but I have a busy life. Is he for real? Should I worry about this?

DEAR FRIEND: Well, the word is not "worry" but do be cautious. It sounds like you want to take things slowly (and you should!) so make plans at your own pace. Also, subconsciously he may be on the "rebound" — trying to replace his ex-wife quickly so he's not lonely, although he's probably just feeling excited to have someone new and wants to grab you while this feeling lasts (and before you get away). If you care for him, then treat him nicely and appreciate what he does for you. You should also make sure you are truthful about your feelings every step of the way. With time, things will even out and you will be able to see if he really does have deep affection for you and you for him. Until then, let him establish a life on his own and learn to do some things for himself (and he should also learn to be patient). Don't let him smother you or draft you into the role of "wife" even before you are one!

DEAR ACCIDENTAL EXPERT: My problem is that I have a friend who is involved with a real jerk. He cheats on her and can be rude and obnoxious. Most of her friends can't stand him, but she will just not leave him. She believes all his lies and thinks he will change. I want to just tell her to smarten up but am afraid. What should I do?

DEAR FRIEND: You are really in a difficult situation and any decision you make may have consequences. What I say is that if she is a good friend and comes to you for advice — tell her the truth, not just what you think, but what you KNOW. Tell her the facts, and then let her make up her own mind. All you can do is be there for your friends if and when they need you — and it sounds like she will need you at some point, but who knows? I once told a friend (who came to me) what I thought of her fiancé who began blatantly cheating on her a week before their wedding — and everyone knew it. When she asked me what to do, of course I had to be truthful, so my answer was "dump him" — but she did not. She carried on with the wedding because "everything was already planned and money was spent." Of course, after the wedding she did not speak to me any longer and he hated me because she told him what I said. And last I saw them, there was a rawness and insensitivity about them which was sad to see. As unfortunate as things turned out, if

I had it to do over, I still would not be able to find it within myself to lie to someone I cared about — no matter what the outcome.

DEAR ACCIDENTAL EXPERT: I met a guy about a week ago while I was out with some friends at a bar. We seemed to hit it off and he took my number and said he'd call. A day or so after we met, he called my cell phone late one night but didn't leave a message (I saw the caller ID and think it was him). Do you think it's okay for me to call him? Do you think he lost my number? Some of my friends tell me to call him and others tell me not to. (edited)

DEAR FRIEND: I know it may be very hard not to pick up that phone, but I don't think you should. If he is interested, he will call again — if he's not, then he won't. And why would he call you in the middle of the night? Why not try to reach you at normal hours and ask you out on a proper date or leave a message? If he was smart enough to dial your phone number once, he can again. Your number is probably obtainable in his cell phone records anyway. So if he really wants to call, well, you know. I say, don't waste your time with losers, liars, game-players or moochers. Get out there and enjoy yourself — try not to make going out with friends about meeting someone — you will meet someone of quality when the time is right.

DEAR ACCIDENTAL EXPERT: I have been with my boyfriend for a very long time and he still goes out and parties a lot without me. I'm left at home a lot while he goes out (drinking) with his friends. How can I make him stop and grow up?!

DEAR FRIEND: I know that men and women mature at different stages, but at some point you have to ask yourself is this what you really want? Do you tell him how you feel about his late nights and being left alone? How does he respond to your talks? First of all you have to let him know how you feel — in a calm, sensible manner, and not in the middle of a fight. Pick a night when you are together to discuss the situation rationally. You have to figure out what each of you really wants — are you a homebody, while he is a party animal? Are you open to going out with him - are you ever invited? After your talk, you have some thinking to do. Carefully consider the reality of the way things are between you and where you think things are heading. If you truly don't see your lives coming together — and if you are unhappy — I say don't waste time. Life is too short. Set some goals, make your plans and move on if things continue like this and if he doesn't care or love you enough to change.

Most Common Complaints by Women about Men

He doesn't listen.

He forgets (probably because he wasn't listening).

He's immature.

He's a sports junkie.

He says inappropriate/hurtful things.

He leaves his stuff all over the place.

He does too much for others (not much left over for me).

He wants sex too much.

Most Common Complaints by Men about Women

She's overly emotional.

She tries to boss me around/thinks she's my mother.

She shops too much.

She's too picky.

She gets jealous.

She talks on the phone constantly (telling her friends our life story).

She's always tired/never wants to have sex.

She always wants to change things about me.

<u>SAMPLE SURVEY 1</u>

Thank you for completing my survey. Your answers can relate to a current relationship, a past relationship or just romantic relationships you have had in general.

Please rate in order of importance:

Honesty___   Faithfulness ___   Sense of Humor ___

Education ___   Passion ___   Kindness ___

Beauty/Fit Body ___   Good Job ___

Please finish these sentences:

The biggest difference between me and my partner/lover is: _____

_____

The nicest thing a partner/lover ever did for me was: _____

_____

The nicest thing I ever did for a partner/lover was: _____

_____

The thing that most irritates me about my partner/lover is: _____

_____

What puts me most in the mood for intimacy is: _____

_____

A surefire way to reach my heart is: _____

_____

If my partner/lover does something to upset me, I usually: _____

_____

The biggest mistake I make (or made) in relationships is:

_____

The one thing I worry most about in a relationship is: _____

_____

The best thing you can do for someone you love is: _____

_____

The thing I would most like the opposite sex to know about my gender

is: _____

SURVEY SAYS…

When I tallied up the results, the *most desirable* qualities in a mate were:

1. **Honesty** (also tied for first was "kindness")
2. **Attractiveness**
3. **A Sense of Humor**
4. **Kindness** (also tied for fourth was "honesty")
5. **Faithfulness**
6. **Passion**
7. **Education**
8. **Job**

<u>SAMPLE SURVEY 2</u>

Please answer these questions as briefly as you can. Thanks.

QUESTION	ANSWER
What do you think men/women want?	
How much and about what do you criticize yourself?	
Do you have a sense of humor? If so, what do you do for fun?	
What makes you feel *not* like having sex?	
How do you feel about his/her ability to remember things?	
How do you feel about strip clubs?	
Does he/she listen to you? To what extent?	
Do you share any hobbies? If so, what.	
Have you ever had a really bad fight? If so, what was it about?	
Do you eat meals together?	

If you could change something about him/her what would it be?	
What has he/she done that was really stupid?	
How do you tell the other that you want to have sex?	
Do you believe in God? Other power?	
Describe your perfect man/woman.	
Who do you think is sexy? (either a type, or cite a celebrity example)	
Have you ever threatened your mate? If so, over what?	
Describe your perfect day.	
Other comments?	

Inspirations from the Masters

"Everything I need to know is revealed to me." ~ Louise Hay

"All that I need comes to me." ~ Louise Hay

"The universe gifts me with courage in all things." ~ Julia Cameron

"Grace is not a strange, magic substance which is subtly filtered into our souls to act as a kind of spiritual penicillin. Grace is unity, oneness within ourselves, oneness with God." ~ Thomas Merton

"If you have a sincere and open heart, you naturally feel self-worth and confidence, and there is no need to be fearful of others." ~ The Dalai Lama

"There's no shop that sells kindness, you must build it within. You can transplant hearts, but you cannot transplant a warm heart." ~ The Dalai Lama

"For one human being to love another: that is perhaps the most difficult of all tasks, the ultimate, the last test and proof, the work for which all other work is but preparation." ~ Rainer Maria Rilke

"Let us give thanks for this beautiful day. Let us give thanks for this life. Let us give thanks for the water without which life would not be possible. Let us give thanks for Grandmother Earth who protects and nourishes us." ~ Daily Prayer of the Lakota

"I will face this day with optimism and hope. Pessimism is not an option." ~ Pamela Leavey

"In life there are always choices. I choose to spend this day cherishing my life and all the people who are in my life." ~ Pamela Leavey

"The only way to have a friend is to be one." ~ Ralph Waldo Emerson

"There's only one corner of the universe you can be certain of improving, and that's your own self." ~ Aldous Huxley

"When I thought I couldn't go on, I forced myself to keep going. My success is based on persistence, not luck." ~ Estee Lauder

"It's so important to believe in yourself. Believe that you can do it, under any circumstances. Because if you believe you can, then you really will. That belief just keeps you searching for the answers, and then pretty soon you get it." ~ Wally "Famous" Amos

"Our true gift to ourselves lies not in what we have but in who we are." ~ Marianne Williamson

What Women Most Want the Opposite Sex to Know

"How come you can't read my mind. You're supposed to know what I want!"

"Stop thinking with your penises!"

"Don't <u>ever</u> say 'You must be saying this/acting this way because you have your period.'"

"The small things count — women have long memories (as men will attest to) and not just for the bad things either..."

"Cuddling and holding and kissing are important without any expectations of sex... It would be nice to be held without thinking, oh God, he's looking for sex again. If they only knew... that kind attention usually does lead to more sex..."

"If a good man shows a good woman that he adores her with actions, not just talk, she will nearly double it with her actions!"

"... they need to LISTEN when we talk to them, not just pretend to!!!"

"I wish they could experience PMS and be more understanding."

"I'd want men to know that there is a happy medium between "trying too hard" and "disinterest." I am attracted to men who are comfortable with themselves. Don't try to impress me. Just be yourself and relax!"

"Don't rush too fast into romance/intimacy. If a relaxed friendship develops, romance may follow and it will be rooted."

"They are very closed when it comes to expressing their feelings — they don't call, they don't initiate contact and they just expect us to know what is going on in their mind. Communication is the key to a successful relationship. Especially at the beginning when it comes to letting the other person know what you're thinking and feeling... I find that communicating is the hardest part because you never know what they are thinking by their actions..."

"I wish they knew when it was time to propose."

"... women were NOT put on earth to serve them."

"Gentle is NOT bad."

"My life doesn't revolve around sex and I don't think of it 24-7 like they do. It's literally all they think about and all they care about and I'm so tired of it!!! Don't get me wrong, sex is great; but I only enjoy it or want it when I'm not totally exhausted. I could be crawling in the house at midnight from exhaustion from a hectic day but that doesn't seem to matter to a man."

"We thought men were the breadwinners and the workers of the family, until we got out into the working world and saw for ourselves — the jig is up."

What Men Most Want the Opposite Sex to Know

"We understand that women don't think the same way about everything that we do (but we're not sure women always understand the same about us)."

"We want the same things you want... happy kids, a nice house... and sex."

"No matter what, I'm always here for you."

"We try our best."

"We don't always do what you want but we still love you."

"Let us be men."

"They're drama queens. They blow everything out of proportion..."

"Stop talking so much. They talk about things that aren't important."

"Women shouldn't stay with men who abuse them... they should cut them off completely and move on... don't stay because that's all you know."

"Not all men are the same... the nice guys seem to suffer because there are a few jerks around..."

"You know what I'm gonna say... we love sex."

"Don't pick on us."

"We really don't need to hear every little thing... just tell us the important parts... and men want sex a lot."

"Why do they have to act like that... they get all upset and stuff... just calm down."

"You women are all alike. It's all what you can get from a guy."

> *Life should NOT be a journey to the grave with the intention of arriving safely in an attractive and well preserved body, but rather to skid in sideways, chocolate in one hand, martini in the other, body thoroughly used up, totally worn out and screaming, "WOO HOO... what a ride!*

Who's Who

Wally "Famous" Amos*: Founder of Famous Amos Chocolate Cookie Co.; originally went to college to become a secretary which led to a clerical job at the William Morris Agency; became the agency's first African American talent agent, working with such people as Diana Ross & the Supremes, Simon & Garfunkel, Marvin Gaye and various other child stars, teen idols and movie stars; attracted clients to the William Morris Agency by sending them chocolate chip cookies along with an invitation to visit him; has written thirteen books, including Watermelon Magic: Seeds of Wisdom, Slices of Life and The Famous Amos Story: The Face That Launched a Thousand Chips; advocated literacy and helped thousands of adults learn to read.*

Marcus Aurelius*: Born to a prominent Spanish family in Rome; was orphaned; by age twelve he was mastering geometry, music, mathematics, painting and literature; became the 14th Roman Emperor; considered one of the most important stoic philosophers; his work Meditations, written on campaign between 170–180, is still revered as a literary monument to a government of service and duty and has been praised for its "exquisite accent and its infinite tenderness."*

James Matthew Barrie*: Scottish author and dramatist, best known for his character Peter Pan. The play Peter Pan (or The Boy Who Would Not Grow Up) was first performed in 1904 and published in 1928. Other plays by Barrie are his parody Ibsen's Ghosts (1891); Quality Street and*

The Admirable Crichton, both of which were first performed in 1902; What Every Woman Knows (1908); Dear Brutus (1917), a play in 3 acts; and The Boy David (1936); knighted in 1913 and the same year he became rector of St. Andrews University where he delivered his famous address on 'courage'.

Kim Basinger: *Born in December, 1953, in Georgia to Don, a jazz musician and loan-company manager, and Ann, a former model, champion swimmer and water ballet performer (her mother performed in some Esther Williams movies); a former fashion model and Academy Award-winning American actor; movie credits include Katie: Portrait of a Centerfold, the 1979 remake of From Here to Eternity; Hard Country, Never Say Never Again, The Man Who Loved Women, 9 1/2 weeks, The Natural and Batman.*

Alexander Graham Bell: *A Scottish-born, Canadian scientist and inventor; worked in telecommunications technology, he was responsible for important advances in aviation and hydrofoil technology. In 1876, at the age of 29, he invented the telephone; in 1877, he formed the Bell Telephone Company; one of his first innovations after the telephone was the "photophone," a device that enabled sound to be transmitted on a beam of light - the principle upon which today's laser and fiber optic communication systems were founded.*

Charlotte Bronte: *An English novelist, the eldest of the three Brontë sisters whose novels have become enduring classics of English literature; published Poems by Currer, Ellis and Acton Bell with her sisters; in 1847, she published her best-known novel, Jane Eyre; married in 1854 and died of complications of pregnancy in 1855. Another novel, Emma, barely begun; The Secret and Lily Hart, were not published until 1978.*

Leo Buscaglia: *Author of a number of New York Times bestselling inspirational books on love and human reticences; his presentations touched viewers' hearts television nearly as effectively as they did in person; called the "granddaddy of motivational speakers;" at one time five of his books were on The New York Times Best Sellers List simultaneously; worked actively to overcome social and mental barriers that inhibited the expression of love between people.*

Julia Cameron: *An award-winning poet, playwright, and filmmaker; writer of twenty-four books, ranging from her widely-praised, hard-hitting crime novel The Dark Room to her volumes of children's poems and prayers; has extensive film and theatre credits, she is best known for her hugely successful works on creativity; credited with having founded a new human potential movement which has enabled millions to realize their creative dreams, Cameron eschews the title "creativity expert," preferring to describe herself simply as an "artist."*

Andrew Carnegie: *A Scottish-born American businessman, a major philanthropist, and the founder of the Carnegie Steel Company which later became U.S. Steel; known for having built one of the most powerful and influential corporations in United States history and giving away most of his riches to fund the establishment of many libraries, schools and universities in Scotland, America and worldwide.*

Coco Chanel: *One of the most influential designers of the twentieth century; not influenced by previous fashion, but had entirely new ideas on how to make a woman look feminine; founder of a couture house, her own textile factory and a line of perfumes that included the famous No. 5. Chanel; was the first to introduce black as a fashion color and her versatile, semi-formal "little black dress" became a Chanel trademark and an enduring fashion standard.*

Henry Clay: *Born in Kentucky in April, 1777; a leading American statesman and orator in both the House of Representatives and Senate; founder and leader of the Whig Party and a leading advocate of programs for modernizing the economy; multiple attempts at the presidency were unsuccessful, however, defined the issues of the Second Party System; known as the Great Compromiser; in 1957 a Senate committee chaired by John F. Kennedy named Clay as one of the five greatest Senators in American history.*

Charles Caleb Colton: *An English cleric, writer and collector, well known for his eccentricities; his books, including collections of epigrammatic aphorisms and short essays on conduct, though now almost forgotten, had a phenomenal popularity in their day, including Lacon, or*

Many Things in Few Words, addressed to those who think, *The Conflagration of Moscow*, and *An Ode on the Death of Lord Byron*; at his death he left an unpublished poem of 600 lines called *Modern Antiquity*.

Mason Cooley: *U.S. aphorist. (Aphorism....short, witty saying, usually making a general observation); a writer of pithy sayings; quoted extensively in various collections of quotations and has his own several-volume collection called, City Aphorisms.*

The Dalai Lama: *Tibetan Buddhists believe the Dalai Lama to be one of innumerable incarnations of Avalokite?vara ("Chenrezig" in Tibetan), the bodhisattva of compassion; between the 17th century and 1959, the Dalai Lama was the head of the Tibetan government; considered the supreme head of Tibetan Buddhism; often called "His Holiness."*

Jean de La Fontaine: *Probably the most widely read French poet of the 17th century; a set of postage stamps celebrating La Fontaine and the Fables was issued by France in 1995; his. Fables are said to be choice in every sense: utterly correct, balanced, exquisite in rhyme, natural and easy, droll, witty, knowing, sage, utterly French; any generations of French students have learned them by heart and can quote the most famous lines which have become part of the common language.*

Catherine Deneuve: *One of the best-respected actresses in the French film industry; born in Paris in October, 1943; made her screen debut at the age of 13 in Les Collegiennes; her breakthrough role was in Les Parapluies de Cherbourg; also in Repulsion in 1965 and Belle de Jour; considered one of the most remarkable and compelling actresses of her generation; chose to avoid Hollywood, limiting her appearances in American films to The April Fools (1969) and Hustle (1975); did a series of commercials for Chanel perfume in the 1970s, which led to the creation of her own perfume a decade later.*

Albert Einstein: *Best known as the creator of the theory of relativity; the most famous scientist of the 20th century; published a paper proposing a "special theory of relativity," a groundbreaking notion which laid the foundation for much of modern physics theory; born in Germany in*

March, 1879; acquired Swiss citizenship in 1901; in 1905 obtained his doctor's degree; 1909 became Professor Extraordinary at Zurich; 1911 Professor of Theoretical Physics at Prague; 1914 he was appointed Director of the Kaiser Wilhelm Physical Institute and Professor in the University of Berlin; became a German citizen in 1914 until 1933 when he renounced his citizenship for political reasons and emigrated to America to take the position of Professor of Theoretical Physics at Princeton*. He became a United States citizen in 1940.

Ralph Waldo Emerson: *Born 1803; an American author, poet, and philosopher; the center of the American transcendental movement; his book, Nature, published in 1836, represented at least ten years of intense study in philosophy, religion and literature, and in his First Series of essays; also wrote Threnody, Representative Men; lectures on the "Natural History of Intellect," English Traits and in 1851 began a series of lectures which would become The Conduct of Life.*

Benjamin Franklin: *Born in Boston in 1706; taught himself simple algebra and geometry, navigation, logic, history, science, English grammar and a working knowledge of five other languages; built a successful printing and publishing business in Philadelphia; was an accomplished diplomat and statesman; helped establish Pennsylvania's first university and America's first city hospital; organized the country's first subscription library; one of the most prominent Founding Fathers of the United States; printer, scientist, inventor, civic activist and diplomat; a major figure in the history of physics for his discoveries and theories regarding electricity; political writer and activist.*

Johannes A. Gaertner: *Born in Berlin in 1923; a well-known professor of art history and a much-admired poet and theologian; his book, Worldly Virtues, sold 20,000 copies around the world.*

Robert Hughes: *An Australian art critic and Author; wrote for The Spectator, The Daily Telegraph, The Times and The Observer; obtained the position of art critic for TIME magazine in 1970; quickly established himself in the U.S. as an influential art critic; 1980 the BBC broadcast The Shock Of The New, Hughes's television series on the development of* *modern art- its insight, wit and accessibility are still widely praised.*

Victor Hugo: *A novelist, playwright, essayist and statesman, recognized as the most influential Romantic writer of the 19th century; best-known works are the novels Les Misérables and Notre-Dame de Paris (The Hunchback of Notre-Dame); was elected in 1841 to the Académie Francaise; also elected to the Constitutional Assembly and to the Legislative Assembly; wrote Les Chatimets (1853) and Les Misérables (1862), an epic story about social injustice; was an elected senator in Paris; died in Paris on May 22, 1885; given a national funeral, attended by two million people and buried in the Panthéon.*

Aldous Huxley: *English writer who emigrated was a member of the famous Huxley family; best known for his novels and wide-ranging output of essays, he also published short stories, poetry, travel writing and film stories and scripts an examiner and sometimes critic of social mores, societal norms and ideals; considered, in many academic circles, a 'leader of modern thought' and an intellectual of the highest rank.*

Ann Landers: *Best known for writing the famous syndicated advice column "Ann Landers" — a regular feature in many newspapers across North America.*

Estée Lauder: *Co-founder (with her husband) of Estée Lauder Companies, a pioneering cosmetics company. She was the only woman on Time magazine's 1998 list of the "20 most influential business geniuses of the 20th century." She was also the recipient of the Presidential Medal of Freedom.*

Pamela J. Leavey: *Starting with a small line of essential and fragrance oil blends (Goddess Potions), herbal incenses, body oils and bath salts, Pamela soon expanded her product line to include natural body lotion and bath & shower gel and other handmade personal care products. She taught herself website design and studied online marketing. Established website (www.aromatherapygoddess.com) which offers pages about women's healing: breast cancer and menopause awareness; a daily affirmations and inspirations page and Goddess lore. Pamela's products* *were designed around many of these themes, stressing natural healing and the power of intent and affirmations. Pamela is now continuing her political activism on with her own blog, TheDemocraticDaily.com, which she recently founded to provide news and information about issues important to Democrats.*

Thomas Merton: *One of the most influential Catholic authors of the 20th century; a Trappist monk of the Abbey of Our Lady of Gethsemani; an acclaimed Catholic theologian, poet, author and social activist; wrote over fifty books, scores of essays and reviews, and is the ongoing subject of countless biographies; a proponent of ecumenism, engaging in spiritual dialogues with such icons as His Holiness the Dalai Lama.*

Norman Podhoretz: *Served as an adviser to the U.S. Information Agency; a member of the Council on Foreign Relations; served as Editor-in-Chief of the American Jewish Committee's monthly magazine Commentary; awarded the Presidential Medal of Freedom, the highest honor the U.S. Government can bestow on a civilian.*

Edith Schaeffer: *With her husband toured Europe on behalf of the American Council of Christian Churches and founded the Children for Christ ministry in 1948 in Lausanne.*

Rainer Maria Rilke: *Generally considered the German language's greatest 20th century poet; wrote in both verse and a highly lyrical prose; two most famous verse sequences are the Sonnets to Orpheus and the Duino Elegies; his two most famous prose works are the Letters to a Young Poet and the semi-autobiographical The Notebooks of Malte Laurids Brigge; also wrote more than 400 poems in French, dedicated to his homeland of choice, the canton of Valais in Switzerland.*

Helen Rowland: *A very quotable American journalist and humorist.*

Samuel Ullman: *Born in Germany in 1840; businessman, poet, humanitarian; best known today for his poem Youth which was a favorite of General Douglas MacAuthur; on Birmingham, Alabama's first board of education; during his 18 years there, he advocated educational benefits for* *black children similar to those provided for whites; also served as president and then lay rabbi of the city's reform congregation at Temple Emanu-El; often controversial but always respected, Ullman left his mark on the religious, educational and community life of Natchez and Birmingham.*

John Wayne*: One of the genuine icons of 20th-century American film; considered a super patriot and was closely associated with conservative political causes; honored with a United States postage stamp released in April of 2004.*

Oscar Wilde*: An Irish playwright, novelist, poet, short story writer and Freemason; one of the most successful playwrights of late Victorian London and one of the greatest celebrities of his day.*

Marianne Williamson*: A spiritual activist, author, lecturer and founder of the Peace Alliance, a grass roots campaign supporting to establish a United States Department of Peace; referred to as a modern-day shaman, a Mother Teresa for the '90s and Hollywood's answer to God; founded the Centers for Living, an organization dedicated to providing home delivered care for people with life-threatening diseases and has participated in fund raising activities for charitable causes; her debut work A Return to Love; teaches love and common sense; earliest renown was for her talks on A Course in Miracles, a step-by-step method for choosing love over fear.*

Xenocrates*: A Greek philosopher and scholar or rector of the Academy from 339 to 314 BC; his earnestness and strength of character won for him universal respect.*

Bibliography

Aborn, Shana. "Steps to Forgiveness." *Ladies Home Journal*, November 2004.

Ali, Muhammad. www.cyber-nation.com.

Amused and Bemused. "The Top Ten Kinds of Women to Avoid." www.netscape.com.

Andrology.com. "Male Menopause — Does it really exist? The truth behind and treatment for Male Menopause." May 2004.

Anonymous. "How to Build Self Confidence; The How-To Manual That Anyone Can Write or Edit." www.wikihow.com.

Bach, George R. and Deutsch, Ronald M. *Stop! You're Driving Me Crazy*. Berkley Publishing Group, 1985.

Barash, David P. and Lipton, Judith Eve. *Making Sense of Sex: How Genes and Gender Influence Our Relationships*. Shearwater Books, 1997.

Barry, Dave. "Science Explains the Male Behavior." *The Daily Beacon Online*, 2003.

Benson, Elisa. "Sopranos Star talks about self-image, eating disorders." Colgate University, September 2004.

Berg, Adriane G. *How to Stop Fighting About Money and Make Some: A Couple's Guide to Financial Success*. Newmarket Press, 1988.

Berk, Lee and Tan, Dr. Stanley. "Therapeutic Benefits of Laughter." *Humor and Health Journal*, October 1996.

Betterwayhealth.com. "Drink to Your Health… With Water! Mother Nature's Healthy 'Cocktail.'"

Boxer, Diana. "Nagging in Families: Why and How It Can Be Handled." *The Journal of Pragmatics*, February 2004.

Brott, Armin. "When Parents Fight." www.gardenandhealth.com.

Cabeza, Robert; Dolcos, Florin; and LeBar, Kevin. "How Brain Gives Special Resonance to Emotional Memories." *Neuron*, June 2004.

Campbell, Nancy. "Can nice men be sexy?" www.ivillage.co.uk, June 2004.

Carlisle, Stephen. "The Top 10 Signs She's Crazy." www.askmen.com.

Carroll, E. Jean and Kerner, Ian. "Gender Wars: Men and Women in the Bedroom." *The Today Show*, June 2004.

Carville, James. www.angelfire.com.

CBS Radio Network. Gratitude Theory. The Osgood File. July 2002.
—. The Osgood File. December 2001.

CBS *48 Hours*. "The Secret Life of Eric Wright." July 2004.

Consumer Credit Counseling Service. "Money and Marriage: Don't let money problems ruin your relationship." 2003.

Coping.org. "Tools for Personal Growth, Becoming Vulnerable." 2006.

Crouse, Janice Shaw, Ph.D. "Women of Faith, Women of Power." The Beverly LaHaye Institute, September 6, 2002.

Daily Affirmations. www.aromatherapygoddess.com.

Dave the Dogman. "Sexual and Behavior Tendencies." www.healthy-dogs.net, May 2004.

Department of Health and Human Services, Centers for Disease Control and Prevention; Questions and Answers. "Can I get HIV from oral sex?" www.cdc.gov.

Dove Campaign for Real Beauty. "Mothers Play Crucial Role in Development of Girls' Self-Esteem."

fi.edu/brain/stress.htm#how. "The Human Brain: How Your Brain Responds to Stress."

Field, Tiffany. Touch Research Institute, University of Miami School of Medicine.

Firfer, Holly. "Study Suggests New Therapy for Impotence." University of Pennsylvania, October 1999.

Fisher, Helen. "Your Brain In Love." *Time*, January 2004.

Foreman, Judy. "Women and Stress." www.myhealthsense.com.

Frank, Monica and Gustafson, Susan. "The Reciprocal Influence of Self-Esteem and Exercise." www.behavioralconsultants.com.

Gajew, Nigel. "9 Reasons Why You're Tempted to Cheat." www.askmen.com, May 2004.

Galician, Mary-Lou. "Sex, Love and Romance in the Mass Media." GPN and Center for Media Literacy, 2006.

Gallagher, Leigh. "Pampering Your Inner He-Man." www.forbes.com, November 2003.

Gandy, Debrena Jackson. *All the Joy You Can Stand*. Three Rivers Press, June 2001.

—. *Sacred Pampering Principles*. Perennial Currents, 1998.

Gneezy, Uri. "Gender and Competition: Do Competitive Environments Favor Men More Than Women?" The University of Chicago Graduate School of Business, September 2004.

Goodwin, Dr. Fred, et al., "The Infinite Mind: Sense of Touch." Lichtenstein Creative Media, Inc., October 2002.

Greer, Jane. "Let's Talk About Sex." www.iVillage.com.

Grenrock, Stacey Woods. "The Sex Column." *Esquire*, August 2004.

Hansen, Katherine. "10 Powerful Career Strategies for Women." www.quintcareers.com.

Hay, Louise. *You Can Heal Your Life*. Hay House, Inc., 1999.

Herper, Matthew. "The Science of Love." *Time*, June 2004.

Hols, Garrett. "Nice Guys Finish Last." www.angelfire.com.

Indiana University School of Medicine Press Release. "NEWS FLASH: Men Do Hear — But Differently Than Women, Brain Images Show." August 2005.

Jayson, Sharon. "Technical virginity becomes part of teens' equation." *USA TODAY*, October 19, 2005.

Journal of Social and Clinical Psychology. "Men, too, are sensitive to media body ideals." February 2004.

Keen, Cathy. "UF Study: Online dating virtually irresistible to some married folks." University of Florida, July 2003.

Klensch, Elsa. "De La Renta heats up winter with fabulous femininity." CNN, November 26, 1997.

LaRoche, Loretta. *Life is Short-Wear Your Party Pants.* Hay House, February 2004.

—. *The Joy of Stress.* Humor Potential, November 1997.

—. *How Serious Is This?* Humor Potential, February 1995.

Lemonsick, Michael D. "The Chemistry of Desire." *Time*, January 2004.

Link, Al and Copeland, Pala. "Sexual Magnetism: Pheronomes — The Scent of Sex." *Urban Male Magazine*, Winter 2001.

Lkwdpl.org; Lakewood Public Library. *Living Vignettes of Women from the Past; Women in History.*

Lydiard, R. Bruce, M.D., Ph.D. "Panic Attacks." Institute of Psychiatry at the Medical University of South Carolina, 2002.

McCraty, Rollin. "Coincidence or Intuition?" Journal of Alternative and Complementary Medicine, February 2004.

Mcnair, Trisha. "Laughter and health." BBC Health, May 2004.

MensHealth.com. "Testosterone in blood linked to better memory." November 2002.

Mendes, Sam. *American Beauty.* Dreamworks Pictures, 1999.

Mitchell, Susan and Christie, Catherine. "Mood-Food Relationships" *I'd Kill for a Cookie - A Simple Six-Week Plan to Conquer Stress Eating.* Plume,1998.

MSNBC/ Sexual Health. "Many Teenage Girls Feel Pressured into Having Sex; Survey finds young women give in out of fear of angering boyfriend." June 2006.

National Council for Research on Women.

National Organization for Women Foundation.

NBC11.com. "Double Take: I Want To Get Married; Marriage Becomes Ultimatum In Two Relationships." 2006.

Nellis, Cynthia. "Easy Figure Fixes." www.fashion.about.com, 2006/2007.

Oliver, Jameson. "Top 10 Reasons Why Men Cheat." www.askmen.com, May 2004.

Oregon Health & Science University. "Estrogen Boosts Memory in Men with Prostate Cancer." June 7, 2004.

Phillips, Katherine A. "Body Image Disorder Affecting More Men." *The Journal of Nervous and Mental Disease*, May, 2002.

Psychosomatic Medicine, January/February 2003.

Relationships Australia. "Fair fighting; Some Conflict in Relationships is Inevitable." 2006.

Remez, Lisa. "Oral Sex Among Adolescents: Is It Sex or Is It Abstinence?" Guttmacher Institute, Family Planning Perspectives. Volume 32, Number 6. November/December 2000.

Riera, Mike. "Let the Kids See You Argue." CBS News, October 2001.

Sawyer, Dianne. "Inside Two Marriages: Kids Caught by Couples at the Crossroads." Primetime Live: Thursday, April 25, 2002 .

Schilling, Dianne. "How Strong Is Your Self-Image?" www.womensmedia.com, June 2004.

Sherman, Neil. "Does Male Menopause Exist?" UCLA's Neuropsychiatric Institute in Los Angeles; www.healthAtoZ.com.

Smalley, Gary and Trent, John. "Keeping Romance in your Marriage," *Love is a Decision*. W Publishing Group, January 2001.

Social Issues Research Center. "The Smell Report; Sexual Attraction." 2006.

Sohn, E. "Male Baboons Get Mellow." *Science News for Kids*, April 2004.

Stepp, Laura Sessions. "Half of All Teens Have Had Oral Sex." *Washington Post*; September 16, 2005.

——. "Parents are alarmed by an unsettling new fad in middle schools: oral sex." *Washington Post*, July 8, 1999.

——. "Talking to kids about sexual limits." *Washington Post*, July 8, 1999.

Sternbach, Harvey M.D. UCLA Neuropsychiatric Institute in Los Angeles, 1998.

Sultanoff, Steven M. "Examining the Research in the Therapeutic Benefits of Humor and Laughter." Association for Applied and Therapeutic Humor, 1999.

Tartarotti, Margaux. "Dressing for your Body." *The Fine Art of Dressing*. Perigee Trade, December 1999.

TheQuotationsPage.com.

Thisisawar.com. "Emotional Abuse."

Topps, Mattie; Van Peer, Jacobien M.; Wijers, Albertus A.; and Korf, Jakob. "Fatigue in women is reduced in stress-related cortisol study." *Medical News Today*, November 2000.

University of Pennsylvania Health System Department of Public Affairs. "Get Your Blood Moving: Increased Blood Flow Could Lead To Healthier Blood Vessels; Findings Show The Force of Blood Flow Has Anti-Inflammatory Effect." January 2003.

Vaknin, Sam. "The Pathology of Love." December 2006.

Vissell, Joyce and Vissell, Barry. "Noticing Others' Small Contributions." www.learningplaceonline.com.

Wallis, Claudia. "A Snapshot of Teen Sex." www.time.com. 2005.

West, Melissa. "Relationships: Work and Blessing - An Interview with Joyce and Barry Vissell." www.personaltransformation.com. 2002.

WHDH.com. "Healing Scents." 2006.

Wolf Hollow. Ipswich, Massachusetts.

Women in Leadership Summit, Linkage, Inc. Boston, Massachusetts: October 2003.

Women's Voices in Leadership. Quotations; Status of Women Council, Northwest Territories. Canada.

Wurtman, J. "Carbohydrate Craving, Mood Changes, and Obesity." *Journal of Clinical Psychiatry*, 1989.

Wurtman, R. J. et al., "Carbohydrate Cravings, Obesity and Brain Serotonin." *Scientific American*, 1988.

Wurtman, R. J. and Wurtman, J. J. "Carbohydrates and Depression." *Scientific American*, 1989.